MULTIJURALISM

This work is the result of a collaboration between the Ministry of Justice of the French Republic and the Department of Justice Canada.

A French language edition of this work is published by Les Editions ESKA, Paris.

Multijuralism

Manifestations, Causes, and Consequences

Edited by

ALBERT BRETON
University of Toronto, Canada

ANNE DES ORMEAUX,
Department of Justice, Canada

KATHARINA PISTOR
Columbia University, USA

PIERRE SALMON
Université de Bourgogne, France

Routledge
Taylor & Francis Group
LONDON AND NEW YORK

First published 2009 by Ashgate Publishing

Reissued 2018 by Routledge
2 Park Square, Milton Park, Abingdon, Oxon OX14 4RN
711 Third Avenue, New York, NY 10017, USA

Routledge is an imprint of the Taylor & Francis Group, an informa business

A Library of Congress record exists under LC control number: 2009025232

ISBN 13: 978-0-815-39057-2 (hbk)
ISBN 13: 978-1-351-15288-4 (ebk)

Contents

List of Figures

Notes on Contributors

Annie Bunting, Associate Professor, Law & Society Program, York University, Toronto.

John H. Currie, Associate Professor, Common Law Section, Faculty of Law, University of Ottawa.

Bénédicte Fauvarque-Cosson, Professor, Université Panthéon-Assas, Paris II.

Marc Favero, General Secretary and Legal Director, Brinks France.

Sébastien Grammond, Dean and Associate Professor, Civil Law Section, Faculty of Law, University of Ottawa.

Gillian K. Hadfield, Professor of Law and of Economics, University of Southern California Law School, Los Angeles.

Alice Pezard, Conseiller à la Cour de cassation, France; Associate Professor, Université Paris-Sud XI.

Elise Poillot, Professor, Université du Luxembourg.

Gareth Sansom, Director, Technology and Analysis, Criminal Law Policy Section, Department of Justice Canada.

Introduction

At one level of generality, multijuralism is the coexistence of two or more legal systems or sub-systems within a broader normative legal order to which they adhere. An obvious example is the existence of both the civil law and the common law systems within the same legal order, as is the case in Canada and the European Union (EU). This traditional and important dichotomy relies on a relatively clear-cut and widely understood set of objects. Even if the terms used to designate them are far from fixed, there is little ambiguity about the objects themselves. It does not really matter whether common law and civil law are designated as systems, as above, or as traditions as is often done in the literature. In the same vein, we could speak of the 'legal systems' of Canada and the EU without changing the meaning we have in mind when employing the term 'legal order' to refer to the same objects. The 'jural' or 'juralism' suffixes in 'multijural' or 'multijuralism' (or, for that matter, in 'monojural' and 'monojuralism') are also unambiguous in that context because they point in a relatively straightforward way to the dominant types or forms of laws and judicial procedures that are deemed to differentiate the common law and the civil law systems or traditions.

But the co-existence of common law and civil law is a macroscopic divide. At a finer level of analysis, multijuralism is a more widespread phenomenon and also a more fluid reality than the distinction suggests. As a consequence, it becomes more difficult to identify the concepts associated with, or underlying, the expression. Multijuralism itself can be defined in a broad way as the coexistence of systems of norms considered binding by a subset of actors, a formulation that calls for some clarification. Which set are we thinking of when speaking of 'subsets'? If we hold to our earlier definition and apply it to the simplified context discussed above, the set may be all the users of the Canadian legal order or system and the subsets may be the users of the civil law and common law components of that order or system. When we take a less aggregated view of the matter and limit ourselves to Canada, the chapters of the book show – explicitly when focused on that country and implicitly when dealing with other countries and with the general phenomenon – the relevance of other subsets of actors and components of the legal order. In some cases, however, the relevant set is much larger than any national state – or, for that matter, than the EU as a whole. Because of the international character of many transactions and of the latitude that private parties to these transactions often have to choose a particular national law and/or a national court, and also because of the emergence in some domains of norms that have no national affiliation, it may be argued that the relevant set, overarching the subsets mentioned in the definition of multijuralism, is something like the legal system of the whole world, or at any rate that of all the countries that are signatories of an international treaty or members of an international organization. These extensive interpretations are sometimes fuzzy but, in the current world, they have a place to occupy in the background of most analyses of the co-existence of subsets of actors and components of legal orders.

Together with the need to adopt a flexible interpretation of legal orders or systems, the analysis of multijuralism at a less aggregated level requires that an extensive content be given to the notions of law and legal procedure. In some highly significant contexts, various types of customs, as well as many unconventional modes of conflict resolution and norm enforcement, must now be covered by these notions in addition to codified laws and statutes, case law, and traditional judicial modes of implementation and enforcement. This has a direct bearing on our interpretation of the 'jural' in 'multijuralism', which, as the following chapters illustrate, must also be given a flexible meaning.

Under that perspective, some of the forms which the phenomenon of multijuralism takes disappear or lose their importance, but other forms emerge or become prominent. The emergence or disappearance of some forms of multijuralism may follow deliberate acts of private or public agents or may be the unintended consequence of such acts. They may also be the consequence of technological, sociological or economic developments that are largely independent of any identifiable decisions. Paradoxically, multijuralism sometimes arises as a consequence of policies aimed at harmonizing the law, or making it more uniform. The reason is that the implementation of harmonized rules often gives rise to new diversity.

The chapters that follow are rooted in that frame of reference, although, of necessity, they concentrate on singular aspects of the phenomenon. Thus, they address some effects on legal systems of globalization and technological innovations, international treaties and EU directives, and the persistence of legal and quasi-legal traditions of minorities such as in Canada's indigenous populations and Muslim communities. We first summarize the chapters and then endeavour to draw out some of the forces and mechanisms that underlie the analyses offered in the chapters.

In the first chapter, John Currie seeks to identify the principal characteristics of domestic legal systems and of international treaties that promote either harmonizing or multijural effects within and across domestic legal systems. The analysis is aimed at identifying and illustrating the principal factors that most directly affect the impact of treaties on domestic legal systems. Currie argues that the harmonizing or multijural effects of a given treaty depend, *inter alia*, on whether the mode of reception has a monist or dualist treaty reception regime and, in the case of the latter, how the political system chooses to adapt the treaty's rules within its domestic legal system. The harmonizing potential of treaties depends also on attributes inherent in a particular treaty: the extent to which the treaty addresses primarily contractual arrangements between states or has a normative character; whether it deals with subject-matter coming within the traditional bounds of domestic legal regulation or addresses traditional state-to-state interests; whether the treaty is multilateral in nature and is, hence, subject to reservations by states adhering to it; and whether the treaty incorporates its own set of secondary obligations, such as a supranational dispute settlement regime. Currie argues that it is necessary to have regard to what he calls the net multijural effect of a given treaty: at one level, a treaty regime may inject foreign legal concepts into domestic legal systems; at another level, overly effective injection of international legal concepts into domestic legal systems may have a harmonizing effect across domestic legal systems.

Sébastien Grammond examines an important dimension of multijuralism or legal pluralism, to wit some interactions, in the Canadian context, of indigenous law and legal practices with the civil law and the common law as practised in the country. The interactions relate to the modes through which indigenous law is received and accepted by relevant bodies. To analyse the interaction among legal systems, in Chapter 2 Grammond makes use of a distinction between 'soft' and 'hard' pluralism and thus helps us understand an important dimension of multijuralism. Soft pluralism obtains when a government – usually the central government – delegates the power to enact in certain domains to other governments or authorities. Grammond examines a variety of interactions that belong to soft pluralism and documents the importance of that mode of interaction. Hard pluralism, on the other hand, prevails when parallel legal orders co-exist. Legal orders can thus exist apart from an official recognition and can even be disputed by one or more governments or authorities. Grammond provides an extensive analytical and descriptive discussion of the obstacles to the reception of indigenous legal systems in Canada. Some of these would seem relatively easy to overcome, while others pose a greater challenge. Whether elements of indigenous law are to be recognized and accorded reception will depend on whether the underlying forces favouring recognition are more powerful than the resilience of the obstacles to recognition.

In her discussion of 'family law's legal pluralism' in Canada, Annie Bunting develops her argument in two complementary steps. A first one comprises an analysis of the evolution and current status of family law in Ontario as it pertains to separation and divorce – economists would be tempted to refer to this analysis as describing the 'supply' side of the separation and divorce institutional setups. Bunting argues that the relevant law in Ontario in practice allows for plurality of choice. The second step – unique in the discussions of multijuralism in this volume – is based on qualitative empirical data derived from interviews. It describes some patterns of actual or possible decision-making among individuals seeking separations and divorces – the 'demand' side of the institutional setup. Bunting's investigation is centred on Muslim religious communities because of her interest in these communities but also because of the opportunities they offer to develop her 'model'. The investigation and the model are surely applicable to other populations. The description of what goes on in the Muslim communities is intrinsically interesting, but the evidence Bunting provides makes it clear that multijuralism or pluralism is driven as much by the 'demand' as by the 'supply' side of the institutional setup. Bunting's analysis of the situation in South Africa is of interest in itself but also for the light it sheds on her analysis of what we have called the 'supply' side both in Africa and in Canada. To be more precise, family law as it pertains to marriage, separation and divorce is not given once and for all but is the product of certain social realities – the present and historical attitudes toward polygamy in South Africa for example – and the way these realities shape and condition the way the law is formulated, interpreted and applied in practice.

The chapter by Alice Pezard is concerned with the implications for multijuralism of the Independent Administrative Authorities (IAAs) that have proliferated in France, as (under different names) in some other countries over the last decades. These authorities have been endowed with, or have gained over time, important powers regarding regulation, enforcement (through sanctions in particular), and dispute resolution. Various forces have led to this development. Some are related to weaknesses in the traditional judicial system, pertaining mostly (but not exclusively, as illustrated by the authority against discrimination) to the technical nature of the standards to be implemented or maintained. In the case of France and other countries belonging to the EU, a major determinant has been the objective, adopted at the EU level as an aspect of the 'deepening of the internal market', of fostering open and fair competition in sectors previously held entirely by public monopolies and in which the public sector would continue to have a major role. In such a context, IAAs seemed the natural way to combine, to the degree required, the necessary characteristics of independence and technical competence. The intense exchanges of experience and coordination, promoted by the EU, between each French IAA and their counterparts in other member countries led to some harmonizing, beyond what the EU directives required explicitly, of the national modes of regulation in the specialized domains. Pezard discusses some of the ways the problems raised by their co-existence with the traditional legal and judicial order are addressed. To mention some of the principles which emerge: given the judicial and in particular the sanctioning powers held by the IAAs, only the legislature (not the executive branch) can create IAAs; their competences should remain clearly circumscribed and at the same time non exclusive; their sanctioning power should respect rights and freedoms, in particular those guaranteed by the Constitution and international treaties (non-retroactivity of penal sanctions, fair trials, and so on); and it may be possible to challenge their rulings at the higher levels of the judicial or administrative orders.

In Chapter 5, Bénédicte Fauvarque-Cosson describes and analyses the efforts undertaken at the EU level to harmonize contract law across member countries. There has been and still exists substantial disagreement and vacillation with regard to the degree to which harmonization should be pursued and about what parts of civil law it should deal with. Progressively, however, an approach has emerged which is currently practiced with the support of the EU Commission and Parliament. One feature of the approach is the involvement of a large number of constituencies, which ensures pluralism in many dimensions – legal traditions, representation of consumer and business firms' interests, academic expertise, judicial practice, EU administration, national interests, and so on.. Another characteristic is the relative modesty or realism of the end result sought in the medium term: a 'common frame of reference' (CFR), defined as a set of model rules at the disposal of contracting parties, with no obligation of adoption, and thus deserving to be called an 'optional instrument'. How should the choice of the CFR by the contracting parties be expressed? Under an opt-out solution, the absence of a specific choice on the part of the contracting parties would entail the *de facto* application of the CFR. Under the opt-in system, an express designation by the parties of the optional instrument instead of one of the national laws would be necessary. Neither solution is devoid of serious problems in practice. But Fauvarque-Cosson argues that the second solution, limited furthermore to contracts having a cross-border dimension, is probably the one that member states should be asked to accept in a first stage. For the time being, future developments could thus be left open.

In Chapter 6, Elise Poillot discusses the ways in which national legislators may transpose EU directives in the area of consumer protection. The adaptation of the internal legislation which is required by the directives may be limited to consumer contract law. This solution respects the scope of harmonization called for by the community legislator but it may have unwanted effects on the internal consistency of the national law. Alternatively, a concern for this internal consistency may inspire an extension of the scope of the directives beyond their explicit domain. The result may then be a kind of creeping harmonization of the domain of civil contract law as a whole. Nested in this main distinction, two other distinctions are formulated by Poillot. When the adaptation is strictly limited to consumer contract law, the directives may be transposed faithfully or the transposition may be only interpretative. Poillot shows, referring to the transposition in English law of the term 'good faith' used in one of the consumer protection directives, that a formally faithful or literal transposition is not a pledge of substantive faithfulness. Conversely, by reference this time to France, she shows that a transposition which is not literal but interpretative may perfectly meet the spirit of a directive. Poillot then turns to the case when the adaptation of the national law goes beyond the domain of consumer protection and she notes that the extension may be achieved by the national legislators or by jurisprudence. She shows, referring again to a French example, that the second path (expansionist jurisprudence) is sometimes more easily borrowed than the first (expansionist legislation) – jurisprudence proving then more innovative and more respectful of both the spirit of EU directives and the coherence of the national legal system than legislation.

In Chapter 7, Gillian Hadfield begins by making the point that the problem of harmonizing legal rules across multiple overlapping legal orders is, in part, a problem of knowledge. This implies, she argues, that if the public goal of harmonization is to promote value in transactions and dispute resolution, a legal regime needs institutions that facilitate the production of multijural human capital; that is, expertise about how legal rules interact with each other and with the environment in which economic actors design transactions and dispute resolution mechanisms. Central to her argument is the point that because much of this expertise is embedded in actors who are involved in transactions and disputes, the production of expertise has to be supported by adequate incentives for these actors to invest in the costly production of information and to bear the cost of transmitting this information to public bodies such as courts and regulators. As an information asset, multijural human capital generates positive externalities with the consequence that there will be underinvestment in its production. To deal with this problem, Hadfield argues that international law firms can internalize some of these externalities and thus increase the production of multijural human capital. Significant obstacles to the cross-border integration of legal practice, however, interfere with the formation of truly multi-jurisdictional law firms and thus hamper the process of effective harmonization in multijural settings.

In Chapter 8, on the basis of a survey involving banks, law offices and business firms operating in France, Marc Favero analyses the way that the relationship between *standard* and *model* contracts on the one hand and financial law, understood as the law of financial instruments, on the other, has evolved in that country and presumably elsewhere. One aspect of the development of financial markets is recourse to sophisticated financial instruments or operations – devised by professionals of finance rather than by lawyers – that the traditional law of contracts could not handle satisfactorily. Standard contracts were introduced mainly by banks as a way to facilitate and organize on a uniform basis a particular type of financial transaction involving the new instruments. Model contracts, on the other hand, were developed mainly by law firms to speed up and make more efficient the supply of contracts to clients. Both kinds have had a profound influence on the way the French legal system has evolved to govern the use of financial instruments. Typically, Favero notes, they have filled many gaps in the existing provisions of that system, sometimes at the cost of introducing in contracts features at odds with the legal system and in the system itself provisions completely foreign to its logic and its principles. The influence of the two categories of contracts on legal systems has also been indirect, enhanced by the internationalization they have brought about or accelerated. One may even argue that the body of law that governs financial instruments is evolving as a quasi autonomous body of principles developed in model and standard contracts.

In Chapter 9, Gareth Sansom provides an analysis of some effects of computer-related crimes on the evolution and administration of criminal law. First, crimes perpetuated through the Internet generate problems related to the detection and pursuit of the criminals responsible for the acts – problems related to the technology of Internet communication. Second, computer-related crimes are often transnational crimes, and in some cases, are transnational organized crimes. Sansom then makes the point that transnational organized crimes are the product of an increasing fragmentation and specialization of criminal activity, and a territorial dispersal of the elements of crimes. He goes on to show that these two phenomena are closely related: 'the increasing fragmentation of the criminal activity further facilitating the territorial dispersal of the elements of the crime'. Sansom then makes the point that the ambit or scope of criminal law is more often than not predicated on the legal notion of territoriality. The Internet, on the other hand, operates in a number of spaces – some physical and some virtual. The chapter then proceeds to analyse what Sansom calls the 'strategies of displacement' whereby through the multiplicity of spaces the territorial jurisdictions are subverted. Sansom uses this framework of analysis to examine in detail the cybercrime of child pornography. That analysis allows the reader to understand the nature of that crime. In the process, he establishes that the framework of analysis is not only robust, but effective.

A mechanism at work in several of the chapters is set in motion by the need for a legal and judicial system to adapt to some requirement generated from outside its existing territorial jurisdiction. That requirement may be related to the implementation of some international agreement, as discussed by Currie or, in the EU setting, to the transposition of some directive, as discussed by Pezard and Poillot. In both cases the needed adaptation may be deemed voluntary in the sense that it follows (more or less directly) from an agreement or acquiescence given earlier at some level by the representatives of the countries concerned. But requirements are also often aspects of processes that may be deemed spontaneous in the sense that they develop without the intervention of government, for instance as a manifestation of the multifaceted phenomenon of globalization. This is what can be observed in different domains, in the analyses developed by Favero, Sansom and Hadfield. In their chapters, the globalization of financial markets, the development of the Internet, or the internationalization of transactions and the expansion of international law firms compel changes in legal arrangements or in the way legal institutions function and influence outcomes that are largely independent of governments.

The distinction between the adaptation required by governmental decisions and that imposed by developments involving mostly private individuals and firms is not a strict one. For instance, one might say that many treaties, in the area of human rights for instance, respond to an increased awareness in some countries of what happens abroad – also a manifestation of globalization. Conversely, if technical progress and innovations are obviously major forces in the adaptations required by 'spontaneous' processes, largely independent of governments, of the kind discussed by Favero (new financial instruments) and Sansom (new possibilities on the Internet), the way technical progress and innovations interact with EU directives is not a negligible determinant of the phenomenon analysed by Pezard; moreover, their influence lies in the background of some of the developments described by Currie.

In any case, as far as the logic of the foregoing mechanism is concerned, the way legal systems adapt to new requirements is largely independent of the origin of these requirements. Whether initiated by the globalization of financial markets or by an international treaty on human rights, the adaptation may be set in motion in the same way by the introduction in national legal systems of provisions and procedures that are relatively similar across countries and thus contribute to a process of harmonization or spontaneous alignment by sectors, but are heterogeneous or disharmonious with other parts of these systems and sometimes with their whole logic. As stressed by Currie, the emergence of such heterogeneity or disharmony does constitute a source of multijuralism within a given legal order. The story does not, however, end there. One may expect forces to arise that will work toward a reduction of the heterogeneity that has been created. The legal system will not only cope with what is required of it by treaties, directives or spontaneous developments, but at a later stage will tend to recover some consistency by adjustments in others of its component parts.

A restoration of consistency may also be sought through an extension of the process of adaptation so that it goes beyond what was required originally. This may take place in isolation within each legal system. In that case the result may be more as well as less diversity across systems. But the extension of the adaptation may also take place in the setting of the relations between different legal systems – between the legal systems of the member states of the EU for instance. In her chapter, Fauvarque-Cosson shows how a process of harmonization or approximation between strictly defined areas of contract law may be progressively extended or enlarged so as to potentially cover a wider set of domains. Given the misgivings that this type of development typically encounters, and the uncertainties about consequences and political constraints that surround it *ex ante*, a progressive and cautious approach seems appropriate. This explains the increasing appeal of the opt-in and opt-out solutions which she discusses in a particular domain but which is also felt in a broader context.

We can be more precise about the dynamics sketched in the foregoing discussion by referring more explicitly to the notions of equilibrium and disequilibrium. The reading of the summaries will have revealed that virtually all chapters describe disequilibrium states of nature. A reading of the chapters themselves should reinforce that perception. Consider, by way of illustration, Pezard's chapter on the introduction and growth of Independent Administrative Authorities in France. What these IAAs can and will do is still very much to be determined and their final *modus operandi* is still in the process of being discovered. In some cases, as Pezard makes clear, the equilibrium states can be perceived, but not in all cases. In his discussion of the effects of treaties on domestic laws, regulations, and behaviours, Currie makes clear that the process of adjustment is often a long drawn-out one and that much time is required before a full appraisal of such changes on the multijural effect of any treaty can be made. One could go through all the chapters and point to the disequilibrium nature of the multijural state of the world they describe.

There are a number of implications of this state of affairs. A first one is that if the subjects analysed in the volume were to be revisited ten or fifteen years hence, the effects of the place and role of the IAAs examined by Pezard and the effects of the treaties considered by Currie would, in all likelihood, be differently configured. A second implication of disequilibrium states is that as the forces which the disequilibria create work themselves out in one particular domain, that working out will have effects on adjustment in other domains. It seems reasonable to think that a general theory of multijuralism would not be that different from a general theory of markets in which what goes on in one market affects what goes on in other markets, including the elimination of some and the complete transformation of others.

Disequilibrium situations in areas that pertain to the law in multijural contexts are characterized by legal tension and stress, but also by economic, social, and possibly political tension and stress. It is therefore sometimes possible to understand the impact of certain changes by analysing what is going on in other areas than the one that seems principally affected. It is instructive to read Poillot's chapter with the foregoing as background as she casts a net wider than that which was initially introduced. The foregoing does not imply that it is possible to do otherwise than what Pezard and Currie have done. An awareness that the situations described are disequilibrium situations does, however, beg for a description of the causes of the changes taking place. One can find more or less elaborate efforts in that direction in all the chapters. In some instances these efforts are quite explicit; in others they are more implied. For example, in Favero's chapter, the drive for financial profits derived from increased efficiency in the use of novel transnational contracts is not very explicit, but there is no way of missing the point in the chapter.

The concern with disequilibria and their implications is very much a concern that is central to the way economists contemplate the real world. But there is another concern which at least two of the chapters bring to the forefront. In summarizing Bunting's chapter, we introduced the notions of supply and demand which have been at the core of economics for more than two centuries. We can be more precise about the use of these concepts in trying to understand multijuralism than we were in summarizing the Bunting chapter.

Bunting, but also Grammond, devote considerable space to a description of the legal setup, how it has in fact changed, and how it could evolve in the years ahead. Bunting's discussion pertains to marriage, separation and divorce in Muslim communities in Ontario; Grammond's relates to legal rules and traditions among the indigenous populations of Canada. These discussions are concerned with the configuration and the working of the supply side of legal institutions. The influence of governments – and thus of politics – is acknowledged and analysed in the two chapters. In democracies, politics – however capricious, lobby-ridden and contorted – somehow always respond to voters and citizens. This is a first manifestation of demand in the shaping of multijural configurations.

But, as we pointed out in our summary of Bunting's chapter, there is another manifestation of demand which is revealed in the data that emerged from the interviews she conducted with Muslim women. The data are only qualitative but still quite eloquent. They show that Muslim women who seek separation and divorce can access venues that are broader than those supplied by a narrow constricted reading of the formal Ontario law. It is hard to resist the thought that this second manifestation of demand is also present in the world studied by Grammond, though he himself does not pay attention to this reality.

To conclude this discussion of disequilibrium outcomes – tensions, stresses, and transitions to other configurations – and of supply and demand, let us assume that the working of supply and demand has been such that an overall equilibrium has been reached. What then? The analyst must take it as granted that 'outside' events – exogenous shocks or disturbances – will have an impact on the system. From the point of view of an understanding of multijuralism, what is really needed is an identification of the external events that are likely to be important over long periods of time and have therefore somewhat of a permanent character; these must be distinguished from those external disturbances that are transitory and therefore have a short-term effect. Events are external when they are not part of the processes of multijural adjustment but only influence these processes. Among the important external events identified in the chapters below are major European integration (such as the Single Act, the European Monetary Union, and enlargements), the growing importance accorded to human rights, the international practice of law, the growth of the Internet, the globalization of markets, and the flow of immigrants.

The October 2006 Conference which is at the origin of the material published in this volume was the second conference sponsored by the Department of Justice of the Government of Canada on issues related to bijuralism and multijuralism.[1] We wish to thank Mr. Michel Bouchard, then Associate Deputy Minister in the Canadian Department of Justice, for his unstinting support throughout the life of this second venture, and for his presence and address at the Conference. We would also like to thank the French Ministry of Justice for accepting to participate in the organization of the Conference and for its financial contribution. We are especially grateful to Claudine Jacob who, as Senior Legal Advisor in the French Ministry of Justice, helped organize the conference and contributed to the background document that defined the content parameters of the conference. For their support and encouragement, we are also grateful to Mr. Bruno Sturlèse, Head of European and International Affairs at the French Ministry of Justice, to Mr. Daniel Jouanneau, Ambassador of France in Canada, and to Mr. Philippe Delacroix, Consul General of France in Toronto. We thank Hart House in the University of Toronto for its hospitality, and especially Stephanie Kern for her attention and efficiency. The smooth progress of the Conference was, in good measure, made possible by the help of Linda Delaney, Isabelle Palad, and Sarah Ulmer of Justice Canada. Special thanks are due to Isabelle Palad for her editorial work on all the chapters in this collection. Without her help, the time-gap between the Conference and the publication of the proceedings would have been even longer than it has been.

Albert Breton,
Anne Des Ormeaux,
Katharina Pistor,
and Pierre Salmon

1 The first conference was held in October 2003 at the University of Toronto. The proceedings are available in Albert Breton and Michael Trebilcock (eds) (2006), *Bijuralism: An Economic Approach*, Aldershot UK: Ashgate Publishing; and in (sous la direction de) Breton and Trebilcock (2007), *Le bijuralisme: Une approche économique*, Paris: Les Editions ESKA.

Chapter 1

International Treaties and Conventions as Agents of Convergence and Multijuralism in Domestic Legal Systems

John H. Currie*

Introduction

Among the mechanisms or processes operating across national legal orders that may produce multijural effects within those legal orders are international treaties or conventions.[1] Treaties are agreements that are legally binding on the parties to them, usually states,[2] pursuant to international law. This means that, in accordance with the cardinal principle of international treaty law, *pacta sunt servanda*, states parties to such treaties or conventions are obliged to perform their terms and obligations in good faith.[3] A corollary of this cardinal principle is that a conflict between the terms of a treaty and a state party's domestic law does not (from the perspective of international law) excuse the state party from its duty

* The author expresses thanks to Adam J. Huff, LL.B. candidate, Faculty of Law, University of Ottawa, for research assistance in finalizing citations.

1 The terms 'treaty', 'convention' and other such designations (for example, 'protocol', 'charter', 'covenant', 'statute', and so on) are all used interchangeably in international law. The generic term 'treaty' will be used throughout this chapter to refer to all international agreements that are binding pursuant to international law.

2 Although certain international organizations, such as the United Nations, also have capacity to enter into treaty relations: see *Vienna Convention on the Law of Treaties between States and International Organizations or between International Organizations*, 21 March 1986 (not yet in force).

3 *Vienna Convention on the Law of Treaties*, 23 May 1969, 1155 U.N.T.S. 331, art. 26 [hereinafter *Vienna Convention*]. Indeed this rule is widely considered to be one of the most fundamental principles of international law, perhaps having the character of *jus cogens*, that is, accepted by the international community as a whole as being of a peremptory character and admitting of no derogation: *see* International Law Commission, 'Report of the International Law Commission on the Work of its 18th Session', in its *Yearbook of the International Law Commission* (1966a), at 210-211; Kelsen (1946), *General Theory of Law and State*, at 369-370; Shaw (2003), *International Law*, at 811-812; Currie (2001), *Public International Law*, at 130 and 151; Janis (1993), *An Introduction to International Law*, at 65-66.

of compliance with, or performance of, the treaty norm.[4] Accordingly, in many (but not necessarily all)[5] cases, good faith performance by a state of its treaty obligations will require amendment of its domestic law with the ostensible goal of harmonizing its domestic and international legal obligations.

While the processes of treaty conclusion and domestic treaty implementation are widely intended and believed to play the harmonizing function just described, such factors as the nature and subject-matter of the treaty regime in question, the processes by which domestic treaty implementation is carried out, and the nature of the domestic legal framework in which this occurs, may in fact produce unintended 'disharmonizing' or 'multijuralizing' effects. The purpose of this chapter is therefore to explore both the potential harmonizing and disharmonizing effects of international treaties within domestic legal systems. In this way, the chapter will examine whether, and in what circumstances or settings, international treaties and conventions either suppress or promote multijural effects.

The interaction of international and domestic law has long preoccupied international legal theoreticians and has produced a copious academic literature. It would therefore be difficult to approach the topic of this chapter without adverting, at least in passing, to this substantial body of scholarship and the conclusions it has drawn. Accordingly, this chapter begins with a brief review of the main theoretical models that have been developed by international lawyers to describe (or perhaps prescribe) the interaction of the international and domestic legal systems. It then proceeds with an examination of various factors that influence the potential domestic multijural effects of treaties. For purposes of discussion, these factors may be grouped into two main categories; the first of these includes factors inhering in domestic legal systems themselves and the second concerns factors arising from the nature and content of particular treaty regimes. Some concluding remarks will then be offered suggesting that the potential multijural effects of treaties within domestic legal systems are the product of complex interactions between these various factors.

Theoretical Approaches to the Interaction of International and Domestic Law

Theoretical approaches to the relationship between domestic and international (or, more specifically for our purposes, treaty) law have traditionally fallen into two principal schools of thought: 'monism' and 'dualism'.[6]

---

4 *Vienna Convention, ibid.*, art. 27; *Treatment of Polish Nationals and Other Persons of Polish Origin or Speech in the Danzig Territory* (1932), at 24.

5 For example, where domestic law is already in line with the relevant treaty norms, or where performance of the treaty does not rely or have an impact on the domestic legal system.

6 For a concise overview of the monist-dualist debate among international lawyers generally, see Fitzmaurice (1957), 'The General Principles of International Law: Considered

Monism

'Monism' is premised on a conception of law as a continuous, organic phenomenon that is an integral part of the fabric of a single, greater human society. In this model, legal systems are not compartmentalized or self-contained regimes, but rather localized adaptations of a broader, universal social phenomenon known as 'law'.[7]

Applying this model to the relationship between domestic legal systems and the international legal system, pure monists posit an essential continuity of and unity between such systems. Thus, while the rules of each domestic legal system might only be applicable to certain classes of persons and transactions (usually those tied, by some theory of jurisdiction, to each such system), and the rules of international law would, similarly, only be applicable to different classes of persons and transactions (that is, international legal persons, such as states, and their interactions), this provides no basis, in the view of monists, for positing the essential separateness of domestic and international law.[8] In other words, drawing such a rigid distinction would be no more justifiable than suggesting that different areas of domestic law constitute essentially separate legal systems merely because they speak to different legal subjects. For example, the fact that Canada's corporate law governs the rights and obligations of corporate rather than natural legal persons, or that Canadian criminal law is concerned with fundamentally different transactions than is Canadian contract law, does not cause us to treat these various bodies of rules as essentially separate systems of law unto themselves. Rather, we merely consider them to be integral elements of a single, broader Canadian legal framework. Monists would carry this analysis over to rules of international law as well and posit a single, global legal framework.

While this might seem a somewhat abstract point of classification, monists would nevertheless argue that conceiving of domestic and international legal systems as one continuous whole has practical implications for their interaction. The first such implication is that they *will* interact. And while there are variations on this theme in the academic literature, the predominant view is that this interactive relationship should be viewed in essentially hierarchical terms. That is, international law, for most monists, should be considered normatively 'superior'

---

from the Standpoint of the Rule of Law', at 68-85. See also Starke (1936), 'Monism and Dualism in the Theory of International Law', at 66; and Currie, *supra* note 3, at 195-99.

7 See, for example, Kelsen (1966), *Principles of International Law*, at 290-301, 553-88. See also Kelsen (1967), *Pure Theory of Law*; and Lauterpacht (1966), *The Function of Law in the International Community*.

8 Indeed the tendency, in the twentieth and twenty-first centuries, for international law to extend its normative reach to individuals and to subject-areas traditionally reserved to domestic legal regulation has only strengthened the monist argument.

to domestic law.[9] This view might be of no consequence as long as international and domestic law purport to govern purely distinct subjects and subject matter. However, where their remits overlap, the practical consequence of the essential continuity of the domestic and international legal systems, coupled with the posited normative superiority of international law, would be to give preeminence to the rule of international law: it would supersede conflicting domestic rules.

The overall, long-term effect of such interaction would therefore be, at least theoretically, the gradual harmonization of domestic law with international law and, given that all states are subject to a single, universal system of international law, the gradual harmonization of domestic law across domestic legal systems. The concomitant long-term result would be the suppression of legal pluralism across domestic legal systems, although, perhaps paradoxically, each such system would in some sense be 'vertically multijuralized' through domestic ingestion of international legal rules, a phenomenon to which we return below.

Dualism

By contrast, the competing 'dualist' school of thought rejects most of the foregoing monist premises and conclusions.[10] In particular, dualists posit, as their starting point, the essential separateness or insularity of domestic legal systems, both from one another and from any supranational sources of law. This view is rooted in the Westphalian[11] notion of the essential sovereignty of the modern nation-state, pursuant to which every state enjoys inherent and exclusive sovereign authority to regulate matters that are of domestic concern. This sovereign authority is subject only to the strictures of international law, which are, by definition, limited to matters of purely international – that is, inter-state – concern.

9 A largely discredited, early variant on this monist model posited the normative superiority of domestic law: see, for example, Wenzel (1920), *Juristiche Grundprobleme – Zugleich eine Untersuchung zum Begriff des Staates und Problem des Völkerrechts*, at 351-59, 385-421.

10 See, for example, Hegel (1975), *Natural Law: The Scientific Ways of Treating Law, its Place in Moral Philosophy, and its Relation to the Positive Sciences of Law*; Anzilotti (1955), *Corso di diritto internazionale*, at 49-63. See also Lauterpacht (ed.) and Oppenheim (1955), *International Law: A Treatise*, at 37-39; Strupp (1934), 'Les règles générales du droit de la paix' at 389-418.

11 The reference to a 'Westphalian' conception of the modern nation-state harkens back to the Peace of Westphalia of 1648, which concluded the Thirty Years' War and announced the emergence of a new socio-political arrangement in Europe. That arrangement was premised upon the essential sovereignty of nation-states rather than their subjection to supranational legal authority, whether imperial, ecclesiastical or otherwise. That conception remains the foundation of the modern state and of modern international law. See generally Currie, *supra* note 3 at 5-16.

In this conception, therefore, the distinction between domestic and international law is not merely that each applies to different subjects and subject matter.[12] It is, rather, that these different subjects and subject matter inhabit fundamentally different legal universes. In other words, for a dualist, the distinction between domestic legal systems and the international legal system is *not* like the differences between domestic law applicable to corporations and that applicable to individuals, or between domestic criminal and contract law. Rather, the entire normative structures of the two types of system – including the sources of the law, its binding effect, the fora in which it is adjudicated, indeed the very nature of the society to which it pertains – are fundamentally different.

The practical consequence of the dualist view of the relationship (or rather, the lack thereof) between the domestic and the international legal orders is the essential insularity of the former. In this model, international, and specifically treaty, law plays no direct harmonizing effect because it has no domestic legal relevance or authority at all. Legal heterogeneity across national legal systems is thus preserved, albeit subject to the prospect that domestic legal systems may continue to experience multijural effects inspired by the entrenched diversity of domestic legal orders, unharmonized by operation of international treaty law. Of course, the extent to which any particular domestic legal system *would* experience such multijural effects (including any of a 'vertical' character, as alluded to above) would depend entirely on whether that legal system *chose*, in the exercise of its sovereign prerogatives, to incorporate foreign – including international – legal concepts within its domestic legal order.

Obviously, each of these theoretical models, to the extent it reflects reality, would have profound implications for the domestic harmonizing or 'multijuralizing' potential of treaty law. The point of this chapter, however, is to show that neither of these theoretical models is an adequate explanation of the real-life interaction of treaty and domestic law or of the multijural significance of the former for the latter. Each model fails to take into account a wide variety of factors that in fact have an impact on whether any given treaty regime will produce harmonizing or multijuralizing effects within domestic legal systems. It is to a discussion of the most important of these factors that we now turn.

Factors Relevant to the Harmonizing or Multijuralizing Potential of Treaties

As suggested above, factors relevant to the potential multijural impact of treaties within domestic legal systems may conveniently be examined from two perspectives: first, factors inherent in domestic legal systems themselves; and second, those rooted in the particular treaty regime being considered. Each is considered in turn below.

---

12 A distinction that is, in any event, waning; see discussion *supra* note 8.

Domestic Receptivity to Treaty Law

Domestic constitutional orders and the reception of treaty law As it turns out, the monist and dualist approaches to the interaction of international and domestic law not only have their theoretical, academic proponents but also their adherents in the real world of state constitutional orders. Each state, in other words, determines the extent to which its domestic legal order is monist – that is, 'open' or subject to international treaties to which it has subscribed – or dualist – that is, insulated from the legal effects of such treaties. This is a major shortcoming of both the monist and dualist theories in the abstract, at least as applied to the interaction of international treaty and domestic law generally: neither in fact reflects the approach to international treaty law taken by states generally, because there is no such general approach. Each state determines, based on a variety of domestic historical, political and constitutional factors, the porosity or impermeability of the membrane that separates its domestic legal order from the effect of treaties to which it is a party.[13]

Thus, some states adopt a rigidly dualist stance. In such a state, the legal effects of a duly ratified treaty are strictly confined to the international legal plane, such that the rules contained in the treaty have no direct legal effect or relevance *within* the domestic legal system. A domestic court faced with an issue the subject matter of which is addressed in a treaty binding on that state need not, and indeed ought not, pay any heed to the treaty provision itself. Until and unless a corresponding rule of domestic law is put in place by some domestic law-making mechanism, the treaty rule remains foreign to, and therefore inapplicable within, the domestic legal system. Strictly speaking, moreover, the treaty rule itself *never* becomes domestically applicable in such a system, even if it is transformed into a domestic rule of law by the domestic law-making authority: in such cases, it is in fact the *domestic* rule of law that has domestic legal effect, and the treaty rule, while the source of inspiration for the corresponding domestic rule, nevertheless remains foreign, inapplicable law.

The classic example of such a system is that of the United Kingdom. Under the British constitution, the conduct of foreign relations, including the conclusion of treaty relations, comes within the royal prerogative powers exercised by the executive branch of government. However, as it is a fundamental rule of the British constitution that the executive branch has no domestic law-making authority of its own, the conclusion of a treaty can have no domestic legal effects *per se*.[14] Performance of treaty obligations dependent on changes to domestic law therefore requires Parliamentary action. Until a statute is enacted giving domestic

13 For informative reviews of the variability of state practice in this area, see, for example, Cassese (2005), *International Law*, at 213-37; and Shaw, *supra* note 3, at 135-162.

14 *The Parlement Belge* (1879), 4 P.D. 129 at 150, 154-55. See also *R. v. Keyn (The Franconia Case)* (1876), 2 Exch. 63 (C.C.R.), per Cockburn C.J.

legal effect to a treaty's provisions, the general rule is that the treaty has no direct application within the domestic legal system.[15] To similar effect are the treaty reception regimes of Israel[16] and Australia,[17] to give but a few examples.

At the other end of the spectrum are states which adopt a decidedly monist stance. In such a state, treaty obligations binding *on* the state as a matter of international law are also considered binding *within* the state as a matter of domestic law. This is so whether or not the treaty rule in question has been 'transformed' into a domestic rule of law by some domestic law-making process. In other words, treaties binding on the state have direct effect within the state, such that a domestic court may and usually must have regard to the provisions of the treaty itself. Moreover, in some such states, treaty-based rules will outrank conflicting rules of domestic origin. For example, the constitutions of France,[18] Germany,[19] Greece,[20] Japan,[21] the Netherlands,[22] Spain[23] and the Russian Federation[24] all provide for automatic, direct effect of binding treaty obligations within their respective domestic legal orders, as well as the supremacy of such treaty rules over conflicting domestic

15 *Maclaine Watson v. Department of Trade and Industry*, [1989] 3 All E.R. 523 at 531 (H.L.), per Lord Oliver. There are some limited exceptions to this general rule: see generally Fatima (2005), *Using International Law in Domestic Courts*, at 283-289; and Shaw, *supra* note 3, at 136-138.

16 Lapidoth (1990), 'International Law Within the Israeli Legal System'; Cassese, *supra*, note 13 at 226; Shaw, *supra* note 3, at 151.

17 See *Minister of State for Immigration and Ethnic Affairs v. Ah Hin Teoh FC* (1995), 128 A.L.R. 353 at 361 (H.C.), per Mason C.J. and Deane J.; see also *Kruger v. Commonwealth of Australia* (1997), 146 A.L.R. 126 (H.C.).

18 *Constitution of the French Republic, 1958*, as amended to 2005, in Blaustein and Flanz (eds) (2005), *Constitutions of the Countries of the World*, Binder XII, art. 55. See also Dupuy (1998), *Droit international public*, at 369ff.

19 *Basic Law for the Federal Republic of Germany, 1949*, as amended by the Unification Treaty of 31 August 1990, and the Federal Statute of 23 September 1990 (*Federal Law Gazette* II, p. 885), s. 59.

20 *Constitution of Greece, 1975*, as amended to 2001, in Blaustein and Flanz, *supra* note 18, art. 28(1).

21 *Constitution of Japan, 1946*, in Blaustein and Flanz, *supra* note 18, art. 98(2). See also Iwasawa (1993), 'The Relationship Between International Law and National Law: Japanese Experiences', at 345.

22 *Constitution of the Netherlands, 1983*, as amended to 2002, in Blaustein and Flanz (eds) (2003a), *Constitutions of the Countries of the World*, Binder XIII, art. 94.

23 *Constitution of Spain, 1978*, as amended to 1992, in Blaustein and Flanz (eds) (2003b), *Constitutions of the Countries of the World*, Binder XVII, art. 96(1).

24 *Constitution of the Russian Federation, 1993*, in Blaustein and Flanz (eds) (2002), *Constitutions of the Countries of the World*, Binder XV, art. 15(4). See also *Federal Law on International Treaties of the Russian Federation, 1995*, s. 5; Butler (2002), *The Law of Treaties in Russia and the Commonwealth of Independent States*.

law.[25] It is, however, a common requirement of such constitutional systems that the treaty be published in the domestic legislative journal or gazette as a condition of such direct effect. It should also be noted that, even in such monistic systems, treaty provisions which are non-self-executing – that is, that require some domestic legislative adaptation for their workable implementation in the domestic legal system – are not generally considered to have direct domestic effect absent such legislative adaptation.[26]

A variation on this approach is to recognize the direct domestic legal effect of validly concluded treaties, but to take a more nuanced position with respect to the issue of precedence in cases of conflict between treaty rules and domestic law. For example, the South African constitution provides that the self-executing provisions of treaties to which South Africa is a party automatically form part of domestic law, provided they do not conflict with the South African constitution or Parliamentary enactments.[27] A slightly more robust and well-known position prevails in the United States, where the self-executing provisions of duly ratified treaties have direct domestic effect as federal law.[28] The result is that such treaty provisions supersede conflicting state law, at least until abrogated by subsequent, conflicting federal law.[29] A common feature of the South African, American and many other domestic systems, however, is a domestic rule of statutory interpretation that seeks to reconcile, if at all possible, the domestic legal effect of treaty provisions and facially conflicting domestic legislation.[30]

There are also states that fall somewhere between the dualist-monist extremes. This is where I would place the Canadian legal system, notwithstanding the

25 Though generally not supremacy over the domestic constitution. An exception here is the Constitution of the Netherlands, which in some circumstances appears to contemplate the supremacy of treaty obligations over the Dutch constitution itself: see *supra* note 22, art. 91(3); Jacobs (ed.) (1987), *The Effect of Treaties in Domestic Law*, at 109; Cassese, *supra* note 13, at 229, 234; Shaw, *supra* note 3, at 156.

26 For a review state practice with respect to non-self-executing treaties, see Cassese, *supra* note 13 at 227.

27 *Constitution of the Republic of South Africa, 1996*, in Blaustein and Flanz (eds.) (2004), *Constitutions of the Countries of the World*, Binder XVI, s. 231(4).

28 *Constitution of the United States of America*, in Blaustein and Flanz (eds.) (1996), *Constitutions of the Countries of the World*, Binder XIX, art. VI(2); *Foster v. Neilson* (1829), 27 U.S. (2 Pet.) 253 (U.S.S.C.); *Edye v. Robertson* (1884), 112 U.S. 580 (U.S.S.C.). For discussion of the distinction between the treatment of self-executing and non-self-executing treaties in U.S. law, see Iwasawa (1986), 'The Doctrine of Self-Executing Treaties in the United States: A Critical Analysis'; and Vázquez (1995), 'The Four Doctrines of Self-Executing Treaties'.

29 *Whitney v. Robertson* (1888), 124 U.S. 190 (U.S.S.C.). See also American Law Institute, *Restatement of the Law (Third): The Foreign Relations Law of the United States*, vol. 1, at 63ff.

30 See, for example, s. 233 of the South African Constitution, *supra* note 27; *U.S.* v. *Palestine Liberation Organization* (1988), 695 F.Supp. 1465 (N.Y. Dist. Ct.).

conventional view that Canada's approach to treaty law is dualist in much the same way as that of the United Kingdom. According to that traditional view, binding treaty commitments entered into by the federal executive branch may be binding on Canada on the international place, but have no direct effect in domestic law until and unless they are expressly 'transformed' into domestic law by statute.[31] If this were a correct characterization, Canada would of course fall into the first category of states described above.

However, I would contend that this is not in fact an accurate picture of the Canadian approach to treaty law. There are three specific reasons why I say so. First, it is well established in Canadian law that Canadian courts are required, to the extent possible, to interpret domestic law in such a way as to avoid conflicts with treaties to which Canada is a party, whether or not those treaties have been transformed into domestic law.[32] Second, it is equally well established that, whether for purposes of applying this reconciliatory rule or otherwise, Canadian courts are to resort directly to the treaty text itself,[33] and to apply international legal rules of treaty interpretation[34] in interpreting, in domestic proceedings, treaties to which Canada is a party.[35] The combination of these two rules is clearly to give some degree of direct and perhaps even, in some circumstances, superseding effect to treaty law within the Canadian legal system, if only by way of interpretive techniques. Third, recent case law in the Supreme Court of Canada has underscored the extent to which Canadian common law courts may derive policy guidance from treaties entered into by the federal executive when incrementally developing the

---

31 *Francis v. Canada*, [1956] S.C.R. 618; *Capital Cities Communications Inc. v. Canadian Radio-Television Commission*, [1978] 2 S.C.R. 141; *R. v. Canada Labour Relations Board, ex parte Federal Electric Corporation*, (1964) 44 D.L.R. (2d) 440 at 453-56 (Man. Q.B.); Brunnée and Toope (2002), 'A Hesitant Embrace: The Application of International Law by Canadian Courts', at 22; R. St.J. Macdonald, 'The Relationship Between International Law and Domestic Law in Canada' in Macdonald, Morris and Johnston (eds) (1974), *Canadian Perspectives on International Law and Organization*, at 88; Currie, *supra* note 3 at 205. The basis for this position is the rule of Canadian constitutional law to the effect that the executive branch has no independent power to enact domestic law, such function being the exclusive preserve of the legislative branch.

32 See, for example, *Daniels v. White and The Queen*, [1968] S.C.R. 517 at 541; *Schreiber v. Canada (Attorney General)*, [2002] 3 S.C.R. 269 at para. 50; Sullivan (2002), *Sullivan and Driedger on the Construction of Statutes*; Côté (2000), *The Interpretation of Legislation in Canada*, at 367-69; Brunnée and Toope, *ibid.* at 21; van Ert (2002), *Using International Law in Canadian Courts*, at 99-136.

33 *National Corn Growers Assn. v. Canada (Import Tribunal)*, [1990] 2 S.C.R. 1324 at 1371.

34 As evidenced in the *Vienna Convention*, *supra* note 3, arts. 31-33.

35 *Pushpanathan v. Canada (Minister of Citizenship and Immigration)*, [1998] 1 S.C.R. 982 at 1019-22.

common law or interpreting domestic statutes or even constitutional texts.[36] This is of course a far cry from cloaking such treaties with direct, binding, domestic effect, but it does show that in Canada a nominally dualist stance with respect to treaty law has in fact given way to an approach that has shades of monism, and that is considerably receptive to the domestic legal effects of treaty rules *per se*.[37] (Indeed, there is evidence of a similar tendency in other nominally dualist jurisdictions, such as the United Kingdom.[38])

Furthermore, notice that the three rules of domestic Canadian law that produce these effects specifically concern the ways in which domestic *courts* may take cognizance of treaty law. The significance of these rules is therefore likely magnified in a domestic legal system – such as the common law system – that attributes binding precedential character, or law-making effects, to such judicial activity. That is, if rules of interpretation are, in essence, modes of (perhaps indirect) treaty reception, and interpretation is in essence a judicial exercise, the domestic normative impact of such judicial interpretive activity can only be enhanced in common law systems.

This is not to say, however, that the predilection of states for either monist or dualist treaty reception regimes is necessarily dictated or predicated upon the nature of their dominant legal tradition – for example whether they follow a common law, civilist or other legal tradition. In fact, there is a wide variation of practice, in terms of domestic receptivity to treaty law, within legal traditions.[39] Thus, the cases reviewed above show that civilist jurisdictions are not uniformly monist in outlook when it comes to the domestic legal effects of treaties. Similarly, common law jurisdictions are not uniformly dualist in outlook, as illustrated by the relatively monist stance taken by the United States, or for that matter, the increasingly monist stance being adopted by the Canadian (and British) courts. Rather, the extent to which any particular domestic legal system is receptive or impervious to the effects of treaty law depends ultimately on the particular provisions of its own constitution.[40]

Given these observations, how is the position occupied by any given state on the monist-dualist spectrum relevant to the potential multijural effects of treaties?

---

36 See, for example, *Reference re Public Service Employee Relations Act (Alta.)*, [1987] 1 S.C.R. 313; *Slaight Communications Inc. v. Davidson*, [1989] 1 S.C.R. 1038 at 1056-57, per Dickson C.J.; *Baker v. Canada (Minister of Citizenship and Immigration)*, [1999] 2 S.C.R. 817 at 861, per L'Heureux-Dubé J.; *Suresh v. Canada (Minister of Citizenship and Immigration)*, [2002] 1 S.C.R. 3 at paras. 59-78.

37 See generally H.M. Kindred, 'The Use and Abuse of International Legal Sources by Canadian Courts: Searching for a Principled Approach' in Fitzgerald (ed.) (2006), *The Globalized Rule of Law: Relationships Between International and Domestic Law*, at 5; A. de Mestral and E. Fox-Decent, 'Implementation and Reception: The Congeniality of Canada's Legal Order to International Law' in *ibid.* at 31; and van Ert, *supra* note 32.

38 See generally Fatima, *supra* note 15, at 290-358.

39 *See* Shaw, *supra* note 3, at 160-161.

40 *Ibid.* at 161.

There are at least two profound multijural implications of a state's constitutional rules governing treaty reception.

The first of these concerns what might be referred to as 'horizontal' multijural effects. A state that accords direct and controlling effect to treaty law within its domestic legal system will necessarily have its domestic law harmonized with that of other states which are parties to the same treaties and which follow the same monist approach to treaty law. The overall result will be the suppression of differences across these domestic legal orders within the subject matter of the treaty. A secondary consequence of this direct harmonization effect, especially in the case of broadly ratified multilateral treaties, will be the gradual suppression of opportunities for multijural cross-pollination between these domestic legal orders. In other words, if variations in domestic law are eliminated through the direct harmonizing effects of treaties, the diversity of the 'stock' of domestic legal approaches to any given legal problem will be commensurately reduced. By reducing this diversity and suppressing future domestic legal innovations inspired by peculiar legal norms in foreign domestic legal systems, the harmonizing effects of treaties are reinforced. All other things being equal, the tendency will therefore be to promote, both directly and indirectly, a form of 'monojuralism'.

By contrast, states adopting more or less dualist stances *vis-à-vis* treaty law preserve their ability to adapt, by way of their domestic transformation or implementation processes, rules of treaty law. This local adaptation or 'filtering' process thus creates opportunities for local variations on the common theme of the underlying treaty regime. The possibility of heterogeneous, local 'translations' of treaty rules is thus preserved, as is the potential, therefore, for future multijural cross-pollination between domestic legal orders that in fact pursue distinctive implementation approaches to common treaty rules.

Paradoxically, however, the potential for what has been referred to above as 'vertical' multijural effects is inversely proportional to that for the horizontal multijural effects just described. A domestic legal system that accords direct domestic effect to treaty rules is of course one that embraces rules of law elaborated by and within another legal system – in particular the international legal system. By definition, therefore, according direct domestic effect to treaties is to inject an element of foreign – that is, international – law into the domestic legal system. Moreover, to the extent that treaty rules themselves are informed and shaped by the domestic legal experiences and imperatives of the various parties negotiating the treaty, domestic constitutional orders that are receptive to treaty law provide vehicles for the direct domestic implantation of foreign *domestic* legal concepts as well.

By contrast, a strictly dualist approach to domestic reception of treaty law, while not necessarily an insurmountable barrier to such vertical multijural effects, does nevertheless present additional hurdles. In particular, a refusal on the part of the domestic law-making branch to receive the treaty rule at all will obviously prevent vertical injection of foreign legal concepts into local legal culture. Such a phenomenon can be expected to be relatively rare, however, given universal recognition of the *pacta sunt servanda* principle and the consensual nature of treaty formation. Beyond this, however, even the process of transforming a treaty rule for purposes of implementing it domestically introduces opportunities for stripping the treaty rule of some or all of its foreign elements, thus minimizing 'contamination' of local law by foreign legal concepts, be they of an international or foreign domestic character. In short, while a dualist system certainly provides opportunities for preserving a degree of heterogeneity across domestic legal systems, it will tend to do so at the expense of the immediate multijuralizing effect that would otherwise be produced by according direct domestic effect to the treaty rule itself. The extent to which this effect may flow, however, depends heavily on the mechanism(s) by which treaty law is in fact transformed into domestic law in dualist systems. We turn now to a consideration of this further domestic legal factor affecting the multijural potential of treaties.

Domestic modes of treaty reception or transformation As suggested in the preceding section, another factor affecting the potential for domestic multijural effects of treaties – one that will be relevant in those states that require some form of domestic transformation or implementation of treaty rules before they can have domestic effect – is the means by which such transformation or implementation is carried out within that domestic legal system.

There are a number of ways in which a rule of treaty law that does not have direct domestic effect may be transformed into domestic law.[41] For example, a straightforward approach is merely to enact a piece of legislation that refers directly to the treaty and provides that it shall have domestic legal effect as though its provisions had been enacted as domestic legislation.[42] This scenario is closest, for purposes of evaluating its multijural implications, to direct domestic legal effect of the treaty itself in a monist state. For all practical intents and purposes, the treaty rule in such a case becomes, in terms, the domestic rule. There is no adaptation of the treaty rule for domestic purposes, and hence no barrier to the effective vertical harmonization of domestic and treaty law, or the horizontal harmonization of the domestic law of states parties sharing this and/or the monist approach to treaty reception.

A different approach to domestic treaty transformation is to enact domestic legislation that repeats, *verbatim*, the rule as articulated in the treaty itself.[43] The effects of this approach will tend to be very similar to those of the 'incorporation by reference' approach just described. There is, however, potential for subtle

41 See de Mestral and Fox-Decent, *supra* note 37, at 42-56 for a survey of implementation techniques.

42 For a discussion of use of this implementation technique in Canada, see J.M. Keyes and R. Sullivan, 'A Legislative Perspective on the Interaction of International and Domestic Law' in Fitzgerald (ed.) (2006), *The Globalized Rule of Law: Relationships Between International and Domestic Law*, at 311-316. For a review of UK practice here see Fatima, *supra* note 15, at 57-61.

43 See Keyes and Sullivan, *ibid.* at 317-318.

differences between the two approaches. For example, in the case of a *verbatim* repetition of the terms of a treaty in a domestic statute, domestic rules of statutory interpretation may apply to the enactment, whereas in the case of incorporation by reference, domestic law may require resort to international rules of treaty interpretation for purposes of construing the referenced treaty text.[44] Another potential difference is that *verbatim* enactment of a treaty's terms will tend to 'freeze' the domestic version of the treaty regime as a domestic statute, whereas the domestic meaning of treaty law incorporated by reference into domestic law may continue to evolve as the treaty regime itself evolves – for example, under the influence of the practice of parties to the treaty.[45] In other words, while the multijural implications of the *verbatim* enactment of treaty rules will in most cases approximate those of incorporation by reference and/or granting direct domestic effect to those rules, this approach nevertheless retains some scope for differentiation between the treaty scheme and the statutory scheme. If exploited, the result may be the introduction of variations across ostensible legislative implementation schemes in various countries. Thus, in addition to the vertical multijural effects inherent in enactment of a domestic implementing statute, a degree of heterogeneity will also be preserved across domestic legal orders. The seeds of future, potential horizontal multijural effects will have been planted.

Finally, domestic transformation of treaty law may take the form of enacting provisions that attempt to capture the essence of the treaty while nevertheless departing from its precise wording. The reasons for doing so may vary. For example, modifying the wording of a treaty for purposes of domestic implementation may in fact be an attempt to faithfully reflect the meaning of the treaty in domestic law, taking into account the fact that domestic law may attribute peculiar legal meanings to some of the terms used in the treaty, meanings that may depart from the intentions of its framers.[46] If this is indeed the goal, and it is achieved, the effect will be to harmonize the domestic legal effect of the treaty with the meaning of the treaty itself, as well as with the expression given to it in other implementing domestic legal systems. Alternatively, departure from the specific terms of the treaty may in fact be driven by domestic legal imperatives other than faithful reflection of the international legal meaning of the treaty. The greater the number and extent of such departures, the greater will be the distinctions that endure as between treaty and domestic law, as well as between various domestic laws purporting to implement the treaty. The treaty's harmonizing effect will accordingly be diminished, again preserving a measure of legal heterogeneity across domestic legal orders.

Indeed, elements of all these approaches can be found within Canadian treaty implementation practice. An example of simple transformation or incorporation by reference in domestic legislation is the *Foreign Missions and International*

---

44 *Ibid.* at 317.

45 A process expressly contemplated in the *Vienna Convention, supra* note 3, art. 31(3)(b). See also Cassese, *supra* note 13, at 222.

46 Keyes and Sullivan, *supra* note 42, at 317.

Organizations Act,[47] which implements in Canada key provisions of the *Vienna Convention on Diplomatic Relations, 1961*[48] and the *Vienna Convention on Consular Relations, 1963*.[49] Other than a few provisions relating to interpretation and the establishment of certain administrative procedures necessary to give effect to the provisions of both conventions, the *Act* simply gives relevant provisions of those conventions legal force in Canadian law.[50] There is no attempt to restate or paraphrase the provisions of the conventions within the implementing statute. Rather, the conventions are simply included as schedules to the *Act*.[51] The potential for variations between the conventions and domestic Canadian law is thus minimized.

A different approach is taken in Canada's *Oceans Act*,[52] which implements Canada's obligations as a party to the 1982 *United Nations Convention on the Law of the Sea* (*UNCLOS*).[53] Rather than merely including *UNCLOS* as a schedule to the *Oceans Act* and conferring domestic legal effect upon its provisions – say, those defining coastal state maritime zones – the *Oceans Act* in fact reproduces, in many instances *verbatim*, those provisions. Thus, for example, the definitions of Canada's territorial sea,[54] its contiguous zone,[55] its exclusive economic zone[56] and its continental shelf[57] borrow language directly from corresponding provisions of *UNCLOS*. To this extent, variations between the legal regime propounded in *UNCLOS* and in Canada's *Oceans Act* are minimized, and Canada's domestic rules governing the extent and nature of its maritime zones are harmonized with those of *UNCLOS* and those of other states either giving direct domestic effect to its provisions or faithfully incorporating its precise terms in domestic implementing legislation. Where there are variations in the text, of course, precisely the opposite

47 *Foreign Missions and International Organizations Act*, S.C. 1991, c. 41.

48 *Vienna Convention on Diplomatic Relations*, 18 April 1961 (in force 24 April 1964).

49 *Vienna Convention on Consular Relations*, 24 April 1963 (in force 19 March 1967).

50 *Foreign Missions and International Organizations Act*, *supra* note 47, s. 3.

51 *Ibid*., Schedules I and II.

52 *Oceans Act*, S.C. 1996, c.31.

53 *United Nations Convention on the Law of the Sea*, 10 December 1982 (in force 16 November 1994) [hereinafter UNCLOS].

54 Compare *Oceans Act*, *supra* note 52, s. 4 with *UNCLOS*, *supra* note 54, arts. 3-4.

55 Compare *Oceans Act*, *supra* note 52, ss. 10-11 with *UNCLOS*, *supra* note 53, art. 33.

56 Compare *Oceans Act*, *supra* note 52, ss. 13-14 with *UNCLOS*, *supra* note 53, arts. 55-57.

57 Compare *Oceans Act*, *supra* note 52, ss. 17-18 with UNCLOS, *supra* note 53, arts. 76-77.

effect obtains, with attendant consequences for the maintenance of a degree of diversity in the domestic legal effects of the treaty.[58]

Finally, an illustration of domestic treaty implementation that paraphrases or draws inspiration from a treaty without relying upon its express terms is Canada's *Crimes Against Humanity and War Crimes Act*.[59] This Act implements Canada's obligations under the *Rome Statute of the International Criminal Court*.[60] In particular, pursuant to the *Rome Statute*'s complementarity provisions,[61] the Act establishes Canadian criminal jurisdiction over the 'core' international crimes of genocide, crimes against humanity and war crimes. Moreover, it defines these crimes for purposes of domestic criminal prosecutions. However, in doing so, it does not slavishly parrot or limit itself to the provisions of the *Rome Statute*. Rather, it seeks to give effect to the underlying intent of the *Rome Statute*, which is to put an end to impunity for perpetrators of the most serious international crimes, whether through their domestic or international prosecution.[62] For example, the Act extends Canadian criminal jurisdiction over core international crimes not only on the basis of the territorial and nationality principles, as does the *Rome Statute*;[63] it also does so on the basis of the passive personality and quasi-universal principles.[64]

---

58 For example, Canada chooses, in the *Oceans Act*, to rely upon a system of geographical coordinates of points joined by geodesics in order to give effect to *UNCLOS's* provisions relating to the use of straight baselines for purposes of establishing the boundaries of a coastal state's maritime zones: see *Oceans Act*, *supra* note 52, ss. 5, 13, 17 and 25, and *UNCLOS*, *supra* note 53, art. 7.

59 *Crimes Against Humanity and War Crimes Act*, S.C. 2000, c. 24 [hereinafter *CAHWCA*].

60 *Rome Statute of the International Criminal Court*, 17 July 1998 (in force 1 July 2002) [hereinafter *Rome Statute*]. Canada's *CAHWCA* was, incidentally, the first comprehensive national legislation implementing the *Rome Statute* adopted anywhere in the world.

61 The *Rome Statute* provides that the Court may only exercise jurisdiction over the core crimes where national legal systems fail or are unable genuinely to do so, clearly making the Court's jurisdiction secondary or 'complementary' to that of national criminal systems: *ibid.*, art. 17.

62 *Ibid.*, Preamble: ' ... *Affirming* that the most serious crimes of concern to the international community as a whole must not go unpunished and that their effective prosecution must be ensured by taking measures at the national level and by enhancing international cooperation, *Determined* to put an end to impunity for the perpetrators of these crimes and thus to contribute to the prevention of such crimes, *Recalling* that it is the duty of every State to exercise its criminal jurisdiction over those responsible for international crimes .... '

63 *Ibid.*, article 12(2).

64 *CAHWCA*, *supra* note 59, s. 8. 'Quasi-universal' jurisdiction refers to the exercise of jurisdiction over crimes having no territorial or national links to Canada other than the presence of the accused in Canadian territory at the time such jurisdiction is exercised. This 'presence requirement' belies accurate classification of such jurisdiction as genuinely 'universal': see *Case Concerning the Arrest Warrant of 11 April 2000 (Democratic Republic*

Similarly, the definitions of genocide, crimes against humanity and war crimes adopted in the Act take as their starting point the very precise definitions of these same crimes in the *Rome Statute*,[65] but go further in defining these crimes in terms of customary or conventional international law as it may exist from time to time.[66] In other words, while ostensibly implementing the *Rome Statute*, Canada's *Crimes Against Humanity and War Crimes Act* adopts a distinctly Canadian approach to fulfilling its treaty obligation to ensure accountability for perpetrators of the most serious international crimes. This approach could be contrasted, for example, with that taken by Australia[67] and Germany[68] (largely verbatim enactment of the *Rome Statute* definitions of crimes, with variations in terminology and some elements of crimes), or by the United Kingdom[69] (direct incorporation by reference of the *Rome Statute*'s definitions of crimes).

It will therefore be seen that the Canadian legal system alone displays considerable variability as to the extent to which it embraces or resists the harmonizing effects of international treaty law. To the extent that other dualist jurisdictions adopt a similarly eclectic approach to the mechanisms by which treaties are transformed into domestic law, one can expect concomitant variability in the domestic harmonizing effects of such treaties.

Nature and Content of Treaty Regimes

Thus far we have focused on features of the particular domestic legal system that either enhance or undermine the potential multijural effects of treaties. We turn now to a consideration of the topic from the opposite perspective. What are the features of treaties themselves that affect their potential for either fostering or suppressing multijural effects?

International treaties and conventions assume different forms and address different types of subject matter, all of which may play a role in their potential multijural effects. For example, treaties may be essentially contractual in character (merely providing for reciprocal rights and obligations of performance) or they may assume a 'law-making' character (for example, codifying or restating certain areas of customary international law, or articulating novel normative regimes of general application). They may also be bilateral (between only two states) or multilateral (between more than two states), and in the latter case may permit

---

of the Congo v. Belgium), [2002] I.C.J. Rep. 5, Joint Separate Opinion of Judges Higgins, Kooijmans and Buergenthal at paras. 41, 45.

65 *Rome Statute, supra* note 60, arts. 6-8.

66 *CAHWCA*, *supra* note 59, ss. 4(4), 6(4).

67 *Criminal Code Act, 1995* (Aust.), No. 12, as amended by the *International Criminal Court (Consequential Amendments) Act, 2002* (Aust.), No. 42, ss. 268.3-268.101.

68 *Act to Introduce the Code of Crimes Against International Law* (Germany), 26 June 2002, ss. 6-12.

69 *International Criminal Court Act, 2001* (U.K.), c. 17, s. 50.

or forbid reservations (that is, unilateral changes) to their terms upon ratification or accession by states parties. They may address subject-matter that is typically the subject of international, rather than domestic, legal regulation, whereas others specifically impose obligations in areas (such as criminal law) that traditionally are of direct concern to each state's domestic legal system. They may also incorporate dispute resolution mechanisms that may themselves be sources of binding legal obligations ancillary to the treaty regime itself. Consideration will therefore be given to the relevance of these various attributes of treaties for their potential multijural effects.

Treaty-contracts vs. 'law-making' treaties The first such feature has to do with the overall character of the treaty regime. International lawyers distinguish here between 'treaty-contracts' on the one hand, and 'law-making' treaties on the other. The first of these, usually taking the form of bilateral treaties, typically involve mutual undertakings that are essentially contractual in nature. That is, they involve specific performance obligations in respect of which a *quid pro quo* is required in return. A simple illustration of such a treaty might be an agreement between two neighbouring states on cooperation in patrolling their common border; or on the joint development of a new defensive system. In many such cases, the nature of the mutual rights and obligations created under the treaty will have little or no significance within the domestic legal systems of either state party to the treaty, particularly in circumstances where performance of the treaty obligations comes within the exclusive purview of the executive branch of each government. In such cases, therefore, the effects of such treaties for the domestic legal systems of either state will be modest or non-existent. In other words, because these treaties are not fundamentally about the creation of rules of law, their potential relevance to issues of domestic multijuralism is minimal. A concrete example of such a treaty would be the recently renewed NORAD agreement between Canada and the United States,[70] performance of which is unlikely to require changes to domestic law in either country and the domestic multijural consequences of which can, accordingly, be expected to be nil.

Law-making treaties, in contrast, typically assume a multilateral format. Indeed, the goal of a law-making treaty is usually to achieve universal participation in the treaty regime so as to approximate, as far as possible, a sort of international statutory effect for the treaty. Further, rather than focusing on mutually enforceable rights and obligations of the parties, law-making treaties tend to set out normative regimes of general application. Examples of law-making treaties include the

70 Agreement between the Government of Canada and the Government of the United States of America on the North American Aerospace Defense Command, 28 April 2006 (in force 12 May 2006), online: http://www.treaty-accord.gc.ca/ViewTreaty.asp?Treaty_ID=105060 (last accessed 30 January 2007).

Genocide Convention;[71] the *Vienna Convention on Diplomatic Relations*;[72] the *International Covenant on Civil and Political Rights*[73] and its sister convention, the *International Covenant on Economic, Social and Cultural Rights*;[74] the *United Nations Convention on the Law of the Sea*;[75] and the *Vienna Convention on the Law of Treaties* itself.[76] The explicit purpose of such law-making treaties is to encourage universal adherence to the norms that they set out, including through adoption, where relevant and necessary, of domestic rules of law consistent with the normative regimes they propound.

Naturally, such law-making treaties, intended as they are to have an impact on the international conduct and, in some cases, domestic practices of states parties to them, are highly relevant to issues of multijuralism. At one level, they are explicitly intended to harmonize domestic law and thus to suppress country-specific or regional variations on legal matters of concern to the international community as a whole. However, at another level, adherence to such a treaty regime generally entails an obligation to adapt one's domestic legal system so as to be able to conform to the law-making treaty regime. As we have seen above, this in itself has multijural effects in that this process involves the injection into each domestic legal system of various foreign legal elements – whether these be conceived of as the rules of treaty law themselves, or the various domestic traditions that may have influenced the final shape of those treaty rules.

Thus, the character of a treaty as either a treaty-contract or a law-making treaty will have a direct bearing on whether it will have domestic juridical effects in general, and pluralizing or harmonizing such effects in particular.

Subject-matter of the treaty Within the broad category of law-making treaties are those that establish legal regimes essentially concerned with inter-state relations or transactions confined in their scope and effects to the international sphere. A prime example of this type of law-making treaty would be the *Vienna Convention on the Law of Treaties*.[77] This widely ratified multilateral convention sets out the basic rules by which treaties between states are negotiated, concluded and brought into force;[78] the circumstances under which treaties may be amended;[79] the grounds

71 *Convention on the Prevention and Punishment of the Crime of Genocide*, 9 December 1948 (in force 12 January 1951).

72 *Vienna Convention on Diplomatic Relations*, 18 April 1961 (in force 24 April 1964).

73 *International Covenant on Civil and Political Rights*, 16 December 1966 (in force 23 March 1976).

74 *International Covenant on Economic, Social and Cultural Rights*, 16 December 1966 (in force 3 January 1976).

75 *UNCLOS*, *supra* note 53.

76 *Vienna Convention*, *supra* note 3.

77 *Ibid.*

78 *Ibid.*, articles 6-18.

79 *Ibid.*, articles 39-41.

upon which treaties may be considered invalid;[80] and the bases upon which treaties may be validly terminated or suspended.[81] While purporting to set out a generally applicable legal regime governing the treaty practices of states, and thus being of relevance to states in their relations *inter se*, the *Vienna Convention* is of little direct relevance for the domestic legal systems of states parties to it.[82] In particular, respect for its provisions does not depend on or require enactment of any particular rules of domestic law. Its subject-matter, in other words, is quintessentially international in character, in that it largely addresses matters of relevance only on the international legal plane.

Another example of such a multilateral law-making treaty is the *Charter of the United Nations*.[83] That treaty establishes a permanent intergovernmental organization; defines the essential attributes of that organization; elaborates the relationship between the organization and its member states; and posits a number of fundamental principles and purposes, such as the general impermissibility of the use of armed force in inter-state relations, that animate the organization and govern the mutual rights and obligations of its members. As with the *Vienna Convention*, therefore, the *Charter of the United Nations* is fundamentally concerned with relations between states on the international plane. Again, respect for its provisions does not critically depend on the shape or content of the domestic laws of parties to it, nor does it expressly contemplate domestic legal action with a view to achieving its purposes.

Because of this central characteristic of treaties such as the *Vienna Convention* and the *UN Charter* – that is, treaties the subject-matter of which concerns exclusively international issues – their potential multijural impact on domestic legal systems will be minimal at best. While such multilateral law-making treaties certainly do aim to harmonize state action at the international level, they do not anticipate or require domestic legal effects or purport to impose obligations of performance *within* domestic legal systems. They are therefore essentially 'value-neutral' in terms of domestic harmonization or multijuralism.

However, another, much broader class of multilateral treaties comprises those that touch upon issues not strictly confined in their scope to traditional inter-state interactions. These range from treaties ostensibly concerned with inter-state relations but which nevertheless impose obligations that require adaptations of domestic law, to those primarily and explicitly concerned with matters traditionally considered to be of domestic legal relevance but in respect of which certain harmonized approaches within domestic law are imposed by the treaty regime.

---

80 *Ibid.*, articles 46-53.

81 *Ibid.*, articles 54-64.

82 A potential exception to this observation is the circumstance where a domestic court or tribunal may have occasion to apply the *Vienna Convention*'s provisions on treaty interpretation in the course of giving the treaty domestic effect, whether directly or indirectly. See further *supra*, discussion accompanying notes 33 to 35.

83 *Charter of the United Nations*, 26 June 1945 (in force 24 October 1945).

An example of the former type of treaty is the recently concluded *United Nations Convention on the Jurisdictional Immunities of States and their Property.*[84] This treaty gives expression to long-recognized rules of customary international law governing the immunities enjoyed by states from the jurisdiction of foreign courts. Thus, while ostensibly seeking to ensure that relations between states are carried on in a manner respectful of their status as sovereign equals in international law, operationalization of this international legal regime necessarily entails certain limitations on exercises of jurisdiction over foreign states by domestic courts. This in turn will require states parties to the *Convention* – once it comes into force – to take necessary steps within their domestic legal orders, such as the enactment of immunities statutes, to give effect to the immunities recognized in the *Convention.* In other words, the subject matter of the legal regime articulated in this *UN Convention* is directly relevant to the domestic legal order of states parties to that *Convention.* It is thus a source of potential multijural effects within those domestic legal orders, either through direct vertical effect (in the case of states with monist reception regimes) or through domestic implementing action (in the case of states following dualist reception regimes).

Examples of treaties with subject matter even more directly relevant to domestic legal regimes abound. For example, most international human rights treaties, such as the *Covenant on Civil and Political Rights*[85] and the *International Covenant on Economic, Social and Cultural Rights,*[86] address the human rights obligations owed by states to individuals, including those within their own jurisdiction. Historically such issues were strictly the preserve of domestic legal orders, but the advent of universal human rights standards, articulated in multilateral human rights treaties, has irrevocably wrested such exclusive jurisdiction over the content of human rights standards from domestic legal orders.

The effect has been both harmonizing and pluralizing within those domestic legal orders. The harmonizing effects have flowed from the very concept of *universal* human rights norms – that is, baseline rules, from which no derogation is permitted, governing all states' conduct *vis-à-vis* individuals.

Conversely, the emergence of such universal standards in international human rights treaty law has had the effect of injecting such standards into domestic legal systems to which they may be foreign. Consider, for example, that international human rights treaties commonly impose express obligations on states parties to take steps within their domestic legal systems to ensure respect of those rights. In other words, these treaties specifically mandate changes to domestic law. For example, article 5 of the *Genocide Convention* provides that states parties shall 'enact … the necessary legislation to give effect to the provisions of the present

84 *UN Convention on the Jurisdictional Immunities of States and Their Property*, 2 December 2004 (not yet in force).

85 *Supra* note 73.

86 *Supra* note 74.

Convention … .'[87] Similarly, article 2(2) of the *International Covenant on Civil and Political Rights* requires each state party to:

> … take the necessary steps, in accordance with its constitutional processes and with the provisions of the present Covenant, to adopt such legislative or other measures as may be necessary to give effect to the rights recognized in the present Covenant.[88]

To the extent that the content of the treaty's human rights standards reflects conceptions of human rights predominantly associated with certain domestic legal traditions – for example, Western liberal democratic notions of the position of the individual in society – their incorporation into widely ratified human rights treaties has in some cases had the multijural effect of disseminating such conceptions to societies founded on other legal traditions.

Similarly, treaties addressing transnational or international criminal activity also touch upon an area of the law that states have historically regarded as coming fundamentally within their domestic jurisdiction. Yet, broadly ratified multilateral treaty regimes have emerged that target certain types of criminal conduct, impose obligations of domestic criminalization of such conduct, and in many cases add obligations of extradition and/or domestic prosecution of such conduct. Examples of such treaties abound. To illustrate, the thirteen international terrorism conventions each require the domestic criminalization of specific terrorism-related activities, the domestic assertion of extended notions of jurisdiction over such activities, and the extradition or prosecution of suspects.[89] Similarly and as we

---

87 *Supra* note 71, art. 5.

88 *Supra* note 73, art. 2(2).

89 *Convention on Offences and Certain Other Acts Committed on Board Aircraft* [hereinafter *Tokyo Convention*], 14 September 1963; *Convention for the Suppression of Unlawful Seizure of Aircraft* [hereinafter *Hague Convention*], 16 December 1970; *Convention for the Suppression of Unlawful Acts Against the Safety of Civil Aviation* [hereinafter *Montreal Convention*], 23 September 1971; *Convention on the Prevention and Punishment of Crimes Against Internationally Protected Persons, Including Diplomatic Agents* [hereinafter *Protected Persons Convention*], 14 December 1973; *International Convention Against the Taking of Hostages* [hereinafter *Hostage Convention*], 17 December 1979; *Convention on the Physical Protection of Nuclear Material* [hereinafter *Nuclear Material Convention*], 3 March 1980; *Protocol for the Suppression of Unlawful Acts of Violence at Airports Serving International Aviation* [hereinafter *Montreal Convention Protocol*], 1988; *Convention for the Suppression of Unlawful Acts Against the Safety of Maritime Navigation* [hereinafter *Maritime Safety Convention*], 10 March 1988, as amended by 2005 Protocol (not yet in force); *Protocol for the Suppression of Unlawful Acts Against the Safety of Fixed Platforms Located on the Continental Shelf* [hereinafter *Maritime Convention Protocol*], 1988, as amended by 2005 Protocol (not yet in force); *Convention on the Marking of Plastic Explosives for the Purpose of Identification* [hereinafter *Plastic Explosives Convention*], 1991; *International Convention for the Suppression of Terrorist*

have seen, the *Rome Statute of the International Criminal Court* encourages states parties to prosecute perpetrators of genocide, crimes against humanity and war crimes – as specifically defined in the *Rome Statute* itself – failing which it requires states parties to surrender suspected perpetrators of such crimes to the Court for prosecution if the alleged crime has occurred within their territory or if the suspect bears the nationality of a state party to the *Rome Statute.*[90] The *Rome Statute* also requires that states parties enact domestic legislation to permit full cooperation, as defined in the *Statute*, with the International Criminal Court.[91]

The domestic implications of such treaty obligations and their concomitant, potential multijural effects may be self-evident, but are also readily illustrated. Consider for example, Canadian criminal law, which, in keeping with its largely British pedigree, traditionally asserts criminal jurisdiction only on the basis of the territorial principle.[92] Canada's *Criminal Code* nevertheless abounds with exceptions to this traditional common law approach, for example asserting jurisdiction over criminal activity on the basis of the nationality, passive personality, security or even the quasi-universal principles of jurisdiction.[93] It largely tends to do so, however, with respect to crimes that are the subject of multilateral treaties authorizing and, in some cases, requiring the assertion of such extended notions of criminal jurisdiction. This is the case, for example, with respect to the extraterritorial jurisdiction asserted by Canada over hijacking and hostage-taking

---

Bombings [hereinafter Terrorist Bombing Convention], 15 December 1997; *International Convention for the Suppression of the Financing of Terrorism* [hereinafter *Financing Convention*], 9 December 1999; *International Convention for the Suppression of Acts of Nuclear Terrorism* [hereinafter *Nuclear Terrorism Convention*], 14 September 2005 (not yet in force).

90 *Rome Statute*, *supra* note 60, art. 86.

91 *Ibid.*, art. 88: 'States Parties shall ensure that there are procedures available under their national law for all the forms of co-operation which are specified under this Part [of the Statute].' Other illustrations of treaty provisions obliging states parties to enact specific provisions within domestic law include art. 49 of the *Geneva Convention for the Amelioration of the Condition of the Wounded and Sick in Armed Forces in the Field*, 12 August 1949; art. 50 of the *Geneva Convention for the Amelioration of the Condition of Wounded, Sick and Shipwrecked Members of Armed Forces at Sea*, 12 August 1949; art. 129 of the *Geneva Convention Relative to the Treatment of Prisoners of War*, 12 August 1949; and art. 146 of the *Geneva Convention Relative to the Protection of Civilian Persons in Time of War*, 12 August 1949, each of which provide that 'The High Contracting Parties undertake to enact any legislation necessary to provide effective penal sanctions for persons committing, or ordering to be committed, any of the grave breaches of the present Convention … '

92 *Criminal Code of Canada*, R.S.C. 1985, c. C-46, s. 6(2); *R. v. Libman*, [1985] 2 S.C.R. 178.

93 See, for example, *Criminal Code*, *ibid.*, s. 7. See also *CAHWCA*, *supra* note 59, ss. 6-8.

offences,[94] offences against internationally protected persons,[95] torture,[96] piracy,[97] and so on. In other words, Canada's presumptive territorial approach to criminal jurisdiction has been heavily influenced by its participation in multilateral treaty regimes providing for, and in some cases requiring, the exercise of domestic criminal jurisdiction on non-territorial bases. Moreover, some such bases, such as the nationality principle of jurisdiction, are prevalent in countries following a civilist legal tradition, whereas others, such as the quasi-universal basis of jurisdiction, are distinctly international legal constructs. Both categories have nevertheless been imported into Canadian criminal law largely through Canada's adherence to and implementation of multilateral treaties.

These instances clearly illustrate that, when the subject-matter of a treaty is directly relevant to matters traditionally coming within the purview of domestic legal regulation, adherence to the treaty will tend to have significant multijural impacts on the shape and scope of domestic law.

Treaties subject to reservations A further factor affecting the potential multijural effects of international treaties arises in the particular case of multilateral treaties. The multilateral law-making treaty became, in the twentieth century, the international community's instrument of choice for clarifying and progressively developing international law. A condition of the successful pursuit of such a law-making agenda was, as alluded to above, the participation of as many states as possible in such multilateral treaty regimes. However, the essentially contractual nature of international treaty law poses a fundamental challenge for the achievement of such universal treaty participation. In particular, a rigidly contractual approach to treaty law would require that each state becoming a party to a given treaty be bound to precisely the same rights and obligations as every other state expressing its consent to be bound by the same treaty. In an international system populated by some 193 states or so, each with its own views as to the desirable content of any given treaty, this approach would in general have one of two consequences: the terms of the treaty would have to be drafted so as to reflect the lowest common denominator of legal commitments acceptable to all states, or less than universal participation in the treaty regime by states would have to be expected and accepted. Neither outcome would be particularly desirable: the former because it would

94 *Criminal Code*, *ibid*., ss. 7(2) and 7(3.1), in implementation of Canada's obligations under the *Montreal* and *Hostage Conventions*, *supra* note 89.

95 *Criminal Code*, *ibid*., s. 7(3), in implementation of Canada's obligations under, *inter alia*, the *Convention on the Privileges and Immunities of the United Nations*, 13 February 1946 (in force 17 September 1946).

96 *Criminal Code*, *ibid*., s. 7(3.7), in implementation of Canada's obligations under the *Convention Against Torture and Other Cruel, Inhuman or Degrading Treatment or Punishment*, 10 December 1984 (in force 26 June 1987).

97 *Criminal Code*, *ibid*., s. 7(3.7), in implementation of Canada's obligations under *UNCLOS*, *supra* note 53, arts. 100, 105 and 107.

allow the content of the treaty regime to be dictated for all by each and every state participating in the negotiations, and the latter because it would defeat the original object of the exercise: universal participation.

The solution to this dilemma in modern treaty practice is the 'reservation'. A reservation is a unilateral declaration made by a state, usually at the time it expresses its consent to be bound by a treaty, which purports to modify specific terms of the treaty in their application to the reserving state.[98] The International Court of Justice and the *Vienna Convention on the Law of Treaties* have confirmed the permissibility of making reservations to multilateral treaties, provided that such reservations are compatible with the object and purpose of the treaty.[99] The effect of such a reservation will depend on the reaction to it by other states parties to the treaty. In particular, the treaty will come into force between the reserving state and those states parties that accept the reservation, subject to reciprocal modification in accordance with the reservation, of the rights and obligations of each such accepting state in its treaty relationship with the reserving state. The mutual rights and obligations of accepting but non-reserving states *inter se* remain, however, unaffected by the reservation. For states parties objecting to the reservation, one of two possibilities will obtain: either the objecting state will object to the formation of any treaty relations at all between itself and the reserving state; or the objecting state will simply object to the coming into force, as between itself and the reserving state, of the provision(s) to which the reservation pertains, but not of the treaty generally. In either case, the treaty relationship between the objecting states parties and other non-reserving parties to the treaty remain unaffected by the reservation.[100]

Naturally, the faculty bestowed by modern treaty law upon states to make unilateral reservations to multilateral treaties has had the effect of greatly increasing the participation rate by states in multilateral law-making treaty regimes. Indeed, this is the whole point of reservations.[101] States that might otherwise choose not to ratify or accede to a given treaty due to some of its specific provisions may nevertheless proceed with ratification or accession if their concern can be addressed by the formulation of a reservation that is compatible with the object and purpose of the treaty. However, this increased participation rate exacts a hefty price in terms of uniformity of the treaty rights and obligations undertaken by states parties to the treaty regime. Reservations, in effect, can shatter the symmetry of states parties' obligations under the treaty with respect to all but its most central features – that

98 *Vienna Convention, supra* note 3, art. 2(1)(d).

99 *Reservations to the Convention on the Prevention and Punishment of Genocide*, Advisory Opinion, [1951] I.C.J. Rep. 15 [hereinafter *Reservations to Genocide Convention Case*]; *Vienna Convention, supra* note 3, art. 19.

100 *Reservations to Genocide Convention Case, ibid.* at 29-30; *Vienna Convention, supra* note 3, arts. 19-23. See also generally Browlie (2003), *Principles of Public International Law*, at 584-586; Shaw, *supra* note 3 at 821-831.

101 *Reservations to Genocide Convention Case, ibid.* at 23-24; Shaw, *supra* note 3, at 822.

is, its object and purpose. In extreme cases, where many parties enter reservations, the treaty may in the end be multilateral in form only: the relations between the various parties to the treaty will effectively be bilateralized.[102]

The multijural consequences of reservations to multilateral treaties will immediately be recognizable. First, at the level of treaty obligations themselves, an ostensibly harmonized set of rules can be tailored, by states formulating reservations, to suit their own particular national interests. Harmonization thus gives way to unilateral customization by reserving states. Moreover, the customizing effects of reservations are magnified by their reciprocal effect (as between reserving and accepting states). The result is a species of multijural, rather than a genuinely multilateral, treaty. And this multijuralized treaty regime in turn has consequences for its domestic harmonizing potential. Evidently, a state that can unilaterally tailor its obligations under a multilateral treaty regime is in a position to protect its domestic legal system from unwanted legal effects of that regime. It can, in other words, stymie the potential harmonizing impact – or, thought of differently, the vertical multijuralizing effect – of the multilateral treaty within its domestic system.

Of course, assessing the net, overall multijural impact of reservations to multilateral treaties also requires consideration of their secondary effects. For example, the reciprocal effect of a reservation means that, at least in its relations with the reserving state, an accepting state also acquires the 'benefit' of the reservation. Assuming that the reservation was initially formulated by the reserving state in order to respond to or preserve some domestic legal interest or imperative, the reciprocal benefit of the reservation for an accepting state means that it too will benefit from preservation of the same domestic legal interest or imperative. In other words, the domestic legal reasons for formulating a reservation may acquire domestic legal relevance for states accepting, but not formulating, the reservation. Another secondary effect of reservations is that resisting the harmonizing effect of a multilateral treaty does tend to preserve the unique features of the reserving state's domestic legal system. This in turn preserves a degree of legal pluralism – an essential condition precedent for future multijural interactions between domestic legal systems – that might otherwise be lost through perfectly uniform endorsement and implementation of a given multilateral treaty regime.

In short, the reservations practices of states subscribing to multilateral treaties will have complex ramifications for the harmonizing or multijuralizing effects of such treaties.

Treaties incorporating mandatory dispute resolution mechanisms A final factor with multijural implications flowing from the nature of the treaty itself is the incorporation (or not) of a mandatory dispute resolution mechanism within the treaty regime. Absent such a mechanism, binding adjudication of disputes arising under the treaty will depend on case-by-case consensual submission thereof, by

---

102 See generally Currie, *supra* note 3, at 125-126.

the parties, to a dispute resolution body of their choice. In the absence of such consent, the dispute will tend to remain unresolved, with few if any multijural consequences for the domestic legal systems of either party.

However, should a mandatory dispute resolution process be established within the treaty framework, several multijural consequences can be expected to follow. First, failure to perform treaty obligations in good faith (including, where applicable, the obligation to enact domestic implementing legislation consistent with the treaty's provisions) will in all likelihood lead to enforcement action by other parties to the treaty. Thus, including mandatory dispute resolution mechanisms within a treaty regime will tend, all other things being equal, to encourage treaty performance and, in particular, more assiduous attempts to harmonize domestic law with that of the treaty (always assuming, of course, that domestic legal harmonization is necessary in order to perform the treaty's obligations). Prime examples of such treaty-based dispute resolution regimes, and of their profound impact on domestic compliance with treaty obligations, are the complex mandatory dispute resolution mechanisms established under the *General Agreement on Tariffs and Trade* and the *North American Free Trade Agreement*.[103]

Second, for states parties recognizing the direct domestic effect of rulings by treaty-based dispute resolution or adjudication mechanisms, either as a general rule[104] or as a result of specific, domestically implemented treaty arrangements providing for such direct effect, such rulings will clearly produce domestic legal effects that are extrinsic, in their origins, to the domestic legal order. The potential for injection of 'foreign', supranational law into the domestic legal system by such a process is self-evident.[105]

Third, even in the absence of provisions recognizing the direct domestic effect of rulings by treaty-based dispute resolution mechanisms, such rulings will nevertheless constitute authoritative pronouncements that will exert normative force on and within states parties. In particular, such rulings will usually clarify the nature of states parties' obligations under the treaty, clarification that would not otherwise be authoritatively available. In this sense, rulings by treaty-based dispute resolution bodies will tend to produce *sui generis* norms, a multijural effect in itself. Moreover, such authoritative rulings, when coupled with compliance

---

103 See *Agreement Establishing the World Trade Organization*, 15 April 1994, Annex 2: *Understanding on Rules and Procedures Governing the Settlement of Disputes* (1997) [hereinafter WTO DSU]; and *North American Free Trade Agreement*, 17 December 1992 [hereinafter NAFTA], Chapter 20. See generally Castel et al. (1997), *The Canadian Law and Practice of International Trade*, at 669-720. See also Johnson (1998), *International Trade Law*, at 283-304.

104 For example, Spain: see *Constitution of Spain, 1978*, *supra* note 23, art. 92.

105 An interesting feature of the NAFTA chapter 20 dispute resolution mechanism provides for authoritative guidance from the NAFTA Commission to domestic courts or administrative tribunals engaged in interpreting or applying NAFTA in domestic proceedings: NAFTA, *supra* note 103, art. 2020; Castel *et al.*, *supra* note 103, at 73.

monitoring processes and direct diplomatic pressure by other states parties, will usually carry considerable weight and tend to foster domestic compliance.[106] These effects will of course be magnified where mandatory dispute resolution provisions in treaties are accompanied by corresponding compliance mechanisms or explicit obligations upon the disputing parties to comply with and give domestic effect to the outcomes of the dispute resolution process.[107]

In short, treaties incorporating mandatory dispute resolution mechanisms will tend to magnify their harmonizing impact on domestic legal systems. As noted at several points in the discussion above, this can be considered at once to enhance and suppress the multijural effects of the treaty. The treaty's multijural effects will be enhanced through the more effective injection of essentially 'foreign' treaty rules into domestic law; whereas they will also be suppressed by promoting harmonization across domestic legal systems, thus depleting the diversity of such systems along with the potential for future multijural interactions between them.

Conclusions

This chapter has sought to identify the principal characteristics of domestic legal systems and of international treaties that will tend to promote either harmonizing or multijural effects within and across domestic legal systems. This analysis has not purported to be exhaustive, but has aimed rather at identifying and illustrating the principal factors that will most directly affect the impact of treaties on domestic legal systems.

In that spirit, we have seen that the harmonizing or multijural effects of a given treaty depend, *inter alia*, on whether the state of reception has a monist or dualist treaty reception regime and, in the case of the latter, how the state chooses to adapt the treaty's rules within its domestic legal system. Moreover, the propensity of states to adhere to a monist or dualist approach, or to follow any particular mode of treaty implementation, is not amenable to ready classification or prediction based on adherence to any particular domestic legal tradition (such as the common or

106 An excellent example of this effect is the exemplary record of compliance, by member states, with rulings of the European Court of Human Rights, established by Protocol 11 to the *European Convention for the Protection of Human Rights and Fundamental Freedoms*, 4 November 1950 (in force 3 September 1953). While there is no formal mechanism for domestic enforcement of the Court's judgments, effective monitoring by the Council of Europe's Committee of Ministers and Parliamentary Assembly Monitoring Committee has encouraged widespread compliance by member states with the Court's rulings: see generally Freeman and van Ert (2004), *International Human Rights Law*, at 438-441; and Shaw, *supra* note 3, at 324-333.

107 As provided, for example, in art. 23 of the WTO DSU, *supra* note 103, or in art. 2018 of NAFTA, *supra* note 103. For discussion of the domestic impact in Canada of various WTO-GATT rulings, see Castel *et al.*, *supra* note 103, at 22-23.

civil law traditions). State practice in these matters varies widely and is primarily driven by the particular constitutional structure adopted within each state.

We have also observed that the harmonizing or multijural potential of treaties very much depends on a number of attributes inherent in the particular treaty itself. Such factors include the extent to which the treaty addresses primarily contractual arrangements between states or, rather, has a normative character; whether it deals with subject-matter coming within the traditional bounds of domestic legal regulation, or rather addresses traditional state-to-state interests; whether the treaty is multilateral in nature and is, hence, subject to reservations by states adhering to it; and whether the treaty incorporates its own set of secondary obligations, such as a supranational dispute settlement regime.

The foregoing discussion has demonstrated, moreover, that it is difficult if not impossible to predict the harmonizing or multijural effects of treaties within and across domestic legal systems by examining any one of these factors in isolation. Indeed all such factors interact in complex ways, sometimes magnifying and sometimes neutralizing their cumulative multijural effects. For example, a treaty that addresses domestically relevant subject matter may have increased multijural relevance within domestic legal systems; but this tendency may be neutralized, in some states, by a rigidly dualist stance; whereas the effects of such a dualist stance will in turn be attenuated by invocation of 'direct' methods of treaty transformation, such as enactment by reference. And so on.

It is also necessary to have regard to what this chapter has referred to as the net multijural effect of a given treaty: at one level, a treaty regime may inject foreign legal concepts into domestic legal systems and, to that extent, be considered a source of multijuralism. However, at another level, overly effective injection of international legal concepts into domestic legal systems may have a harmonizing, and thus homogenizing, effect across domestic legal systems. The net result may thus be a long-term depletion of diversity across domestic legal systems, with attendant consequences for future multijural exchanges between them.

References

American Law Institute (1987). *Restatement of the Law (Third): The Foreign Relations Law of the United States*, volume 1, St. Paul: American Law Institute.

Anzilotti, Dionisio (1955). *Corso di diritto internazionale*, volume 1, 4th edition, Padua: Dedam.

Blaustein, Albert P. and Gisbert H. Flanz (eds) (1996). *Constitutions of the Countries of the World*, Binder XIX, New York: Oceana Publications.

Blaustein, Albert P. and Gisbert H. Flanz (eds) (2002). *Constitutions of the Countries of the World*, Binder XV, New York: Oceana Publications.

Blaustein, Albert P. and Gisbert H. Flanz (eds) (2003a). *Constitutions of the Countries of the World*, Binder XIII, New York: Oceana Publications.

Blaustein, Albert P. and Gisbert H. Flanz (eds) (2003b). *Constitutions of the Countries of the World*, Binder XVII, New York: Oceana Publications.

Blaustein, Albert P. and Gisbert H. Flanz (eds) (2004). *Constitutions of the Countries of the World*, Binder XVI, New York: Oceana Publications.

Blaustein, Albert P. and Gisbert H. Flanz (eds) (2005). *Constitutions of the Countries of the World*, Binder XII, New York: Oceana Publications.

Browlie, Ian (2003). *Principles of Public International Law*, 6th edition, Oxford: Oxford University Press.

Brunnée, Jutta and Stephen J. Toope (2002). 'A Hesitant Embrace: The Application of International Law by Canadian Courts', *The Canadian Yearbook of International Law*, **XL**: 3–60.

Butler, William E. (2002). *The Law of Treaties in Russia and the Commonwealth of Independent States*, Cambridge: Cambridge University Press.

Cassese, Antonio (2005). *International Law*, 2nd edition, Oxford: Oxford University Press.

Castel, Jean-Gabriel, William C. Graham, Armand L.C. de Mestral, Mark A.A. Warner and Susan Hainsworth (1997). *The Canadian Law and Practice of International Trade*, 2nd edition, Toronto: Emond Montgomery.

Côté, Pierre-André (2000). *The Interpretation of Legislation in Canada*, 3rd edition, Scarborough: Carswell.

Currie, John H. (2001). *Public International Law*, Toronto: Irwin Law.

Dupuy, Pierre-Marie (1998). *Droit international public*, 4th edition, Paris: Dalloz.

Fatima, Shaheed (2005). *Using International Law in Domestic Courts*, Oxford: Hart Publishing.

Fitzgerald, Oonagh (ed.) (2006). *The Globalized Rule of Law: Relationships Between International and Domestic Law*, Toronto: Irwin Law.

Fitzmaurice, Gerald (1957). 'The General Principles of International Law: Considered from the Standpoint of the Rule of Law', *Recueil des Cours*, **92**(2): 1–227.

Freeman, Mark and Gibran van Ert (2004). *International Human Rights Law*, Toronto: Irwin Law.

Hegel, Georg L. (1975). *Natural Law: The Scientific Ways of Treating Law, its Place in Moral Philosophy, and its Relation to the Positive Sciences of Law*, trans. T.M. Knox, Philadelphia: University of Philadelphia Press.

International Law Commission (1966a). 'Report of the International Law Commission on the Work of its 18th Session', *Yearbook of the International Law Commission*, vol. II: 172-363, at: http://untreaty.un.org/ilc/documentation/english/a_cn4_191.pdf

International Law Commission (1966b). *Yearbook of the International Law Commission*, volume I, part II, New York: United Nations Publications, at: http://untreaty.un.org/ilc/publications/yearbooks/Ybkvolumes(e)/ILC_1966_v1_p2_e.pdf

Iwasawa, Yuji (1986). 'The Doctrine of Self-Executing Treaties in the United States: A Critical Analysis', *Virginia Journal of International Law*, **26**: 627–692.

Iwasawa, Yuji (1993). 'The Relationship Between International Law and National Law: Japanese Experiences', *British Year Book of International Law*, **64**: 333–390.

Jacobs, Francis G. (ed.) (1987). *The Effect of Treaties in Domestic Law*, London: Sweet & Maxwell.

Janis, Mark W. (1993). *An Introduction to International Law*, 2nd edition, Boston: Little, Brown.

Johnson, Jon R. (1998). *International Trade Law*, Toronto: Irwin Law.

Kelsen, Hans (1946). *General Theory of Law and State*, Cambridge: Cambridge University Press.

Kelsen, Hans (1966). *Principles of International Law*, 2nd edition, New York: Holt, Rinehart & Winston.

Kelsen, Hans (1967). *Pure Theory of Law*, trans. Max Knight, Berkeley: University of California Press.

Lapidoth, Ruth (1990). 'International Law Within the Israeli Legal System', *Israel Law Review*, **24**(3-4): 451–484.

Lauterpacht, Hersch (ed.) and Lassa Oppenheim (1955). *International Law: A Treatise*, volume 1, 8th edition, London: Longmans.

Lauterpacht, Hersch (1966). *The Function of Law in the International Community*, Hamden: Archon Books.

Macdonald Ronald St. J., Gerald L. Morris and Douglas M. Johnston (eds) (1974). *Canadian Perspectives on International Law and Organization*, Toronto: University of Toronto Press.

Shaw, Malcolm N. (ed.) (2003). *International Law*, 5th edition, Cambridge: Cambridge University Press.

Starke, Joseph G. (1936). 'Monism and Dualism in the Theory of International Law', *British Year Book of International Law*, **17**: 66–81.

Strupp, Karl (1934). 'Les règles générales du droit de la paix', *Recueil des Cours*, **47**(1): 259–595.

Sullivan, Ruth (2002). *Sullivan and Driedger on the Construction of Statutes*, 4th edition, Markham: Butterworths.

Van Ert, Gibran (2002). *Using International Law in Canadian Courts*, The Hague: Kluwer Law International.

Vázquez, Carlos Manuel (1995). 'The Four Doctrines of Self-Executing Treaties', *The American Journal of International Law*, **89**(4): 695–723.

Wenzel, Max (1920). *Juristiche Grundprobleme – Zugleich eine Untersuchung zum Begriff des Staates und Problem des Völkerrechts*, Berlin: F. Dümmlers.

International Conventions and Agreements

Charter of the United Nations, 26 June 1945, United Nations, Canada Treaty Series, vol. 1945, no. 7.

Convention on the Privileges and Immunities of the United Nations, 13 February 1946, United Nations Treaty Series, vol. 1, p. 15.

Convention on the Prevention and Punishment of the Crime of Genocide, 9 December 1948, United Nations Treaty Series, vol. 78, p. 277.

Geneva Convention for the Amelioration of the Condition of the Wounded and Sick in Armed Forces in the Field, 12 August 1949, United Nations Treaty Series, vol. 75, p. 31.

Geneva Convention for the Amelioration of the Condition of Wounded, Sick and Shipwrecked Members of Armed Forces at Sea, 12 August 1949, United Nations Treaty Series, vol. 75, p. 85.

Geneva Convention Relative to the Treatment of Prisoners of War, 12 August 1949, United Nations Treaty Series, vol. 75, p. 135.

Geneva Convention Relative to the Protection of Civilian Persons in Time of War, 12 August 1949, United Nations Treaty Series, vol. 75, p. 287.

European Convention for the Protection of Human Rights and Fundamental Freedoms, 4 November 1950, European Treaty Series No. 005.

Vienna Convention on Diplomatic Relations, 18 April 1961, United Nations Treaty Series, vol. 500, p. 95.

Vienna Convention on Consular Relations, 24 April 1963, United Nations Treaty Series, vol. 596, p. 261.

Convention on Offences and Certain Other Acts Committed on Board Aircraft, 14 September 1963, United Nations Treaty Series, vol. 704, p. 219.

International Covenant on Civil and Political Rights, 16 December 1966, United Nations Treaty Series, vol. 999, p. 171.

International Covenant on Economic, Social and Cultural Rights, 16 December 1966, United Nations Treaty Series, vol. 993, p.3.

Vienna Convention on the Law of Treaties, 23 May 1969, United Nations Treaty Series, vol. 1155, p. 33.

Convention for the Suppression of Unlawful Seizure of Aircraft, 16 December 1970, United Nations Treaty Series, vol. 860, p. 105.

Convention for the Suppression of Unlawful Acts Against the Safety of Civil Aviation, 23 September 1971, United Nations Treaty Series, vol. 974, p. 177.

Convention on the Prevention and Punishment of Crimes Against Internationally Protected Persons, Including Diplomatic Agents, 14 December 1973, United Nations Treaty Series, vol. 1035, p. 167.

International Convention Against the Taking of Hostages, 17 December 1979, United Nations Treaty Series, vol. 1316, p. 205.

Convention on the Physical Protection of Nuclear Material, 3 March 1980, United Nations Treaty Series, vol. 1456, p. 246.

United Nations Convention on the Law of the Sea, 10 December 1982, United Nations Treaty Series, vol. 1833, p. 3.
Convention Against Torture and Other Cruel, Inhuman or Degrading Treatment or Punishment, 10 December 1984, United Nations Treaty Series, vol. 1465, p. 85.
Vienna Convention on the Law of Treaties between States and International Organizations or between International Organizations, 21 March 1986, UN Publications.
Protocol for the Suppression of Unlawful Acts of Violence at Airports Serving International Aviation, 24 February 1988, United Nations Treaty Series, vol. 1589, p. 474.
Convention for the Suppression of Unlawful Acts Against the Safety of Maritime Navigation, 10 March 1988, United Nations Treaty Series, vol. 1678, p. 221.
Protocol for the Suppression of Unlawful Acts Against the Safety of Fixed Platforms Located on the Continental Shelf, 10 March 1988, United Nations Treaty Series, vol. 1678, p. 304.
Convention on the Marking of Plastic Explosives for the Purpose of Identification, 1 March 1991, 30 I.L.M. 721.
North American Free Trade Agreement, 17 December 1992, Canada Treaty Series, vol. 1994, no. 2.
Agreement Establishing the World Trade Organization, World Trade Organization, 15 April 1994, Dobbs Ferry: Oceana Publications.
International Convention for the Suppression of Terrorist Bombings, 15 December 1997, United Nations Treaty Series, vol. 2149, p. 256.
Rome Statute of the International Criminal Court, 17 July 1998, UN Doc. 2128, United Nations Treaty Series, vol. 90.
International Convention for the Suppression of the Financing of Terrorism, 9 December 1999, United Nations Treaty Series, vol. 2178, p. 197.
UN Convention on the Jurisdictional Immunities of States and Their Property, 2 December 2004, United Nations General Assembly, Res. A/59/38.
International Convention for the Suppression of Acts of Nuclear Terrorism, 14 September 2005, at: http://untreaty.un.org/English/Terrorism/English_18_15.pdf.
Agreement between the Government of Canada and the Government of the United States of America on the North American Aerospace Defense Command, 28 April 2006, at: www.treaty-accord.gc.ca/ViewTreaty.asp?Treaty_ID=105060.

Legal Cases

Permanent Court of International Justice

Treatment of Polish Nationals and Other Persons of Polish Origin or Speech in the Danzig Territory, PCIJ, Ser. A/B, No. 44, 1932

International Court of Justice

Reservations to the Convention on the Prevention and Punishment of Genocide (advisory opinion), [1951] I.C.J. Rep. 15
Case Concerning the Arrest Warrant of 11 April 2000 (Democratic Republic of the Congo v. Belgium), [2002] I.C.J. Rep. 5

American Cases

Foster v. Neilson (1829), 27 U.S. (2 Pet.) 25
Edye v. Robertson (1884), 112 U.S. 580
Whitney v. Robertson (1888), 124 U.S. 190
U.S. v. Palestine Liberation Organization (1988), 695 F.Supp. 1465 (N.Y. Dist. Ct.)

Australian Cases

Minister of State for Immigration and Ethnic Affairs v. Ah Hin Teoh FC (1995), 128 A.L.R. 353
Kruger v. Commonwealth of Australia (1997), 146 A.L.R. 126

British Cases

R. v. Keyn (The Franconia Case) (1876), 2 Exch. 63 (C.C.R.)
The Parlement Belge (1879), 4 P.D. 129
Maclaine Watson v. Department of Trade and Industry, [1989] 3 All E.R. 523

Canadian Cases

Francis v. Canada, [1956] S.C.R. 618
R. v. Canada Labour Relations Board, ex parte Federal Electric Corporation, (1964) 44 D.L.R. (2d) (Man. Q.B.)
Daniels v. White and The Queen, [1968] S.C.R. 517
Capital Cities Communications Inc. v. Canadian Radio-Television Commission, [1978] 2 S.C.R. 141
R. v. Libman, [1985] 2 S.C.R. 178
Reference re Public Service Employee Relations Act (Alta), [1987] 1 S.C.R. 313
Slaight Communications Inc. v. Davidson, [1989] 1 S.C.R. 1038
National Corn Growers Assn. v. Canada (Import Tribunal), [1991] 2 S.C.R. 1324
Pushpanathan v. Canada (Minister of Citizenship and Immigration), [1998] 1 S.C.R. 982.
Baker v. Canada (Minister of Citizenship and Immigration, [1999] 2 S.C.R. 817
Schreiber v. Canada (Attorney General), [2002] 3 S.C.R. 269
Suresh v. Canada (Minister of Citizenship and Immigration), [2002] 1 S.C.R. 3

Legislation

Act to Introduce the Code of Crimes Against International Law, 2002 (Germany)
Basic Law for the Federal Republic of Germany, 1949, as amended by the Unification Treaty, 31 August 1990 and the Federal Statute of 23 September 1990, *Federal Law Gazette*, II: 885 (Germany)
Crimes Against Humanity and War Crimes Act, S.C. 2000, c. 24
Criminal Code Act, 1995 (Australia), No. 12, as amended by the *International Criminal Court (Consequential Amendments) Act, 2002* (Australia), No. 42.
Criminal Code of Canada, R.S.C. 1985, c. C-46
Federal Law on International Treaties of the Russian Federation, 1995 (Russia)
Foreign Missions and International Organizations Act, S.C. 1991, c. 41 *Oceans Act*, S.C. 1996, c. 31
International Criminal Court Act, 2001, c. 17 (United Kingdom)

Chapter 2
The Reception of Indigenous Legal Systems in Canada

Sébastien Grammond

Introduction: The Hidden Face of Bijuralism

In Canada, the concept of plurality of legal systems is usually thought to refer to the coexistence in the country of the common law and of the civil law. The overlapping of these two European legal traditions, often presented as the main characteristic of Canadian law, tends to eclipse almost completely another form of legal dualism, that which combines European-inspired and indigenous legal systems. Currently, the reception of indigenous legal systems is a phenomenon known only to a few specialists. Although the great majority of Canadian law professionals are aware of the existence of civil law and common law systems and are at least able to identify the points that are common to both, they are generally unaware of the relevance of indigenous legal traditions. Indeed the legal rules governing the indigenous peoples are usually considered to be part of Canadian law and to come under its theory of sources: legislation, jurisprudence, contractual agreements, and so on.[1] This obvious gap in Canada's legal discourse with regards to the indigenous peoples is especially surprising given that recognition of local law is a characteristic of British imperial law, which has influenced Canadian constitutional law. Moreover, the residual sovereignty of the indigenous peoples has always been recognized in the United States, which has allowed some native groups to set up tribal courts that enforce indigenous law.

Several factors justify the renewal of interest in indigenous legal traditions, as evidenced in a recent discussion paper from the Law Commission of Canada.[2] The wider reception of these systems carries the promise of greater autonomy for native peoples. This autonomy would provide better ways to adapt the law to the social reality of aborigines. Beyond this instrumental interest, the law is part of a people's identity, and increased recognition of their legal systems can help reinforce their identity. If the 1992 Charlottetown Accord proposed to recognize that, within the Canadian Constitution, the civil law was one of the elements making Quebec a distinct society (Tremblay, 1995, p. 463), why could not the

1 For an introduction to this area of law, see Grammond (2003).

2 Law Commission of Canada (2006), *Justice within: Indigenous Legal Traditions*; see also Law Commission of Canada (2007).

same reasoning apply to the law of indigenous peoples? And finally, current or emerging international law norms protect the rights of the indigenous peoples to promote, preserve and develop their legal systems.[3]

As part of a larger research project on the interactions between legal systems, the purpose of this chapter is to shed light on the reception of indigenous legal systems in Canadian law. In other words, under what conditions does Canadian law recognize the existence of standards, values or processes emanating from indigenous legal systems? What are the main theoretical and prescriptive issues that arise out of the will to recognize indigenous law?

Contrary to civil law/common law bijuralism, which involves legal traditions that are in fact quite similar, one cannot talk about the reception of indigenous legal systems without an adequate theoretical basis. In the next section we will introduce the concept of legal pluralism, providing several examples of its application to indigenous law. In the third section we will analyse the main aspects in which the indigenous conception of law differs from the Western conception, and we will identify the challenges this creates when considering the reception of indigenous standards in Canadian Law. The fourth section focuses on the prescriptive issues raised by the reception of indigenous law, including in terms of culture and individual rights.

A word of caution before we get to the heart of the matter: the purpose of this chapter is mainly to discuss the current situation and identify the various issues raised by the reception of indigenous legal systems. Indeed we feel that a thorough understanding of the situation is crucial before reforms are proposed. This is not an attempt to develop a legal rationale, including a constitution-based one, in favour of the reception of indigenous legal systems or self-government; others have already undertaken this task.[4]

The Legal Pluralism Perspective

The issue examined in this chapter revolves around the concept of 'multijuralism', which designates the different modes of interaction between public or private legal systems. For our purpose, we prefer to use the well-known concept of legal pluralism[5] to analyse the interaction between Canadian law and indigenous legal

---

3 *Convention (No. 169) concerning Indigenous and Tribal Peoples in Independent Countries*, adopted by the World Trade Organization on June 27, 1989, reproduced in Schulte-Tenckhoff (1997), p. 197 and following, art. 8 and 9; *United Nations Declaration on the Rights of Indigenous Peoples*, U.N. G.A. Res. 61/295, art. 34.

4 See Borrows (2005), pp. 201-207; Royal Commission on Aboriginal Peoples (1993), *Partners in Confederation: Aboriginal Peoples, Self-Government, and the Constitution.*

5 On the theory of legal pluralism, see, among others: Griffiths (1986); Kleinhans and Macdonald (1997); von Benda-Beckmann (2002); Vanderlinden (2005).

systems. This choice is justified by the number of studies that exist on the problem of indigenous law that refer specifically to the theory of legal pluralism.[6]

The theory of legal pluralism involves two main components, depending on whether one is looking at the plurality of law sources inside or outside the State. In the following pages, we will show how the reception of indigenous legal systems in Canadian law falls in one or the other category.

'Soft' or Intra-State Pluralism

There are two radically opposed perspectives on the plurality of law sources. The first, which can be referred to as soft or hierarchical pluralism, ascribes the recognition to an ultimate source of law, usually the sovereign State. Soft pluralism arises from the fact that this sovereign State delegates to subordinate bodies, either territorially (for example the Canadian provinces), either in a social realm that exercises a certain autonomy (for example professional orders), the power to enact certain categories of norms. The term pluralism in this case simply means that different rules of law are applicable to different individuals or situations.

When it comes to the *interaction* between various legal orders, this conception of pluralism emphasizes concepts that do not formally question the State's prescriptive monopoly or the established hierarchy of formal sources of law. The analysis of interactions between legal orders is then centered on the concept of *validity:* the indigenous norms will be valid if they are recognized, one way or another, by the State, but invalid (or at least non-legal, meaning that they are not cognizable by the courts) in the opposite case. In other words, a rule that does not ultimately come from the State cannot be legal. The challenge of the research then becomes to determine the validity (or recognition) criteria that are applied or should be applied. In fact, from a legal point of view, this form of pluralism essentially raises questions as to the exercise of a delegated power, which usually comes under administrative law.

The concept of soft pluralism is similar to the concept of 'bijuralism' in Canada. This concept is used to describe the fact that in Canada, there is a territory (Quebec) where private law is different from what it is in the rest of the territory. However, bijuralism does not call into question the supremacy of the Canadian Constitution which, in the end, determines the respective spheres of application of the two systems, or even the possibility for the federal Parliament to change civil law rules applicable in Quebec when these come under its jurisdiction.

Interactions deriving from a delegation Canadian law provides several examples of a delegation of power in favour of indigenous peoples, that is intra-State pluralism

6 For example: *Lajoie et al.* (1996); *Melançon* (1997); *Lajoie et al.* (1998).

situations. Thus, for a long time now, the *Indian Act*[7] has granted band councils[8] regulatory powers to deal with local native interests. These powers, similar to those of a municipality, cover areas such as road regulations, road construction, alcohol consumption, zoning, residence on the reserve, and so on. More recently, as part of agreements on native self-government, the federal Parliament enacted a law that grants much broader powers to First Nations in the Yukon.[9] These legislative powers, similar to those of a province, extend to areas such as education, health, adoption, and so on. In both cases, indigenous peoples may adopt, in areas that come under the jurisdiction recognized to them under Canadian law, rules that are different from those which apply to non-natives. However, one should not exaggerate the scope of these powers. Indeed the concerted use of these powers often depends on the granting of adequate funding, which does not always happen in reality.[10] The recent Nisga'a Treaty illustrates another type of limit: some of the legislative powers recognized to the Nisga'a government are subject to very specific limits. For example, any Nisga'a legislation concerning youth protection must include standards that are similar to provincial standards in the same area.[11] Freedom of action is therefore considerably reduced for aborigines.

Interaction through borrowings Without questioning the supremacy of the State, 'soft' pluralism can also designate the diversity of general law principles that underpin the application of formal standards. It can be referred to as a borrowing. For example, a Quebec civil law rule can be interpreted using common law principles and *vice versa* (LeBel and Le Saunier, 2006). The same type of borrowing can occur between a Western legal system and an indigenous legal system. Even in the absence of explicit reference to the rules of the indigenous order, Canadian law can evolve through its perception of the indigenous legal tradition.

The most well-known examples of this are probably found in criminal law.[12] Faced with the very high rate of incarceration in the native population and the cultural inadequacy of the current system for natives, criminal justice authorities have attempted to organize the system in a way that would better meet their aspirations. Thus a judge sentencing an aboriginal offender can hold a 'sentencing circle'.[13] He would invite

7 *Indian Act*, R.S.C. 1985, c. I-5, art. 81, 83 and 85.1.

8 Band councils are usually elected bodies that represent the members of an 'Indian band', that is, a local native community.

9 *Yukon First Nations Self-Government Act*, S.C. 1994, c. 35.

10 See Dacks (2004).

11 *Nisga'a Final Agreement*, ch. 11, art. 89.

12 For a history of the adaptation of criminal law to the indigenous peoples, see Jaccoud (2002); for an analysis of the application of criminal law to the indigenous peoples from a pluralist perspective, see Melançon, *loc. cit.*, note 6.

13 See Green (1998). For a description of a sentencing circle, see, for example, *R. v. Naappaluk* (1993), 25 C.R. (4th) 220, J.E. 93-1681, [1994] 2 C.N.L.R. 143 (C.Q.), or *R. v. Morin*, [1995] 4 C.N.L.R. 37, 101 C.C.C. (3d) 124 (Sask. C.A.); *R. v. Johnson* (1994), 91 C.C.C. (3d) 21, [1995] 2 C.N.L.R. 158 (Yukon C.A.).

the victim's family, the family of the accused, community elders and other interested parties to get together and express what they feel would be an appropriate sentence. The purpose of this exercise is to devise a sentence that focuses more on rehabilitating the accused and restoring harmony in the community than on punishment, denunciation and deterrence; these objectives are closer to indigenous conceptions of criminal justice, often descried as being founded on reparation rather than punishment.[14]

A borrowing can also occur when a Canadian tribunal, having to interpret a written norm adopted by a native government, considers the values of the indigenous legal tradition in the interpretative process. Thus the Yukon Supreme Court concluded that the elders from the Ta'an Kwäch'an First Nation traditionally had the power to appoint an interim leader when this position became vacant without a successor having been designated. According to the Court, this traditional rule could be used to fill a gap in the written constitution of this First Nation, which did not provide for this specific situation.[15]

In its landmark decisions on aboriginal rights, the Supreme Court also stated that concepts must be borrowed as much from civil law and from common law as from indigenous legal traditions to define the aboriginal title or ancestral rights. Thus even when defined by Canadian courts, aboriginal land rights would be defined taking into account the 'perspective of aboriginal peoples';[16] they would originate from the 'relationship between common law and pre-existing systems of aboriginal law'.[17] We have to recognize, however, that in subsequent decisions, the Court paid little heed to the guideline it had set for itself and never considered aboriginal rules of land occupation.[18] As we will see, the function of the announced borrowing, which never took place, is probably to legitimize the Court's jurisprudence.

'Hard' or Extra-State Pluralism

The second conception of legal pluralism, which can be called hard, or sociological, or extra-State pluralism, does not presume the supremacy of a legal order over the others, but rather highlights the multiplicity of the sources of normativity that become superimposed in a given society and that can influence or determine individual conduct.[19] The emphasis is no longer on the validity of norms, but rather on their effectiveness: the legal sociologist is seeking to demonstrate the existence of parallel legal orders and the fact that individuals can feel more

---

14 Kwochka (1996), 'Aboriginal Injustice: Making Room for a Restorative Paradigm', quoted among others in *R. v. Gladue*, [1999] 1 S.C.R. 688, at 726-727.

15 *Harpe v. Ta'an Kwach'an Council*, [2006] 2 C.N.L.R. 70 (Yukon S.C.), notably at par. 100.

16 *R. v. Van der Peet*, [1996] 2 S.C.R. 507, at 550-551.

17 *Delgamuukw v. British Columbia*, [1997] 3 S.C.R. 1010, at 1082.

18 See Otis (1999), pp. 611-619; Bankes (2006); see also comments by Justice LeBel in *R. v. Marshall*; *R. v. Bernard*, [2005] 2 S.C.R. 220.

19 Griffiths, *loc. cit.*, note 5; Kleinhans and Macdonald, *loc. cit.*, note 5.

strongly bound by these legal orders than by those of the State. Such legal orders can therefore exist apart from any official recognition and even be overtly disputed by the State. They remain no less effective if part of the population obeys their prescriptions.

The purpose of an analysis of interactions between legal orders, from this perspective, is not to decide which legal order should win out in a given situation or what a tribunal should do when a litigant invokes a rule from a non-State order. Rather, it seeks to observe the respective effectiveness of the various competing legal orders and their modes of interaction, but does not seek to draw out prescriptive conclusions *per se*.[20]

The concept of extra-State pluralism can also be used to describe the interactions between indigenous and Canadian legal orders, when the State is not seeking to define the indigenous norm or to subject it to its internal controls. In other words, extra-State pluralism exists when the Canadian State merely *recognizes* an indigenous norm, without trying to *empower* an indigenous individual or entity to adopt this norm. The situation is similar to what exists in private international law: the legal system of a country recognizes the legal rules of another State, but without giving them validity.

Hard pluralism in the courts Canadian law contains the seed of this form of pluralism. The 'doctrine of reception', which explains the importing of English law into Canada, has a place not only for civil law as it was applied before the British conquest, but also to indigenous legal systems (Walters, 1999). The Supreme Court has accepted the principle of indigenous law survival by affirming, in the *Mitchell* decision, that 'aboriginal interests and customary laws were presumed to survive the assertion of sovereignty, and were absorbed into the common law as rights'.[21] However, the courts have applied this doctrine only in limited cases, such as the recognition of aboriginal marriages.

The famous *Connolly* v. *Woolrich* case,[22] heard by the Superior Court of Quebec in 1867, is a prime example of extra-State pluralism. William Connolly, a citizen of Lower Canada (today the province of Quebec), left Montreal in 1803 to go into the fur trade. He travelled to Western Canada, at a time when the presence of non-natives was reduced to a few trading posts, and married the daughter of a Cree chief, remembered only as Suzanne in history. They lived happily and had many children, but their story took a dramatic turn in 1832 when William, who had made his fortune and returned to Montreal, decided to consider his marriage to Suzanne invalid and abandoned her in order to marry her cousin, one Julia Woolrich. Many years later, the eldest son of William and Suzanne sued Julia, who had inherited from William, maintaining that as William's legitimate child, he was

20 See, for example, *Lajoie et al.* (1996) and *Lajoie et al.* (1998) *loc. cit.*, note 6.

21 *Mitchell v. M.R.N.*, [2001] 1 S.C.R. 911, at par. 10.

22 *Connolly v. Woolrich* (1867), 11 L.C.J. 197, 1 C.N.L.C. 70 (Sup. Ct.), *Connolly v. Woolrich and Johnson et al.* (1867), 17 R.J.R.Q. 75.

entitled to a portion of the inheritance. His right to sue hinged upon the validity of the marriage between William and Suzanne and the Court had to rule on this matter. Judge Monk, in passages which have been extensively quoted, declared that the introduction of English law in the Hudson Bay territory had not abolished Cree legal rules, including those pertaining to marriage, and that the validity of the marriage between William and Suzanne had to be evaluated based on the law in effect in that region at that time, that is, Cree law. Since, according to witnesses heard by the Court, William and Suzanne's union was indeed considered a marriage by the Cree, judge Monk recognized the validity of this marriage under Canadian law.

The Court of Appeal confirmed this decision, although the motives supporting its conclusion were more restricted and were limited to the need to recognize the status of marriage to unions entered into in places where no priest was available to officiate.[23] In addition, in a subsequent case, at a time where Mrs. Woolrich's lawyer had himself been appointed as judge at the Court of Appeal, the latter refused to recognize the validity of an aboriginal marriage entered into under similar circumstances,[24] which could mean that the *Connolly* decision had thus lost any precedential value. Yet the case has continued to be cited as an authority on native law recognition, including in cases involving marriage and adoption. For example, in a landmark decision rendered in 1993, the British Columbia Court of Appeal stated that, in general, the effects of aboriginal legal rules concerning personal status should be recognized in Canadian law.[25]

Hard pluralism in legislation The courts are not the only ones to engage in extra-State pluralism exercise. In some cases, the legislator and the government refer specifically to norms emanating from indigenous legal systems, without defining these norms, thus preserving, at least in theory, the normative autonomy of the indigenous peoples.

A first example of this comes from the *Indian Act*. In the *Act*, the definition of the word 'child', under article 2, 'includes a legally adopted child and a child adopted in accordance with Indian custom'. This means that under the rules regarding the transmission of Indian status (articles 6 and 7 of the *Act*), adoption under indigenous law is on an equal footing with the adoption under applicable provincial legislation. In addition, article 2 defines the 'council' of an Indian band as being, in some cases, 'the council chosen according to the custom of the band'. Bands governed by this provision therefore are not subject to the electoral process set out in articles 74 and following of the *Act*, but rather have the power to define

23 *Johnstone v. Connolly* (1869), 17 R.J.R.Q. 266, 1 C.N.L.C. 151 (Q.B.).

24 *Fraser v. Pouliot et al.* (1885), 13 R.L.O.S. 520, 2 C.N.L.C. 163 (Q.B.); the Supreme Court, disposing of the appeal in this case, did not deem it necessary to rule on the validity of the marriage: *Jones v. Fraser* (1886), 13 S.C.R. 342. On this topic, see Sanders (1975).

25 *Casimel v. Insurance Corp. of British Columbia* (1993), 106 D.L.R. (4th) 720 (B.C.C.A.); see also Zlotkin (1984).

their own method of choosing leaders, ostensibly in agreement with their own political traditions. We will see however how the Canadian government and the courts have largely influenced the content of the 'band custom', in most cases imposing the Western democratic elective process.

The Nunavut Accord[26] provides another example of extra-State pluralism. This agreement is a 'modern treaty', that is, an agreement between the Canadian government and the Nunavut Inuit which spells out the land rights and political participation rights recognized to this native people of Canada's North and the financial compensation accorded them by the government. In this context, it is necessary to identify persons considered to be Inuit who are entitled to benefit from the Agreement. Article 35.3.1 of the Agreement states that a person who 'is an Inuk as determined in accordance with Inuit customs and usages', 'identifies himself or herself as an Inuk and who is associated with Nunavut' is considered a benficiary. Thus the Agreement relies entirely on Inuit law to define the status of Inuit. Canadian law does not attempt to interfere in this determination.

Hard pluralism rooted in aboriginal rights Constitutional recognition of aboriginal rights, including the rights related to the development of certain natural resources, also opens the door to a form of pluralism. Given the collective nature of aboriginal rights, several authors claim that recognizing these necessarily implies a self-regulation space: thus, indigenous peoples would have the power to authorize some of their members to develop resources and could decide on the timing and quantities harvested or other such issues (Otis, 1999, pp. 611-619). Thus, a subjective right would give rise, so to speak, to a right to govern. However, this hypothesis, founded on the collective nature of aboriginal rights, has rarely been realized in practice, since the courts do not require these indigenous rules of resource management to be proven in trials involving the practice of traditional activities such as hunting or fishing.[27] There is however a decision by the Court of Appeal of British Columbia which recognizes the power of an indigenous group to invite members of another community to exercise its aboriginal rights.[28] It is also possible that certain indigenous groups in fact exercise this normative autonomy in the absence of any official recognition by the government. Thus the Uashat mak Mani-Utenam band has

26 *Agreement between the Inuit of the Nunavut Settlement Area and Her Majesty the Queen in right of Canada*, (1993); see also the similar provisions of articles 3.1.1 and 3.2.2 of the *Labrador Inuit Land Claims Agreement*, (2004), and the new chapter 3A of the *James Bay and Northern Quebec Agreement* inserted Complementary Agreement No. 18, concerning the Nunavut Inuit; see Grammond (2008).

27 In this regard, the decision in *R. v. Marshall*, [2004] 1 C.N.L.R. 211 (N.S.C.A.), at 224, appears to be an exception; this decision was overturned for other reasons in *R. v. Marshall; R. v. Bernard*, [2005] 2 S.C.R. 220.

28 *R. v. Jack* (1995), 131 D.L.R. (4th) 165, [1996] 2 C.N.L.R. 113 (B.C.C.A); see also *R. v. Meshake*, [2007] 3 C.N.L.R. 326, 85 O.R. (3d) 575 (C.A.); *R. v. Shipman*, [2007] 3 C.N.L.R. 375, 85 O.R. (3d) 585 (C.A.).

adopted a fishing code to regulate the exercise of aboriginal rights by its members. Although this code has no basis in federal or provincial legislation, the regime it has established seems to be tolerated by the government.

One aspect of this self-regulation space which still seems promising is the self-definition of rules of membership in Métis communities. The Canadian Constitution recognizes aboriginal rights for the Métis, but no rules in Canadian law define who the Métis are. The Supreme Court has had to issue guidelines to determine who should be considered a Métis.[29] One element of these guidelines is the acceptance of the individual concerned by the community, which supposes that it is up to the Métis communities themselves and their representative organizations to set out these membership rules. In fact in 2002 the Métis National Council had already proposed a definition of the Métis identity, which is implemented using Métis citizenship registries kept by the Métis associations in the different provinces.[30] A word of caution, however: the Supreme Court has also indicated that membership status in a Métis organization did not constitute conclusive evidence of Métis identity within the meaning of the Canadian Constitution. Thus the Court is prepared to include individuals who would participate in the community's activities without having membership status and also indicates that a Métis organization cannot confer the membership status to a person who has 'no demonstrable ancestral links with the historic community'. The Canadian State therefore, through its courts, imposes a subtle form of control over the indigenous norms it is prepared to recognize.

'Parallel' governments and hard pluralism The persistence of an indigenous legal system can sometimes go hand in hand with the existence of a traditional indigenous government, in parallel with band councils established under the *Indian Act.* One striking example is the Six Nations: they have preserved their traditional mode of government, based on the Great Law of Peace, even though in 1923 the federal government imposed an elective band council.[31] Both councils, that is, traditional and elective, work in parallel and often in cooperation. Still they obey different legitimacies: the elective council comes under Canadian law, whereas the traditional council is solidly based in the native legal order.

The courts sometimes recognize this duality. The *Gitga'at*[32] case opposed two factions of an indigenous community who fought for control of a community business. Basing himself on the incorporation documents of this business and on the discussion that had surrounded its creation, the judge concluded that control

29 *R. v. Powley*, [2003] 2 S.C.R. 207, notably at par. 33.

30 See the definition on the Métis National Council website at: http://www.metisnation.ca/who/definition.html (accessed November 9, 2006), and the Métis Nation of Ontario website at: http://www.metisnation.org/registry/home.html for a sample registry (accessed November 9, 2006); see Grammond (2009).

31 Grammond, *op. cit.*, note 1, at 76.

32 *Gitga'at Development Corp. v. Hill*, 2006 BCSC 686, reversed by (2007), 66 B.C.L.R. (4th) 349 (C.A.).

belonged to the hereditary chiefs, and not the band council elected under the *Indian Act*. Still the judge made the decision power of the hereditary chiefs conditional to the collective will of the members of the community. The ultimate legitimacy, in this case, was neither Canadian law nor indigenous traditions as such, but rather the consent of community members.

The Conceptions of Law and the Challenges of Reception

To accept to receive elements from indigenous legal systems in Canadian law is not only to recognize the plurality of the ultimate sources of law, but also to consider very different conceptions of what is understood by the concept of 'law' itself. What is of a legal nature to natives may not be so to non-natives, or *vice-versa*. It is even said sometimes that law is a Western concept, which has no specific equivalent in native societies.[33] Perhaps in the end the place of 'law' for natives does not have much to do with its role or function in Western societies.

There is often a tendency to minimize these crucial theoretical distinctions when examining the interaction between Canadian law and indigenous law. Some decisions look at the issue as if it were a matter of private international law, that is, the application of the rules of law of one country by the courts of another country. In this case, as indicated in article 2809 of the *Civil Code of Québec,* the court that must apply foreign law must require that proof be made of such law by expert testimony on the subject, that is, the testimony of lawyers from the country concerned. This is what Judge Monk did in the *Connolly v. Woolrich* case: he essentially deemed that Northern Alberta should be considered as a foreign country at the beginning of the nineteenth century and he heard testimony on the content of this law, more specifically on the content of rules governing Cree 'marriage'. He then applied these rules to the situation before him, to then deduce the consequences arising therefrom, *according to the law of successions of Lower Canada,* regarding John Connolly's right to a portion of the inheritance left by his father, William.

Even when two Western countries are involved, say France and England, this type of exercise poses difficulties that are well-known to comparative law specialists. It is not always possible to find, within a system, a rule or institution that is the exact equivalent of a rule or institution in the other system. The classic example of this is the trust in English law, an institution that does not have an equivalent in French law. Comparatists therefore have to replace a rule of law or a legal institution within its more general context in order to understand its function and logic.

33 See Glenn (2000), pp. 65-66; Vanderlinden, *loc. cit.*, note 5, at 346, 363; see also Lacasse (2004) at 23, 47-50, 71.

The Westernization of Aboriginal Law

These problems are exacerbated when radically different legal systems are involved. Take the *Connolly* case: the exercise undertaken by Judge Monk supposes that the Cree society at the beginning of the nineteenth century had a 'marriage' institution that was more or less identical to Western marriage, that is, the voluntary and indissoluble union between a man and a woman. Judge Monk indeed noted the similarities between Cree marriage and Christian marriage to justify recognition: 'it would be sheer legal pedantry and pretension, for any man, or for any tribunal, to disregard this Indian custom of marriage, inspired and taught, as it must have been by the law and the religion of nature among barbarians, who, in this essential element of a moral life, approach so near to the holy inculcations of Christianity'.[34] He also assumes that this institution is governed by precise rules that can determine who is or is not married. Finally he bases himself on the premise that these rules are legal in nature in that they have certain characteristics usually associated with law in Western societies: enunciation by a competent human authority, general application, mandatory nature, degree of stability.

Justice seems to have been done in this case and Judge Monk today passes for a particularly enlightened spirit for his time. However, one can criticize the fact that he sees indigenous law as a copy of Western law. To illustrate this, we refer to the decision rendered in 1995 by Judge Muldoon in the *Sawridge*[35] case, although it was overturned on appeal, a new trial has been ordered and we are probably still very far from the final outcome of this case. The Sawridge Band claimed it had an ancestral right, protected under the Canadian Constitution, to set its own membership rules. More specifically, the band claimed that under traditional legal rules, a woman who married a foreigner lost her band member status. If the Band was right on this point, it could render inoperative Bill 'C-31' adopted by federal Parliament in 1985, designed to give women their Indian and band member status back, from which they had been deprived by a century-old provision of the *Indian Act*.

To justify its rejection of the band's claims, Judge Muldoon incorporated in his rationale the report by anthropologist Alexander von Gernet, who testified for the government. Von Gernet claimed that the Sawridge band had never had rules to determine membership since, according to him, the fact that these so-called rules were not uniformly followed showed that they were not considered mandatory, and therefore were not legal. The parentage system observed by the anthropologists was not legal either, since it emanated from environmental constraints rather than the expression of human will. Von Gernet was of the opinion, rather, that native individuals could freely decide to associate themselves with a group or another, and could change affiliations in the process. He concluded thus:

---

34 *Connolly v. Woolrich and Johnson et al., supra*, note 22, at 115 (R.J.R.Q.).

35 *Sawridge Band. v. Canada*, [1996] 1 F.C. 3 (F.C.T.D.); this decision was overturned on appeal for apparent partiality on the part of the trial judge: *Sawridge Band v. Canada*, [1997] 3 F.C. 580 (F.C.A.).

> On the whole, membership appears to have been primarily a function of economics and not blood relationships. There are no indications that the leadership made decisions about the exclusion of new or returning members. In fact, in what has been described as the 'anarchistic individualism of the Plains', the leader had relatively little power; it was only after treaty that the government invested the chief with a local authority he did not previously enjoy.[36]

Actually, while recognizing the specific characters of indigenous normativity, Von Gernet and Judge Muldoon reserve the term 'legal' for a normative system which obeys the principles of Western law: it must proceed from a human authority and consist in rules of general application, otherwise these can be only 'economic or environmental constraints', outside of the legal field:

> The identification of decision-maker(s) or an adjudicating authority is essential, not only in light of the allegations about 'membership' made in the statement of claim, but also if the term 'law' is to be regarded as an acceptable description of the alleged tribal regulations [...].[37]

Paradoxically, a heightened sensitivity to native methods of social regulation led Judge Muldoon to deny the legal character of these. Who is right? Should one try, rather, as did judge Monk in the *Connolly* case, to force indigenous law into a Western mould, allowing the transposing of its rules to Canadian law?

Actually, both Judge Monk and Judge Muldoon claim implicitly that indigenous rules of law cannot be given recognition if they do not fit the Western conception of law. Judge Monk concluded that Cree law had a rule on marriage that was quite similar to the Canadian rule. As for Judge Muldoon, he deemed that the membership standards in the Sawridge Band did not coincide with a Western conception of law because they were not mandatory and had not been enacted by a human authority. Therefore he refused to admit them in Canadian law.

Exploring a Law Beyond Positivism.

To gain a better understanding of the relationships between Western-inspired Canadian law and indigenous law, one must therefore be aware of the fact that what the indigenous peoples today present as their law or their legal tradition stems from a conception of law that is very different from what Western lawyers are used to. Pluralism-leaning lawyers had already noticed this. The adoption of a pluralist perspective (that is, 'hard' or extra-State pluralism) on law usually leads one to consider legal systems that more or less depart from the Western conception of law that underpins civilist and common law traditions. According to a positivistic conception of law, still widespread

36 *Ibid.*, at 126-127.
37 *Ibid.*, at 126.

among law professionals, the law represents the normative activity of the State, that is, the rules enacted and sanctioned by the State for its citizens. Hard pluralism, breaking with the State's exclusive authority, necessarily leads to a transcending of the positivistic conception centred on it. Thus looking at the interaction between the law of the State and that of a religious group (for example concerning marriage), one is forced to admit that there exists, among this group, a system of norms or conflict resolution that can be called law, whether or not it is recognized as such by the State.

Consequently, it is evident that in order not only to examine indigenous normativity in a significant manner, but also to make decisions regarding the reception of this normativity while doing justice to indigenous peoples, a conception of law must be adopted which sufficiently reflects what aborigines themselves consider as law in their own tradition.[38] For example, the Law Commission of Canada, in a recent discussion chapter on the subject, largely inspired by the work of aboriginal lawyer John Borrows, states that 'Indigenous laws typically are non-prescriptive, non-adversarial and non-punitive. They generally promote values such as respect, restoration and consensus and are closely connected to the land, the Creator and the community.'[39] This quote gives an idea of the main components of the Western conception of law that must be questioned in order to study the indigenous legal systems satisfactorily.

First, indigenous societies did not have official or professional lawmaking bodies.[40] Therefore it is necessary to admit that a legal standard may be valid even if it has not been enacted (or at least enunciated) by a competent authority, as demanded by the positivistic theory. This is not to say, however, that indigenous legal systems were pure systems of diffuse social control. Indigenous law was carried by an oral tradition made of relatively solidified elements, which could be articulated during ceremonies or in wampums.

Second, it would seem that indigenous law is made up of a set of values rather than specific norms. Thus Borrows, in the above excerpt, mentioned respect, restoration and consensus. These values were turned into action, into decisions about concrete cases. They could be conveyed through stories or tales designed to gain the support of the listener. For example, Borrows tells a traditional story about the Anishinabe people in which the hero, Nanabush, uses ruse to kill a deer, then, through his own negligence, allows wolves to eat the carcass. Nanabush's subsequent tribulations show that he abused the resources at his disposal and did not treat the deer with respect. According to Borrows, this story conveys an important principle of the Anishinabe environmental law.[41]

---

38 See, for example, Borrows (2005), pp. 176-179.

39 Law Commission of Canada (2006), *Justice Within: Indigenous Legal Traditions*, p. 4.

40 *Ibid.*, at 189-193.

41 Borrows (1996), pp. 649-652; see also Borrows, *loc. cit.*, note 4, at 193-195; Mills (1994), pp. 156-161.

The emphasis on values also explains how indigenous legal traditions are often considered to focus on conflict resolution (or reconciliation) processes rather than on the standards themselves (Rouland, 1988, pp. 70-73). Values are implemented in concrete cases. There is no inflexible 'rule' *per se*. The only thing that can be observed from the outside is the conflict resolution process. Many anthropologists have studied how indigenous peoples deal with conflict, including those caused by an action which Westerners consider criminal.[42] Some authors who studied Asian law have stated that law founded on flexible values rather than on rigid universal rules was better adapted to a society that privileges community ties over the individual;[43] this conclusion could possibly be extended to indigenous peoples.

Consideration of these differences leads to more fundamental questions: in indigenous societies, was the law separate from other sources of normativity (moral ethics, social pressure, spirituality, religion)? Can one really understand what is presented as law without taking into account the general context of these societies, including their spirituality?

The premise, mentioned among others by Glenn,[44] that indigenous societies did not differentiate between the law and other sources of normativity casts a shadow on any willingness to receive 'indigenous law' in Canadian law. There would be no way then to solve the dilemma posed by the *Connolly* and *Sawridge* cases: to determine the borders of indigenous law and identify its rules. In fact, the decision of the Canadian judge (or of the legislator) as to whether or not to recognize elements of indigenous law then shows its true colours: it is a *political choice,* which is not dictated by a neutral observation of legal phenomena in the indigenous society, but rather by the conception that non-natives have of what is an acceptable degree of autonomy for the indigenous peoples.

An Approach Focused on Power Relations

Analysed as a power relationship, the reception of indigenous law raises epistemological problems that resemble the debate surrounding the integration of 'traditional ecological knowledge', or 'TEK', in the environmental evaluation processes dominated by Western science.[45] Some authors claim that this indigenous knowledge is compatible with the positivist epistemology of Western science.[46] Others, on the other hand, maintain that the appropriation of this knowledge by State representatives leads to their denaturation, since they are then separated from

---

42 See Rouland (1988), at 308 and following.

43 See Mayeda (2006), 'Appreciate the Difference: The Role of Different Domestic Norms in Law and Development Reform; Lessons from China and Japan'.

44 See note 33 above.

45 Thus, article 16.1 of the *Canadian Environmental Assessment Act*, S.C. 1992, c. 37, stipulates that aboriginal ancestral knowledge may be considered when conducting an environmental assessment.

46 An example to illustrate this view is Tsuji and Ho (2002).

the context of the indigenous society, including spirituality, and that the State's intervention thus finds itself legitimized, since the State gives the impression of having taken native concerns into account.[47]

A few recent examples illustrate the power relationships that underlie the decisions of Canadian courts regarding reception of indigenous law. These examples will also illustrate the problems of evidence which, for a jurist, stem from the adoption of a theory of the sources of law that is radically different from that which underlies written laws and the extraction of general rules from the decisions (also written) of the courts.

Who declares the law? The most obvious way in which Canadian law distributes legal power to the indigenous peoples resides in the designation of the authorized enunciators of their law. The case is simple when a self-government agreement specifies that certain designated bodies of an indigenous people have the power to adopt written legislative instruments which must be included in a register accessible to the public.[48] Lawmaking powers are then clearly attributed to these bodies. The same applies when an indigenous government body is given power to publish the customary laws of this people.[49]

Things get more complicated, however, when the Canadian law does not identify the authorized source of the indigenous law it purports to receive. Such is the case, for example, when the *Indian Act* directs the election of the band council to take place according to 'band custom' without defining or identifying what this custom is, or when judges recognize traditional marriage or adoption.[50] Faced with such uncertainty, the receiving judge has several options that reflect divergent conceptions of the very concept of law.

The judge may first look for a form of popular consensus within the people concerned, regarding the norm to be identified. This is what the Federal Court does regarding 'electoral custom'. Pressed by opposing factions to define the custom of certain bands, the Court first stated that it would attempt to identify the rules over which there was a consensus within the band concerned.[51] However, in a subsequent decision, the Court seemed to slip, confusing consensus and majority decision, as evidenced by this statement by Judge Reed: 'I am of the

---

47 See Simpson (2004).

48 See, for example, *Yukon First Nations Self-Government Act*, S.C. 1994, c. 35, art. 10.

49 *Labrador Inuit Agreement*, art. 17.5.

50 See also the definition of 'child' in article 2 of the *Indian Act*, which includes a 'a child adopted in accordance with Indian custom' or the similar definition in *An Act respecting Cree, Inuit and Naskapi Native persons*, R.S.Q. c. A-33.1, art. 14, as well the procedures to recognize a native adoption in the *Adoption Act*, R.S.B.C. 1996, c. 5, art. 46, and in the *Aboriginal Custom Adoption Recognition Act*, S.N.W.T. 1994, c. 26.

51 *Bigstone v. Big Eagle*, [1993] 1 C.N.L.R. 25 (F.C.T.D.), at 34; *Bone v. Sioux Valley Indian Band No. 290 Council*, [1996] 3 C.N.L.R. 54 (F.C.T.D.).

view that approval by a majority of the adult members of the Band is probably a safe indication of a broad consense […]'.[52] Yet, for the indigenous peoples, the concept of consensus is opposed to a simple majority decision. More recently, the Federal Court of Appeal gave precedence to a written electoral code over any subsequent custom or practice.[53] In practice, it amounts to a Western method of defining majority rule. The law is then conceived as a rule that human action can change at will, as is the case with Western systems.

However, the law can also be conceived as existing independently from any human intervention, meaning that the enunciator does not create the law, but enunciates a pre-existing law, whether this law emanates from custom, social practice or a form of revelation. A Canadian jurist must then be able to identify a person or a group of persons (elders, for example), within an indigenous people, who can give access to this knowledge. In a judicial context, this usually takes the form of testimony either by elders or by anthropologists who summarize the teachings of the elders. Usually, there are no written sources, forcing the courts to base themselves on testimonial evidence, which usually carries less probative strength than written documents. The example of the *Sawridge* case mentioned above shows that this situation gives the judge extensive discretionary powers to decide whether or not an indigenous norm will be recognized and to define its content.

It is also possible for a Canadian jurist to be confronted with differing opinions within the indigenous people concerned. It is especially difficult to decide in such conflicts, especially when they involve a so-called traditionalist minority opposing a decision taken by a majority. The democratic principle leads one to favour the majority, whereas an idealized vision of indigenous peoples could lead to favour those who invoke tradition. If we look at the principles of the *Van der Peet* decision,[54] one could even be tempted to say that only 'traditional' norms, which reflect the cultural specificity of the people concerned, warrant recognition.[55] In any case, it is never easy for an outsider to determine what constitutes the tradition of an indigenous people and, as we will see, such determination is liable to freeze this tradition.

Betraying indigenous law? In addition to deciding who enunciates the law on behalf of an indigenous people, Canadian judges can even assume the power to enunciate the content of such law themselves. Thus in British Columbia and the

52 *McLeod Lake Indian Band v. Chingee* (1998), 165 D.L.R. (4th) 348 (F.C.T.D.); *Francis v. Mohawk Council of Kanesatake*, [2003] 4 F.C. 1133 (T.D.), §36-37.

53 *Bruno v. Samson Cree Nation*, 2006 FCA 249, §39; see also *Harpe v. Ta'an Kwach'an Council*, [2006] 2 C.N.L.R. 70 (Yukon S.C.), §84.

54 *R. v. Van der Peet*, [1996] 2 S.C.R. 507.

55 The criteria of cultural specificity, or of the 'integral part of a distinctive culture', was amply criticized (Barsh and Henderson, 1997; Schulte-Tenckhoff, 1997, pp. 155-157; Niezen, 2003), to a point where the Supreme Court, in a recent decision (*R. v. Sappier*; *R. v. Gray*, [2006] 2 S.C.R. 686, §42-47), recognized the validity of this criticism and reformulate the criteria based on the indigenous 'lifestyle' from the first contact era.

Northwest Territories, the law provides expressly for the recognition of custom adoption.[56] Now the courts have begun developing their own criteria for what constitutes a custom adoption: it is the voluntary placement of a child, with the consent of the natural and adoptive parents, with indigenous adoptive parents, where there is a justification that is compatible with custom, for example the mother's young age.[57]

In the same manner, the decision of what constitutes a band's electoral custom has been strongly influenced by the policy of the Indian Affairs Department, which authorizes a band to free themselves of the constraints of the *Indian Act* and to 'return to custom' only on condition that this custom be elective.[58] One should not be surprised that a good number of native peoples today present an elective system as being their 'custom'.

Finally, a rather funny but yet revealing example comes from the Supreme Court decision in *Sundown*,[59] which pertained to the right of a native man to build a hunting camp on public land, as an accessory of the right to hunt recognized under a treaty. Without being asked, Justice Cory cited the collective nature of aboriginal rights to hold that the camp built by Mr. Sundown did not belong to him:

> Any interest in the hunting cabin is a collective right that is derived from the treaty and the traditional expeditionary method of hunting. It belongs to the Band as a whole and not to Mr. Sundown or any individual member of the Joseph Bighead First Nation. It would not be possible, for example, for Mr. Sundown to exclude other members of this First Nation who have the same treaty right to hunt in Meadow Lake Provincial Park.

This opinion is not based on any evidence concerning the content of the indigenous legal system of the people concerned. Yet, shrouded in the authority of a Supreme Court decision, there is a high risk that it will pass for the definitive enunciation of an indigenous rule. This case illustrates the well-known risk related to the reception of 'customary law' by Western legal orders (Zorn and Care, 2002, pp. 631-634). The authority of the judge, when he enunciates the custom, inevitably eclipses that of the traditional enunciators of this custom. In addition to bending the legal system of the people concerned, sometimes based on stereotypes (as in the *Sundown* case), this process contributes to making it more rigid. Indeed, the authority of the precedent linked to judicial decisions, especially in common law

---

56 *Aboriginal Custom Adoption Recognition Act*, S.N.W.T. 1994, c. 26; *Adoption Act*, R.S.B.C. 1996, c. 5, art. 46.

57 *Re Tagornak Adoption Petition*, [1984] 1 C.N.L.R. 185 (N.W.T.S.C.); *Re B.C. Birth Registration No. 1994-09-040399*, [1998] 4 C.N.L.R. 7 (B.C.S.C.).

58 See information sheet on the Department of Indian Affairs website: http://www.ainc-inac.gc.ca/ps/lts/nelts/ele/index_f.html (accessed on January 5, 2007); see also Otis (2004), pp. 401-402.

59 *R. v. Sundown*, [1999] 1 S.C.R. 393.

systems, prevents any subsequent evolution of the 'custom'. The people concerned then lose control over their own legal system to the benefit of the judiciary.

The scope of the reception The decision to receive elements of indigenous law that are relevant to the solution to a dispute often poses the question of the scope of such reception. The *Connolly* case again is a good illustration of this problem. Having received in Canadian law the Cree rules regarding marriage, did Judge Monk also have to receive divorce rules? The repudiation of Suzanne by William having taken place in Montreal, the judge easily ruled that it was governed by Lower Canadian law, which at the time did not recognize divorce.[60]

In this case, recognizing marriage but not divorce was equivalent to imposing a Western (and Christian) conception of family life. But there is more: Judge Monk had to isolate Cree marriage and take it out of its cultural context. The rest of the relationships between the members of the Connolly family were governed by the rules of Lower Canada law, including rules concerning succession. The judge did not attempt to understand family relationships in the wider scope of indigenous thought and values.

It is not always so. A Northwest Territories court ruled that a customary adoption entailed the application of all indigenous legal rules regarding the effects of customary adoption.[61] Thus the natural parents could continue to have obligations toward the child given up for adoption, whereas in Canadian law, this would be impossible, since adoption completely dissolves the legal ties between a child and its natural parents.

In this regard, it may appear ironic that the French *Cour de cassation* provides the model to follow, in a decision on the scope of application of the Kanake custom in New Caledonia.[62] Indeed, the organic law of this territory states that the inhabitants of Kanak customary status are governed by Kanak custom in matters of civil law. The Court of Cassation ruled that this reference encompassed educative assistance (what is called youth protection in Canada), even though Kanak law contained no rule on this subject, since this institution is foreign to it. This reference to customary law, in fact, translates into the recognition of indigenous autonomy to decide, in future, of the content of these rules, even if this means adopting the rules of French law in whole or in part.

The reception, real or feigned, of indigenous law in Canadian law can also have the effect, if not the objective, of *legitimizing* the latter's intervention in aboriginal communities. Take the example of sentencing circles, in which the judge called upon to sentence an offender consults with the members of the community as to the kind of sentence that would serve the needs of the community and restore harmony.

---

60 *Connolly v. Woolrich and Johnson et al., supra* note 22, at 145 (R.J.R.Q.).

61 *K. (S.K.) v. S. (J.)*, [1999] N.W.T.J. No. 94 (N.W.T.S.C.); on this topic, see also Baldassi (2006).

62 French Court of Cassation, Court notice 005-011, December 16, 2005, note Deumier and Encinas de Munagorri (2005).

By giving natives the illusion of having regained control of the criminal justice system, the process hides the fact that the judge, who is a member of the Canadian legal system, retains the entire power to amend or ignore the recommendations of the circle's participants. In reality, the adaptations made to the criminal justice system are relatively minor. The courts have in fact often repeated that sentences handed down to aboriginal offenders found guilty of serious offences would be the same as those imposed to non-natives.[63]

Likewise regarding aboriginal rights, reference to the indigenous perspective or to indigenous legal systems hardly masks the fact that it is the Supreme Court, in the end, that decides the scope of aboriginal rights, and that it seems intent on doing it in such a way as to allow natives to exploit natural resources for domestic purposes, but not commercial purposes.[64]

Legal Pluralism: Normative Aspects

So far, we have examined examples of the reception of indigenous law and identified their impact. However, legal pluralism also raises normative issues, that is, not only issues relating to the mechanisms of interaction between two legal systems and their effects, but also to the desirability of such interactions.

These normative issues can be examined from the perspective of self-government. The normative autonomy that stems from the reception of indigenous law (and corresponding withdrawal of Canadian law) is a facet of self-government long claimed by indigenous peoples and recognized since 1995 by the federal government. Autonomy usually raises questions regarding its relationship with culture and respect for individual rights. We will see in the following pages that culture is often used to define the *scope* of autonomy – in what areas can the indigenous people adopt their own laws? – whereas individual rights are often invoked as a *limit* to this autonomy – why certain indigenous laws should not be recognized.

Normative issues of course cannot be examined absent a theoretical framework justifying the recognition, within a State, of specific rights to a portion of the population. It is not possible to present the ins and outs of this debate in an exhaustive manner in this chapter. Suffice it to say that there are two main schools of thought

63 *R. v. Gladue*, [1999] 1 S.C.R. 688, §79; *R. v. Wells*, [2000] 1 S.C.R. 207, §42; *R. v. J. (C.)*, [1998] 4 C.N.L.R. 198, 119 C.C.C. (3d) 444 (Nfld. C.A.); *R. v. Laliberté*, [2000] 4 W.W.R. 491, 143 C.C.C. (3d) 503 (Sask. C.A.), at 532, 537; *R. v. Casimir*, 2001 BCCA 310; *R. v. Vermette*, [2001] 8 W.W.R. 10, 154 C.C.C. (3d) 193 (Man. C.A.); *R. v. Fox* (2001), 277 A.R. 298 (C.A.); *R. v. Francis* (2001), 240 N.B.R. (2d) 159 (C.A.); *R. v. Sutherland* (2001), 156 C.C.C. (3d) 264 (Ont. C.A.); *R. v. Carrière* (2002), 158 O.A.C. 36 (C.A.); *R. v. Moccasin*, [2006] 2 C.N.L.R. 243 (Sask. C.A.), at 253.

64 This is what seems to come out of the juxtaposition of recent decisions in *R. v. Marshall*; *R. v. Bernard*, [2005] 2 S.C.R. 220, and *R. v. Sappier*; *R. v. Gray*, [2006] 2 S.C.R. 686.

on this topic. The first, which we can call the 'theory of multiculturalism',[65] justifies the rights of minority groups, including the indigenous peoples, by the *de facto* inequities suffered by individuals whose culture is not that of the majority or dominant group. It is not surprising that it ties recognition of autonomy with culture and insists on respect for individual rights. The second, known among other things as 'treaty federalism', insists rather on the original sovereignty of the indigenous peoples and relationships of colonial domination implemented by the State.[66] It usually serves to justify a greater degree of autonomy, is more critical regarding the requirements of cultural specificity posed by Canadian law and considers that the protection of individual rights should be the responsibility of indigenous peoples themselves and not that of the Canadian State.

Indigenous Culture and the Reception of Law

When examining cultural issues, lawyers often use a 'popular' conception of culture which generally refers to art or folklore. Now modern anthropology sees culture in a completely different perspective.[67] Culture indeed is a very broad concept: it designates all the gestures, practices or customs that have a meaning within society; therefore it is a system of thinking, of values, of beliefs. Culture is made up of such varied areas as food customs, economic system, history, leisure, law, and so on. Based on a modern conception, any human activity is cultural.

Of course, too broad a definition risks being useless. This is why, when talking about culture, one usually refers to the regularity likely to be observed in certain human activities within a given society. This tendency to generalize holds a trap, however, into which many jurists have fallen. This is to look for certain practices that would constitute essential elements in a people's culture and in the absence of which a person would not authentically participate in this culture. Today, this conception, called 'essentialism', is rejected. It is of course admitted that cultures evolve over time, but also that the practices that make up this culture vary from one individual to the next and that it is not possible, from the outside, to decide that such and such a practice is essential. Cultural groups are not homogenous, fixed or static: quite the contrary. Moreover, there is continuity, rather than rupture, between different cultural groups. This means that it is not possible to trace a tight border between such groups, as there will inevitably be individuals who will cross the border to adopt cultural practices originating from either group.

If one admits, with the theorists of multiculturalism, that policies concerning the indigenous peoples should aim at the promotion of culture, one is tempted to

65 See, among others, Kymlicka (1995); Raz (1994); Taylor (1994); Mesure and Renaut (2002); Schulte-Tenckhoff (ed.) (2002); Dieckhoff (2004); regarding the application of the justifications to the indigenous peoples, see Macklem (2001), pp. 46-75.

66 See, among others, Tully (1995); Macklem, *op. cit.*, note 65, at 107-159; Turner (2006); Henderson (1994).

67 For a good introduction to this problem, Cuche (2004).

deduce that indigenous legal norms should only be received in Canadian law if they are tied to indigenous cultural specificity. The equation appears logical, but in reality, it hides several of the traps illustrated above, including the risk of reducing culture to folkloric stereotypes.

Thus the Ontario Court of Appeal recently had to rule in a case concerning the governance of a corporation created by an aboriginal community to administer its commercial enterprises. The Court summarily dismissed the relevance of an alleged indigenous norm and gave to understand that it was difficult to find a specifically indigenous aspect to the management of a corporation.[68] The result could have been different if the dispute had been dubbed as relating to the governance of the community, which is more easily tied to indigenous culture.[69] In fact, there is a similarity between this and other decisions, including regarding aboriginal rights,[70] tax exemption[71] or labour relations[72] where the courts dissociated indigenous cultural specificity and the participation of the indigenous peoples themselves in the economy. This approach could undermine the economic autonomy of the indigenous peoples.

Following a similar reasoning, one could be tempted to impose a requirement of 'cultural authenticity' to the reception of indigenous law, that is, that this law would be received only in situations where interested parties follow the cultural traditions of their people. Thus, even if family law is the privileged domain of reception of indigenous law, some judges have refused to recognize an indigenous marriage or adoption since the parties did not follow a traditional lifestyle and the relationships concerned were closer to a common law marriage in contemporary Western society or the simple transfer of custody of a child.[73]

Such cases show that to make reception of indigenous law conditional upon proof of cultural specificity could degenerate quickly into a judgement of what constitutes authentic indigenous culture. The concept of culture is difficult to handle as an operative concept in law. Even if we recognize that reception of indigenous law pursues cultural objectives, it is preferable not to ask jurists carrying out this exercise to assess cultural evidence and pass judgements on this topic. The scope of the reception of indigenous law and ensuing autonomy must therefore be determined using other means. It is probably inevitable that this scope be established through an agreement between the government and the indigenous peoples or, failing that, by a federal law.[74]

---

68 *Wasauksing First Nation v. Wasausink Lands inc.*, [2004] 2 C.N.L.R. 355 (Ont. C.A.), at par. 94-98; see also *Gitga'at Development Corp. v. Hill* (2007), 66 B.C.L.R. (4th) 349 (C.A.).

69 *Gitga'at Development Corp. v. Hill*, 2006 BCSC 686.

70 For example, *R. v. Van der Peet*, [1996] 2 S.C.R. 507; *R. v. N.T.C. Smokehouse Ltd.*, [1996] 2 S.C.R. 672.

71 *MacDiarmid Lumber Ltd. v. God's Lake First Nation*, 2006 SCC 58, §27; Grammond, *op. cit.*, note 1, at 384-387; Marshall (1998).

72 *Mississauga of Scugog Island First Nation v. National Automobile, Aerospace, Transportation and General Workers Union of Canada* (2007), 287 D.L.R. (4th) 452 Ont. C.A.), §36.

73 *Manychief v. Poffenroth*, [1995] 2 C.N.L.R. 67, [1995] 3 W.W.R. 210 (Alta. Q.B.); *Prince v. Duncan (Public Trustee of)*, [2000] 4 C.N.L.R. 249 (B.C.S.C.).

74 See a proposal in this regard from Borrows, *loc. cit.*, note 4.

Individual Rights and Good Governance

Whereas culture is often used to define the scope of reception of indigenous law, individual rights can justify limits to this reception. Indeed the traditional norms of a cultural group can sometimes be perceived as an impairment on the fundamental rights of some of its members. Reconciling the collective interests of the group and the individual rights of its members is one of the main challenges of the theories on minority rights.[75] This problem is often presented as an intractable conflict between the fundamental rights and the autonomy of cultural groups, and the question is which, of fundamental rights or autonomy, should prevail. Given their relationship with liberal philosophy and individual autonomy, multiculturalism theories usually give primacy to charters of rights,[76] although some theorists accept that they may be enforced by institutions other than State courts, or to recognize some flexibility in the concrete scope of protected rights, in order to echo the important elements of indigenous culture.[77] As for the reception of indigenous legal systems, this means that the adoption of a liberal perspective leads to the imposing of conditions to the recognition of indigenous legal norms, in order to ensure they are compatible with individual rights. Some examples follow.

The rights of women For the indigenous peoples as for other minorities all over the world, one major friction point is the question of women's rights. Until 1985, the rules regarding Indian status in Canada discriminated against women,[78] including women who married non-natives, and some aboriginal groups today are still trying to perpetuate the sexist distinctions by claiming that their purpose is the protection of the culture.[79] In addition, aboriginal women's groups often denounce the fact that self-government policies lead to male domination and do not take sufficient account of women's interests.[80]

In 1985, the Federal Parliament tried to solve this problem with so-called Bill 'C-31', which restored Indian status to women who had lost it due to old discriminatory

75 See, among other things, Eisenberg and Spinner-Halev (eds) (2005); Shachar (2001); Otis, 'La gouvernance autochtone avec ou sans la Charte canadienne?' in G. Christie (ed.) (2006), *Aboriginality and Governance: A Multidisciplinary Perspective*.

76 Kymlicka, *op. cit.*, note 65, at 35-44.

77 For an in-depth analysis of this issue, see Otis, *loc. cit.*, note 75.

78 S.M. Weaver, 'First Nations Women and Government Policy, 1970-92: Discrimination and Conflict', in Burt, Code and Dorney (eds.) (1993), *Changing Patterns: Women in Canada*; Moss (1990); Lawrence (2004); Macklem, *op. cit.*, note 65, at 227-233.

79 *Sawridge Band v. Canada*, [1996] 1 F.C. 3 (F.C.T.D.), new trial ordered: [1997] 3 F.C. 580 (F.C.C.A.); *Scrimbitt v. Sakimay Indian Band Council*, [2000] 1 F.C. 513, [2000] 1 C.N.L.R. 205 (F.C.T.D.); *McIvor v. Canada (Registrar, Indian and Northern Affairs)*, [2007] 3 C.N.L.R. 72 (B.C.S.C.) aff'd (2009), 306 D.L.R. (4th) 193 (B.C.C.A.); see also Dick (2006).

80 Native Women's Association of Canada, *An Aboriginal Charter of Rights and Freedoms: Addressing Aspects of Human Dignity*, 1992, online at <http://www.nwac-hq.org/AnAboriginalChaterRightsFreedoms.pdf> (accessed May 30, 2006).

rules, and to their children, and which recognized the power of Indian bands to adopt their own 'membership codes', that is, to decide who was a member of a band.[81] However, to prevent bands from exercising this normative autonomy to deprive reintegrated women from most of the rights tied to their status, Parliament inserted a provision protecting the acquired rights of these women, thus imposing a minimum content to membership codes. Some bands used schemes, which were condemned by the courts, to avoid recognizing these acquired rights.[82]

Although the issue cannot be fully debated in this chapter, the rejection of so-called sexist traditions and the priority given to women's rights by Canadian law[83] seem fully justified. This does not mean that compromise solutions cannot be considered. Aboriginal lawyer John Borrows suggests that indigenous legal standards can evolve in the direction indicated by fundamental rights.[84] He invokes therefore a progressive vision of indigenous culture and law. This approach is reflected in a recent decision by the Yukon Supreme Court, in which the judge ruled that an indigenous group's custom regarding the election of its chief had evolved in such a way as to allow the election of a woman as much as that of a man.[85]

The rights of children For several decades now, there have been laws allowing government officials to take custody of children whose development would be compromised if left in the custody of their parents and to place them with foster families, who eventually adopt them.[86] The application of this system had disastrous consequences for indigenous peoples, who saw a great number of their children adopted by non-aboriginal parents. The concept of the best interest of the child, which is the paramount consideration in decisions concerning children, is often interpreted based on Western standards regarding the role of parents, resulting in more frequent intervention in native families.[87]

To try and reverse this disturbing trend, several provinces changed their laws to take into account the interest of the aboriginal child in remaining in his or her own community. Administrative or even normative autonomy was also recognized for certain indigenous groups, ostensibly to keep aboriginal children in their communities. Such systems underline once again the discrepancy between the interests of the child and those of the group: some will claim that an aboriginal

81 *Indian Act*, R.S.C. 1985, c. I-5, art. 5 and following.

82 *L'Hirondelle v. Canada*, [2003] 4 F.C. 748 (T.D.), confirmed by [2004] 3 F.C. 274 (C.A.); *Scrimbitt v. Sakimay Indian Band Council*, [2000] 1 F.C. 513, [2000] 1 C.N.L.R. 205 (F.C.T.D.) ; *Omeasoo v. Canada (Minister of Indian Affairs and Northern Development)* (1988), 24 F.T.R. 130, [1989] 1 C.N.L.R. 110.

83 See among other things section 35(4) of the *Constitution Act, 1982*, R.S.C. 1985, app. II, No. 44, which specifies that aboriginal and treaty rights are guaranteed equally to male and female persons.

84 See Borrows (1994); Borrows, *loc. cit.*, note 4, at 219.

85 *Harpe v. Ta'an Kwach'an Council*, [2006] 2 C.N.L.R. 70 (Yukon S.C.), at par. 85-91.

86 For example the *Youth Protection Act*, R.S.Q., c. P-34.1.

87 See Kline (1992); Grammond, *op. cit.*, note 1, at 391-397.

child will be better treated in a non-aboriginal family and that to keep him or her in the community serves a collective purpose to the detriment of the child's best interest. This issue was also raised regarding customary adoption which, according to some, does not adequately protect the child's interests.[88]

Several mechanisms have been put in place to limit the normative autonomy of the indigenous peoples in the area of youth protection. For example, the Nisga'a Treaty states that Nisga'a youth protection laws must comply with the principle of the child's best interest.[89] Similarly, the Quebec *Youth Protection Act* allows the government to enter into an agreement with an indigenous people in order to set up a parallel youth protection system, but the general principles of the law, including the child's best interest, must continue to apply.[90]

The rights of victims As we have seen above, criminal law is an area where many experiences have been attempted to adapt and integrate indigenous normativity, especially with respect to sentencing. Such experiences often result in lighter sentencing for the offender.[91] Some women's groups maintain that this approach is not a sufficiently firm solution to the violence to which aboriginal women fall victim. In addition, it seems that the victims often feel social pressure to take part in a sentencing circle, where the real objective is allegedly to keep the offender out of jail. These factors have prompted some aboriginal women to criticize the adoption of an indigenous conception of criminal justice as being detrimental to women and trivializing the violence against them.[92] Moreover, in the case of violent offenders, some native communities even oppose lighter prison sentences,[93] because they have to reintegrate these offenders sooner, without being able to use traditional methods of reconciliation: in other words, the worst of both worlds.

The rights of citizens More generally, the purpose of limiting the reception of indigenous law can also be to protect aboriginal citizens from abuse, real or imagined, by their governments. Thus the jurisprudence of the Federal Court regarding electoral custom insists on the principle of assent by a majority of band members as a criterion to identify the custom of the band in question.[94] The

88 Baldassi, 2006; see also, for a denunciation of customary adoption practices, Commission des droits de la personne et de la jeunesse du Québec (2007), *Investigation into child and youth protection services in Ungava Bay and Hudson Bay*, online: http://www.cdpdj.qc.ca/fr/publications/docs/rapport_Nunavuk_francais.pdf (accessed January 15, 2008) or *X (In the matter of)*, [2006] R.J.Q. 2513, [2007] 1 C.N.L.R. 168 (Quebec Ct.).

89 Nisga'a Final Agreement, ch. 11, art. 96.

90 *Youth Protection Act*, R.S.Q., c. P-34.1, art. 37.5.

91 For an extreme example, see *R. v. Sackanay* (2000), 47 O.R. (3d) 612 (C.A.).

92 E. La Rocque, 'Re-examining Culturally Appropriate Models in Criminal Justice Applications', in Asch (ed.) (1997), *Aboriginal and Treaty Rights in Canada*.

93 See, for example, the decision in *R. v. Amitook*, [2006] C.N.L.R. 249 (Quebec Ct.), §73-77, which quotes a resolution by the Makivik Corp. denouncing overly clement sentences.

94 See note 52 *supra*.

courts therefore pose as guardians of the democratic legitimacy of indigenous governments and refuse to recognize a standard that would not be accepted by a majority of community members. As stated by a British Columbia judge: 'The inherent legitimacy of the hereditary clan governance can only be justified if it preserves consensus building and decision making by the community.'[95]

Likewise, the *Yukon First Nations Self-Government Act*[96] recognizes the validity of the constitutions adopted by the peoples concerned, subject to certain requirements to ensure the democratic legitimacy of their governments. Thus these constitutions must protect the rights and freedoms of citizens, provide accountability measures and a mechanism to control conformity of the laws to the constitutions and contain a formula for constitutional amendment by citizens, allowing them to retain ultimate control over their government.

The rights of others Finally, the protection of the interests of the non-indigenous population can also explain some of the limits imposed on the reception of indigenous legal systems. The courts are sensitive to the consequences that their decisions could have on society in general, whether because of the undue competitive advantage that the reception of certain indigenous rules could create or because of the expenditure of public funds that would result from it.

As we have already mentioned, the *Powley*[97] decision recognized the power of Métis communities to decide on their own membership rules. However, the Supreme Court set certain limits to the recognition of such rules. A Métis community cannot confer membership status to a person who does not have a genealogical tie with a historical Métis community, nor to a person who does not identify themselves as Métis, or whose self-identification appears too recent and purely opportunistic. By this the Court wants to avoid the recognition of Métis rules that would confer rights upon persons who cannot legitimately call themselves Métis, which could lead to an abuse of public funds or of rare resources.

Conclusion: A Provisional Assessment

The reception of indigenous law by Canadian courts is a delicate enterprise, especially given the lack of familiarity of non-aboriginal lawyers with the content of this law and the issues surrounding its reception. As we have seen, the promise of greater autonomy associated with the recognition of indigenous legal systems could be quashed if it is only a pretext for greater control by Canadian lawyers on indigenous knowledge, leading to a denaturation of this knowledge.

95 *Gitga'at Development Corp. v. Hill*, 2006 BCSC 686, §52, reversed by (2007), 66 B.C.L.R. (4th) 349 (C.A.).

96 *Yukon First Nations Self-Government Act*, S.C. 1994, c. 35, art. 8.

97 *R. v. Powley*, [2003] 2 S.C.R. 207, including at par. 31-34.

For a successful reception of indigenous law, it is crucial that it be the work of aboriginal peoples themselves. They must decide the relevance of such a project, and the respective proportions of tradition and modernity of the law that they wish to give themselves. It is possible that they will opt for the written legal technique, integrating indigenous traditional values.[98] It is also important that indigenous law be interpreted and applied first and foremost by indigenous authorities, which would tend to minimize the reception problems analysed in this chapter. Finally, it would be good for non-indigenous Canadian jurists to receive training to better understand the issues surrounding the reception of indigenous law and to have at least a general idea of its content.

References

Baldassi, Cindy L. (2006). 'The Legal Status of Aboriginal Customary Adoption Across Canada: Comparisons, Contrasts and Convergences', *University of British Columbia Law Review*, **39**(1): 63–100.

Bankes, Nigel (2006). '*Marshall and Bernard*: Ignoring the Relevance of Customary Property Laws', *University of New Brunswick Law Journal*, **55**: 120–134.

Barsh, Russel L. and James Youngblood Henderson (1997). 'The Supreme Court's *Van der Peet* Trilogy: Naïve Imperialism and Ropes of Sand', *McGill Law Journal*, **42**(2): 993–1009.

Borrows, John (1994). 'Contemporary Traditional Equality: The Effect of the Charter on First Nations Politics', *University of New Brunswick Law Journal*, **43**: 19–48.

Borrows, John (1996). 'With or Without You: First Nations Law (in Canada)', *McGill Law Journal*, **41**(3): 629–665.

Borrows, John (2005). 'Indigenous Legal Traditions in Canada', *Washington University Journal of Law and Policy*, **19**: 167–223.

Cuche, Denys (2004). *La notion de culture dans les sciences sociales*, 3rd ed., Paris: La Découverte.

Dacks, Gurston (2004). 'Implementing First Nations Self-Government in Yukon: Lessons for Canada', *Canadian Journal of Political Science*, **37**(3): 671–694.

Department of Indian and Northern Affairs Canada (1993). *Agreement between the Inuit of the Nunavut Settlement Area and Her Majesty the Queen in right of Canada*, at: http://www.ainc-inac.gc.ca/pr/agr/pdf/nunav_e.pdf.

Department of Indian and Northern Affairs Canada (2004). *The Labrador Inuit Land Claims Agreement*, at: http://www.ainc-inac.gc.ca/pr/agr/labi/labi_e.pdf.

98 See, for example, Teslin Tlingit Council (2005), the 'Ha Kus Teyea' draft declaration of the Teslin Tlingit Nation of Yukon: http://www.ttc-teslin.com/pdf/ha%20kus%20teyea.pdf (accessed January 22, 2007).

Department of Indian and Northern Affairs Canada (2007). *Information Sheet: Lands and Trust Services – Elections*, at: http://www.ainc-inac.gc.ca/ps/lts/nelts/ele/index_f.html.

Deumier, Pascale and Rafael Encinas de Munagorri (2005). 'Sources du droit interne – Faut-il différer l'application des règles jurisprudentielles nouvelles?', *Revue trimestrielle de droit civil*, **1**: 83–88.

Dick, Caroline (2006). 'The Politics of Intragroup Difference: First Nations' Women and the Sawridge Dispute', *Canadian Journal of Political Science*, **39**(1): 97–116.

Dieckhoff, Alain (2004). *La constellation des appartenances: nationalisme, libéralisme et pluralisme*, Paris: Presses de Sciences Pô.

Eisenberg, Avigail and Jeff Spinner-Halev (eds) (2005). *Minorities within Minorities: Equality, Rights and Diversity*, Cambridge: Cambridge University Press.

France. Court of Cassation (2005). Court notice No. 005-011, 16 December, at: http://www.courdecassation.fr/jurisprudence_publications_documentation_2/avis_15/classes_par_239/2005_410/16_decembre_2005_0050011p_411/005_0011_309.html.

Glenn, H. Patrick (2000). *Legal Traditions of the World*, Oxford: Oxford University Press.

Grammond, Sébastien (2003). *Aménager la coexistence: les peuples autochtones et le droit canadien*, Bruxelles/Montréal: Bruylant/Yvon Blais.

Grammond, Sébastien (2008). 'L'appartenance aux communautés inuit du Nunavik: un cas de réception de l'ordre juridique inuit?', *Canadian Journal of Law and Society*, **23**: 93–117.

Grammond, Sébastien (2009). *Identity Captured by Law: Membership in Canada's Indigenous Peoples and Linguistic Minorities*, Montreal and Kingston: McGill-Queen's University Press.

Green, Ross G. (1998). *Justice in Aboriginal Communities*, Saskatoon: Purich Publishing.

Griffiths, John (1986). 'What is Legal Pluralism?', *Journal of Legal Pluralism and Unofficial Law*, **24**: 1–55.

Henderson, James Youngblood (1994). 'Empowering Treaty Federalism', *Saskatchewan Law Review*, **58**: 241–329.

Jaccoud, Mylène (2002). 'La justice pénale et les Autochtones: d'une justice imposée au transfert de pouvoirs', *Canadian Journal of Law and Society*, **17**(2): 107–121.

Kleinhans, Martha-Marie and Roderick A. Macdonald (1997). 'What is a *Critical* Legal Pluralism?', *Canadian Journal of Law and Society*, **12**(2): 25–46.

Kline, Marlee (1992). 'Child Welfare Law, "Best Interests of the Child" Ideology, and First Nations', *Osgoode Hall Law Journal*, **30**(2): 375–425.

Kwochka, Daniel (1996). 'Aboriginal Injustice: Making Room for a Restorative Paradigm', *Saskatchewan Law Review*, **60**(1): 153–187.

Kymlicka, Will (1995). *Multicultural Citizenship*, Oxford: Oxford University Press.

Lacasse, Jean-Paul (2004). *Les Innus et le territoire: Innu tipenitamun*, Québec: Septentrion.

Lajoie, Andrée, Jean-Maurice Brisson, Sylvio Normand and Alain Bissonnette (1996). *Le statut juridique des peuples autochtones au Québec et le pluralisme*, Cowansville: Éditions Yvon Blais.

Lajoie, Andrée, Henry Quillinan, Roderick A. Macdonald and Guy Rocher (1998). 'Pluralisme juridique à Kahnawake?', *Les Cahiers de Droit*, **39**(4): 681–716.

La Rocque, Emma (1997). 'Re-examining Culturally Appropriate Models in Criminal Justice Applications', in Michael Asch (ed.), *Aboriginal and Treaty Rights in Canada*, Vancouver: UBC Press.

Law Commission of Canada (2006). *Justice Within: Indigenous Legal Traditions*, Ottawa: Law Commission of Canada.

Law Commission of Canada (2007). *Indigenous Legal Traditions*, Vancouver: UBC Press.

Lawrence, Bonita (2004). *"Real" Indians and Others: Mixed-Blood Urban Native Peoples and Indigenous Nationhood*, Vancouver: UBC Press.

LeBel, Louis and Pierre-Louis Le Saunier (2006). 'L'interaction du droit civil et de la common law à la Cour suprême du Canada', *Les Cahiers de Droit*, **47**(2): 179–238.

Macklem, Patrick (2001). *Indigenous Difference and the Constitution of Canada*, Toronto: University of Toronto Press.

Marshall, Murray (1998). 'Business and Investment Income under Section 87 of the *Indian Act*: *Recalma v. Canada*', *Canadian Bar Review*, **77**(3/4): 528–548.

Mayeda, Graham (2006). 'Appreciate the Difference: The Role of Different Domestic Norms in Law and Development Reform; Lessons from China and Japan', *McGill Law Journal*, **51**(3): 547–598.

Melançon, Hugues (1997). 'Une analyse pluraliste des conceptions juridiques autochtones devant les tribunaux de juridiction pénale au Canada', *Canadian Journal of Law and Society*, **12**(2): 159–186.

Mesure, Sylvie and Alain Renaut (2002). *Alter ego: Les paradoxes de l'identité démocratique*, Paris: Flammarion.

Métis Nation of Ontario (2006). *The MNO Registry*, at: http://www.metisnation.org/registry/home.html.

Métis National Council (2006). *Who Are The Métis? National Definition of Métis*, at: http://www.metisnation.ca/who/definition.html.

Mills, Antonia (1994). *Eagle Down is our Law: Witsuwit'en Law, Feasts and Land Claims*, Vancouver: UBC Press.

Moss, Wendy (1990). 'Indigenous Self-Government in Canada and Sexual Equality Under the Indian Act: Resolving Conflicts Between Collective and Individual Rights', *Queen's Law Journal*, **15**(2): 279–305.

Native Women's Association of Canada (1992). *An Aboriginal Charter of Rights and Freedoms: Addressing Aspects of Human Dignity*, at: http://www.nwac-hq.org/en/documents/AboriginalCharterofRightsandFreedoms.pdf.

Niezen, Ronald (2003). 'Culture and the Judiciary: The Meaning of the Culture Concept as a Source of Aboriginal Rights in Canada', *Canadian Journal of Law and Society*, **18**(2): 1–26.

Otis, Ghislain (1999). 'Les sources des droits ancestraux des peuples autochtones', *Les Cahiers de Droit*, **40**(3): 591-620 .

Otis, Ghislain (2004). 'Élection, gouvernance traditionnelle et droits fondamentaux chez les peuples autochtones du Canada', *McGill Law Journal*, **49**(2): 393–417.

Otis, Ghislain (2006). 'Aboriginal Governance with or without the Canadian Charter?', in Gordon Christie (ed.), *Aboriginality and Governance: A Multidisciplinary Perspective*, Penticton, B.C.: Theytus Books.

Raz, Joseph (1994). *Ethics in the Public Domain*, Oxford: Clarendon Press.

Rouland, Norbert (1988). *Anthropologie juridique*, Paris: P.U.F.

Royal Commission on Aboriginal Peoples (1993). *Partners in Confederation: Aboriginal Peoples, Self-Government, and the Constitution*, Ottawa: Supply and Services.

Sanders, Douglas (1975). 'Indian Women: Their Roles and Rights', *McGill Law Journal*, **21**: 656–672.

Secrétariat aux Affaires autochtones Québec (2006). *James Bay and Northern Quebec Agreement and Complementary Agreements*, 2nd ed., Québec: Publications du Québec.

Shachar, Ayelet (2001). *Multicultural Jurisdictions: Cultural Differences and Women's Rights*, Cambridge: Cambridge University Press.

Schulte-Tenckhoff, Isabelle (1997). *La question des peuples autochtones*, Bruxelles/Paris: Bruylant/L.G.D.J.

Schulte-Tenckhoff, Isabelle (ed.) (2002). *Altérité et droit: Contributions à l'étude du rapport entre droit et culture*, Bruxelles: Bruylant.

Simpson, Leanne R. (2004). 'Anticolonial Strategies for the Recovery and Maintenance of Indigenous Knowledge', *American Indian Quarterly*, **28**(3/4): 373–384.

Taylor, Charles (1994). 'The Politics of Recognition', in Amy Gutmann (ed.), *Multiculturalism*, Princeton: Princeton University Press.

Teslin Tlinglit Council (2005). *Ha Kus Teyea – The Tlingit Way: Declaration and Charter of Teslin Tlingit Nation*, Sixth Discussion Draft, 1 June, at: http://www.ttc-teslin.com/pdf/ha%20kus%20teyea.pdf.

Tremblay, André (1995). *La réforme de la constitution au Canada*, Montréal: Thémis.

Tsuji, Leonard, J.S. and Elise Ho (2002). 'Traditional Environmental Knowledge and Western Science: In Search of Common Ground', *Canadian Journal of Native Studies*, **22**(2): 327–360.

Tully, James (1995). *Strange Multiplicity*, Cambridge: Cambridge University Press.
Turner, Dale M. (2006). *This Is Not a Peace Pipe: Towards a Critical Indigenous Philosophy*, Toronto: University of Toronto Press.
United Nations General Assembly (2007). *Resolution 61/295 – United Nations Declaration on the Rights of Indigenous Peoples*, 2 October, at: http://daccessdds.un.org/doc/UNDOC/GEN/N06/512/07/PDF/N0651207.pdf?OpenElement.
Vanderlinden, Jacques (2005). 'À la rencontre de quelques conceptions du pluralisme juridique', *Revue de la common law en français*, 7(1/2): 303–388.
von Benda-Beckmann, Franz (2002). 'Who's Afraid of Legal Pluralism?', *Journal of Legal Pluralism and Unofficial Law*, **47**: 37–82.
Walters, Mark D. (1999). 'The 'Golden Thread' of Continuity: Aboriginal Customs at Common Law and Under the *Constitution Act, 1982*', *McGill Law Journal*, **44**(3): 711–752.
Weaver, Sally M. (1993). 'First Nations Women and Government Policy, 1970-92: Discrimination and Conflict', in Sandra D. Burt, Lorraine Code and Lindsay Dorney (eds.), *Changing Patterns: Women in Canada*, 2nd ed., Toronto: McClelland and Stewart.
Zlotkin, Norman (1984). 'Judicial Recognition of Aboriginal Customary Law in Canada', *Canadian Native Law Reporter*, **4**: 1–17.
Zorn, Jean G. and Jennifer Corrin Care (2002). "Bravara Tru': Judicial Approaches to the Pleading and Proof of Custom in the South Pacific', *International and Comparative Law Quarterly*, **51**(3): 612–639.

Legal Cases

Connolly v. Woolrich and Johnson et al. (1867), 17 R.J.R.Q. 75
Connolly v. Woolrich (1867), 1 C.N.L.C. 70 (Sup. Ct.), 11 L.C.J. 197 (Que. Sup. Ct.)
Johnstone v. Connolly (1869), 17 R.J.R.Q. 266, 1 C.N.S.C. 151 (Q.B.)
Fraser v. Pouliot et al. (1885), 13 R.L.O.S. 520, 2 C.N.S.C. 163 (Q.B.)
Jones v. Fraser (1886), 13 S.C.R. 342
Re Tagornak Adoption Petition, [1984] 1 C.N.L.R. 185 (N.W.T.S.C.)
Omeasoo v. Canada (Minister of Indian Affairs and Northern Development) (1988), 24 F.T.R. 130, [1989] 1 C.N.L.R. 110
Bigstone v. Big Eagle, [1993] 1 C.N.L.R. 25 (F.C.T.D)
Casimel v. Insurance Corp. of British Columbia (1993), 106 D.L.R. (4th) 720 (B.C.C.A.)
R. v. Naappaluk (1993), 25 C.R. (4th) 220, J.E. 93-1681, [1994] 2 C.N.L.R. 143 (C.Q.)
R. v. Johnson (1994), 91 C.C.C. (3d) 21, [1995] 2 C.N.L.R. 158 (Yukon C.A.)
Manychief v. Poffenroth, [1995] 2 C.N.L.R. 67, 3 W.W.R. 210 (Alta. Q.B.)
R. v. Jack (1995), 131 D.L.R. (4th) 165, [1996] 2 C.N.L.R. 113 (B.C.C.A.)
R. v. Morin, [1995] 4 C.N.L.R. 37, 101 C.C.C. (3d) 124 (Sask. C.A.)

Bone v. Sioux Valley Indian Band No. 290 Council, [1996] 3 C.N.L.R. 54 (F.C.T.D.)
R. v. N.T.C. Smokehouse Ltd., [1996] 2 S.C.R. 672
R. v. Van der Peet, [1996] 2 S.C.R. 507
Sawridge Band v. Canada, [1996] 1 F.C. 3 (F.C.T.D.), [1997] 3 F.C. 580 (F.C.A.)
Delgamuukw v. British Columbia, [1997] 3 S.C.R. 1010
McLeod Lake Indian Band v. Chingee (1998), 165 D.L.R. (4th) 348 (F.C.T.D.)
R. v. J. (C.), [1998] 4 C.N.L.R. 198, (1997) 119 C.C.C. (3d) 444 (Nfld. C.A.)
Re B.C. Birth Registration No. 1994-09-040399, [1998] 4 C.N.L.R. 7 (B.C.S.C.)
K. (S.K.) v. S. (J.), [1999] N.W.T.J. No. 94 (N.W.T.S.C)
R. v. Gladue, [1999] 1 S.C.R. 688
R. v. Sundown, [1999] 1 S.C.R. 393
Prince v. Duncan (Public Trustee of), [2000] 4 C.N.L.R. 249 (B.C.S.C.)
R. v. Laliberté, [2000] 4 W.W.R. 491, 143 C.C.C. (3d) 503 (Sask. C.A.)
R. v. Sackanay (2000), 47 O.R. (3d) 612 (C.A.)
R. v. Wells, [2000] 1 S.C.R. 207
Scrimbitt v. Sakimay Indian Band Council, [2000] 1 F.C. 513, 1 C.N.L.R. 205 (F.C.T.D.)
Mitchell v. M.R.N., [2001] 1 S.C.R. 911
R. v. Casimir, 2001 BCCA 310
R. v. Fox (2001), 277 A.R. 298 (C.A.)
R. v. Francis (2001), 240 N.B.R (2d) 159 (C.A.)
R. v. Sutherland (2001), 156 C.C.C. (3d) 264 (Ont. C.A.)
R. v. Vermette, [2001] 8 W.W.R. 10, 154 C.C.C. (3d) 193 (Man. C.A.)
R. v. Carrière (2002), 158 O.A.C. 36 (C.A.)
Francis v. Mohawk Council of Kanesatake, [2003] 4 F.C. 1133 (T.D.)
L'Hirondelle v. Canada, [2003] 4 F.C. 748 (T.D.), [2004] 3 F.C. 274 (C.A.)
R. v. Powley, [2003] 2 S.C.R. 207
R. v. Marshall, [2004] 1 C.N.L.R. 211 (N.S.C.A.)
Wasauksing First Nation v. Wasausink Lands inc., [2004] 2 C.N.L.R. 355 (Ont. C.A.)
R. v. Marshall; *R. v. Bernard*, [2005] 2 S.C.R. 220
Bruno v. Samson Cree Nation, 2006 FCA 249
Gitga'at Development Corp. v. Hill, 2006 BCSC 686, rev'd (2007), 66 B.C.L.R. (4th) 349 (C.A.)
Harpe v. Ta'an Kwach'an Council, [2006] 2 C.N.L.R. 70 (Yukon S.C.)
MacDiarmid Lumber Ltd. v. God's Lake First Nation, [2006] 2 S.C.R. 846
R. v. Amitook, [2006] 3 C.N.L.R. 249 (Quebec Ct.)
R. v. Moccasin, [2006] 2 C.N.L.R. 243 (Sask. C.A.)
R. v. Sappier; R. v. Gray, [2006] 2 S.C.R. 686
X (In the matter of), [2006] R.J.Q. 2513, [2007] 1 C.N.L.R. 168 (Quebec Ct.)
Dubé v. The Queen, 2007 TCC 393, aff'd 2009 FCA 109
McIvor v. Canada (Registrar, Indian and Northern Affairs), [2007] 3 C.N.L.R. 72 (B.C.S.C.), aff'd (2009) 306 D.L.R. (4th) 193

Mississaugas of Scugog Island First Nation v. National Automobile, Aerospace, Transportation and General Workers Union of Canada (2007), 287 D.L.R. (4th) 452 (Ont. C.A.)
R. v. Meshake, [2007] 3 C.N.L.R. 326, 85 O.R. (3d) 575 (C.A.)
R. v. Shipman, [2007] 3 C.N.L.R. 375, 85 O.R. (3d) 585 (C.A.)

Legislation

Aboriginal Custom Adoption Recognition Act, S.N.W.T. 1994, c. 26
Adoption Act, R.S.B.C. 1996, c. 5
An Act respecting Cree, Inuit and Naskapi Native persons, R.S.Q. c. A-33.1
Canadian Environmental Asssessment Act, S.C. 1992, c. 37
Constitution Act, 1982, R.S.C. 1985, app. II, No. 44
Indian Act, R.S.C. 1985, c. I-5
Youth Protection Act, R.S.Q., c. P-34.1
Yukon First Nations Self-Government Act, S.C. 1994, c. 35

Chapter 3

Family Law's Legal Pluralism: Private 'Opting-Out' in Canada and South Africa

Annie Bunting

Introduction

When we think of multijuralism – overlapping legal jurisdictions – we often think of the combination of national, regional and international laws (as in Europe for example) or of two separate national legal systems potentially applying to the same dispute (as in private contract law). Multijuralism could be described as vertical in nature in the former case and horizontal in the latter. Less often, it seems, do we think of multijuralism in terms of the interaction of state law with non-state law or state law with religious legal principles such as those found in Islamic or Rabbinical law.[1] But just as in the case of certain financial instruments,[2] the diamond industry and other commercial enterprises,[3] and Aboriginal nations,[4] religious communities may establish mechanisms for resolving disputes 'in the shadow of the law' (Mnookin and Kornhauser, 1979). While these mechanisms will not always be embodied in formal institutional procedures and structures, they have an impact on individuals for whom those non-state values are also important and persuasive. 'Laila', for example states:

> ... if there['s] anything in the civil that gives me more than Islamically, then I wouldn't take it. No, like here they give half on property and in Islam it is not the case. And really again I am accountable in front of God and not the Canadian system. So I would do what would make me happy with God especially [as] I have read the Quran and I know what is in it.[5]

---

1 The concern over non-state legal systems and their interaction with state law is of course the subject of the rich legal pluralism literature in the field of law and society. I draw on that literature in this chapter. See, for example, Drummond (2005); Engle Merry (1990); Griffiths (1986); von Benda-Beckmann (2002).

2 See Favero (Chapter 8, this volume).

3 See, for example, Bernstein (1992 and 1998).

4 See Grammond (Chapter 2, this volume)

5 'Laila', Interview by author, 16 June 2005, Scarborough, Ontario.

This chapter will explore the place of multijuralism in family law, which I refer to as family law's legal pluralism. As I will argue, it is not just religious couples or immigrant families who may choose to opt out of the statutory family law scheme available in Canada. Many couples at the time of separation and divorce seek out alternative resolution of their disputes to avoid the expense, publicity and time associated with court cases. And in their separation agreements, individuals may contract out of the statutory minimums. In other words, couples may customize their separation negotiations through the choice of venue and through the content of the agreement – indeed the provincial family statute encourages private choice in this respect.

I focus on Muslim religious communities for two related reasons. First, since the announcement in 2003 of the creation of the Islamic Institute for Civil Justice in Ontario to perform family arbitrations there has been heated public debate about the place of faith-based 'opting out' in family law in Canada. Secondly, it is during private arbitrations and mediations that spouses articulate competing values explicitly in terms of multiple legal norms. Therefore, it is in the negotiations of separation agreements and other domestic contracts, very private and intimate affairs, that multijuralism is at play.

If one were to examine only the reported cases where judges are asked to assess the weight of religious legal principles or the binding character of religious domestic contracts on the parties, multijuralism would appear to be a very minor occurrence in family law. Qualitative research which includes interviews with arbitrators, mediators, religious individuals, and community leaders, by contrast, yields a more complete picture of how various legal norms have an impact on individuals' decision-making. Qualitative research is also necessary in order to ascertain the frequency with which individuals are availing themselves of the assistance of community members, mediators, or arbitrators as opposed to or at the same time as, consulting a lawyer or family court. While it is trite to say that not all separation and divorce cases appear as reported decisions, it is important to explore why people approach the law as well as what role the law plays even when it is not formally invoked.

Katherine Brown (2006, 418) argues that it is through the complex negotiations of identities and rights that British Muslim women act: 'The identities of Muslim women are understood here as contextual and relational *positionings*, and it is suggested that the articulation of an Islamic identity may support Muslim women in the strategic negotiations over the realization of their rights'. Brown grounds her work in qualitative research, in particular on interviews about Muslim women's rights with non-governmental organizations in the UK, and on secondary research based on the 1998 to 2002 Southampton Asian Women's Oral History Project. Like Brown, I attempt to present the complex reasons why Muslim women may negotiate their entitlements and responsibilities on separation and divorce according to a variety of legal norms, including non-state religious norms.

I also explore the relationship between community-based mediation, religion, and the family law standards found in statutes. Little academic research exists in

Canada on the interaction of Islamic law (or *Shari'a*) on marriage and divorce and statutory law[6]; informal mediation of family disputes is a fertile place to explore these intersections. Further, little is known about the perception by Muslim Canadians of family law in general, and mediation in particular.[7] Finally, only recently have family mediators addressed cultural issues such as cross-cultural communication, culturally specific childrearing practices, religious instruction for children, alternative healing, and the experiences of recent immigrant families. Court-annexed mediation or formal mediation does not reflect the diversity of the Canadian population. In the words of Edward Kruk (1998, 197):

> The extent to which Canadian family mediation is largely a White, middle-class phenomenon is notable: Ethnocultural communities accounted for an average of only 13.4% of clientele [in the survey of 250 practising family mediators].

This chapter is part of a larger project on cross-cultural conflicts in Canadian family law. One goal of the project is to ascertain, through a variety of methods, the reasons why some people may choose to mediate their marriage breakdown with an Imam, a counsellor at a community-based organization, a feminist social worker, or non-religious criminal lawyer. What role does the religious or cultural paradigm play and what role does state law play in these negotiations?

I draw on research conducted before the announcement in 2003 of the establishment of the Islamic Institute for Civil Justice for business and family arbitration according to Islamic law. In the first stages of the research project I conducted interviews with community-based mediators in Muslim communities in and around Toronto. After the public announcement of the Islamic Institute, I attended public meetings, academic conferences, and consultations in response to the initiative. I then interviewed women who might choose to avail themselves of religious arbitration in the province should that be possible, whether sanctioned by the provincial government or not. I discuss this research with particular reference to why Muslim women and men may choose to opt out of the provincial statutory scheme.

The third section of the chapter examines debates over religious marriage and divorce in South Africa and also includes qualitative research – based on interviews in 2006 with Muslim social welfare providers at the Muslim Judicial Council and the Islamic Social Welfare Agency in Cape Town (Western Cape), as well as with Muslim women. The South Africa research, however, is not primarily qualitative; it is based on case law and academic commentary on religious marriage and divorce, including the *Islamic Marriages Bill*. Finally, close studies of multijuralism in action

---

6 The same observation was made by Qaisi (2000, 68) in respect of the American context.

7 Connie Beck (Law & Society Conference, May 30, 2002) concluded her review of divorce mediation literature with the observation that we do not know how 'ethnic communities' perceive mediation. See also Beck and Sales (2001).

in private family law negotiations reveal the way in which statutory provisions are interpreted and applied in relation to other socio-legal norms. I argue that this is a natural extension of the balance between private ordering and minimum standards in both the Canadian and the South African family law contexts. I first consider the recent law reform in Ontario before discussing the research from Ontario and South Africa.

Faith-based Family Arbitration in Ontario

Socio-Legal Framework

On February 15, 2006 the Ontario Legislature passed the *Family Statute Law Amendment Act*,[8] bringing two and a half years of public debate to a close – or one chapter of the debate to a close. Introduced into the provincial Legislature only three months earlier, the new law makes any religious arbitration of family disputes unenforceable in Ontario, and requires that all family arbitrations conform to provincial statutory requirements.[9] Henceforth, a family arbitration decision will be enforceable only if the arbitrator applies Ontario law or that of another Canadian jurisdiction. Arbitrators may not apply, for example, New York State law or Talmudic law or Islamic law. I asked participants in this research, mostly religious Muslim women, about their views on religious arbitration and family-dispute resolution concerning issues including marriage contracts, *mahr* (dower), custody, support, and divorce.

Most of the women agreed that for religious women it is important to have religious mediation of their separation agreement and to secure a religious divorce that would be recognized in Canada or in a Muslim country. At the same time, women I spoke to had divergent opinions about the desirability of having religious arbitrators making *binding* decisions that would be enforced by Ontario courts. Indeed, there was considerable misunderstanding among the respondents about the binding nature of mediated agreements and arbitration decisions generally. While most of the women with whom I spoke saw themselves as capable of upholding their own rights, either through their choice of arbitrators or their inclination to

---

8 *Family Statute Law Amendment Act*, 2005 – an Act to amend the Arbitration Act, 1991, the Child and Family Services Act and the Family Law Act in connection with family arbitration and related matters, and to amend the Children's Law Reform Act in connection with the matters to be considered by the court in dealing with applications for custody and access.

9 Arbitrations differ from mediation in that in the former, the parties to the arbitration agreement confer decision-making power upon the arbitrator while in mediations, the parties come to an agreement with the assistance of the mediator. In other words, in theory, parties to mediation retain the decision-making power while the parties to an arbitration retain only the power to choose the arbitrator.

challenge what they considered to be patriarchal interpretations of Islamic law, they felt that there were other women in the Muslim community, particularly new immigrants, who would be more vulnerable. For example, Azmat made the following statement:

> If a woman goes for arbitration and she doesn't know her rights, what is she asking for? She will have to listen to whatever they are going to give to her. If a woman goes well informed, then they can negotiate and they can say, 'Hey, you can't say this to me, because this is not the Islamic law,' because we lose the negotiating power right there when we are not informed.[10]

Elsewhere she asserted:

> ... I would like to say to these women [they] should study the Islam more and learn about the religion more before they are so scared or insecure. If they really don't know about the religion of course they are going to be scared of something they don't know, so they are not knowledgeable enough because in their country the man usually dominates the society and they were the ones who implemented the laws and kind of made it from the male perspective, not from the women's side, and that's what is causing problems. It's not the law, it's the people who are implementing the law.[11]

The announcement two and a half years ago of the establishment of an Islamic arbitration service in Ontario, and the response to this public statement, has brought into sharp focus how little we know about religious tribunals in the province and how little we know from the people who may choose to avail themselves (with or without community and family pressure) of the services offered at existing mosques or proposed arbitration tribunals. As the public debate over *Shari'a* tribunals and their consequences for women's rights unfolded, the lack of research in this area was noteworthy as was the lack of a diversity of voices in the debate.[12]

The Ontario government commissioned a review of family law arbitration by former Attorney General Marion Boyd. The Report (2005) included the results of consultations between June and September 2004. Her conclusions echoed my own finding that many people who responded to her consultation had previously been unaware that arbitration was available in family law and that religious communities, most notably the Rabbinical Courts, had been in operation in Ontario for some time.[13] Moreover,

---

10 Azmat, Interview by author, 16 June 2005, Toronto, Ontario.

11 *Ibid.*

12 The debate was largely dominated by spokespersons representing women's rights groups and more secular Muslim organizations voicing opposition to the proposal and elite male religious figures voicing support for it.

13 Boyd (2005, 29).

> because the arbitration process was private, and indeed chosen by many because it kept their personal disputes out of the public limelight, no mechanism was set up to monitor or track the use of arbitrations for these issues. Therefore, the Review was faced with considerable difficulty in determining the extent to which arbitration is used for resolving family law disputes. We had to rely on lawyers and arbitration practitioners who volunteered to share information with us.[14]

Interestingly, very few arbitration settlements (whether based on statutory or religious laws) are judicially reviewed or enforced through the courts.[15]

The Ontario *Family Law Act* puts in place a set of basic rights and obligations to which everyone is entitled as a 'default position.' It then accords great value to private autonomy by permitting couples to contract out of its provisions. The Act recognizes private agreements if they meet the formal requirements stipulated in the act for 'domestic contracts.'[16] If there is a conflict between a domestic contract and statutory rights – if, for example, a domestic contract states that a wife is entitled to less than half of the family property, the amount she would be entitled to under the Act – the Act provides that the provision of the domestic contract will prevail over the rights and obligations set out in the Act.[17] As a result, couples routinely rely upon, and courts routinely enforce, private agreements that depart significantly from the 'default position' set out in the Act. The scope permitted by the Act for private contracting out of statutory rights puts the lie to the myth, propagated during the *Shari'a* tribunal debates, that there is one family law for all Ontarians. The law permits privatized legal pluralism.

In Ontario, mediation is mandatory in most kinds of civil litigation: family law, however, is excluded. Family mediation is thus a voluntary process in Ontario; the courts may order mediation of family disputes only on the consent of the parties.[18] A successful mediation results in a negotiated agreement. Like agreements reached through other means, mediation agreements may take the form of 'domestic contracts' that are binding on the parties and prevail over any inconsistent provisions of the *Family Law Act*, subject to the limitations on the enforceability of private contracts described above.

---

14 Boyd (2005, 35).

15 See Fournier (2006), 'In the (Canadian) Shadow of Islamic Law: Translating *Mahr* into a Private Bargaining Endowment', *Osgoode Hall Law Journal,* 44(4), p. 649-677.

16 *Family Law Act,*, R.S.O. 1990, c. F.3, Part IV.

17 *Family Law Act*, s.2(10).

18 *Family Law Act*, s.3(1). As stated above, in theory, mediators are not to influence the outcome of decisions but rather are to assist parties to come to a mutually agreeable solution. In practise, in particular in cases of informal mediation where the mediator is a religious leader in the community, mediators may play a more decisive role.

The result of the 2006 amendments is that family arbitration decisions are brought within the complex set of provisions in the *Family Law Act* that seek to respect private autonomy and secure some basic civic entitlements. Family arbitrations that are not based on Canadian law – for example, those based on religious principles or foreign law – have no legal effect.

One key theme that arose in interviews prior to the change in the law was the perception amongst participants that an arbitrated decision would not be binding and enforceable in a 'Canadian court.'[19] One woman stated that she would use *Shari'a* tribunals if they were available in her area 'because I am a Muslim and *Shari'a* is my Koran book. If I am not happy about the *Shari'a* decision I have the right to choose Canadian law.'[20] Another woman said she would use religious tribunals 'only as a last resort before going to family law.'[21] A third woman, Fazia, described arbitration as 'counselling, the step before going to court.'[22] Interestingly, after the 2006 amendments to the law, religious arbitrations conducted according to an Islamic legal code would indeed just be 'counselling' and not binding in an Ontario court. Generally, I found there was a lack of legal literacy, or understanding, about the nature of mediation and arbitration in our interviews and in public discussion about the issue. Couples may still arrange their affairs after separation on the basis of religious principles by entering into a separation agreement that is not based on an arbitration decision. In such a separation agreement, they may choose, for example, not to abide by the provisions for equal division of family property found in the statute or the spousal support obligations set out therein. Separation agreements other than arbitration agreements are not affected by the new law. They may be based on any laws or principles the parties choose, and are legally binding subject to the general limitations described above.

The arbitral door to creating binding agreements based on religious principles has been firmly shut by the 2006 amendments. But parties determined to settle their family rights and obligations on the basis of religious principles in a legally binding manner have other options open to them. They can create separation agreements by any means other than binding arbitration. Negotiated separation agreements, even those concluded with the assistance of informal advisors, mediators, or arbitrators (so long as the latter's awards are 'advisory' only or not legally binding), can be based on religious principles and are legally binding under the *Family Law Act*. Thus, the government's denial of legally binding force to family arbitration based on religious principles is, it turns out, a matter of legal form rather than normative substance. The formal obstacle to binding religious arbitration of family matters

19 On the other hand, a few women commented that it would be desirable to have decisions enforced by the family courts, sanctioned by government.

20 Interview by author, 16 June 2005, Toronto, Ontario.

21 Interview by author, 16 June 2005, Toronto, Ontario.

22 Interview by author, 24 June 2005, Toronto, Ontario.

is easily evaded, if the parties so desire, by embodying the results of advisory religious arbitration decisions in negotiated separation agreements.

Placing family-arbitration decisions based on religious principles 'beyond the law' does not mean, of course, that such arbitrations will cease to take place. For the reasons described above, the content of any such decisions may still become legally binding if the parties take the step of embodying them in separation agreements. The recent amendments leave untouched the *Family Law Act*'s balance between private contractual autonomy and statutory entitlements.[23]

In discussing whether she would go to a private, religious arbitrator or to a provincial family court for a separation agreement, 'Laila', a schoolteacher in an Islamic school in Toronto, does not say that she would avoid the civil courts. Rather, she is clear that she would opt in or opt out depending on whether the remedy conformed with her reading of the Quran.[24] Like other women with whom I have spoken over the past four years, she is aware of some details of her entitlements under the provincial family law scheme as well as her entitlements under Islamic law. And while she has not had a dispute with her husband that necessitated such advice, she can imagine going to either a religious/ community leader or the courts or both.[25] Indeed this is consistent with what informal mediators in the Muslim community in Toronto said: couples are often working with a court-annexed family law mediator or their case is in front of the courts while they are simultaneously negotiating informally.[26]

As mentioned above, informal dispute resolution has long been taking place in Canadian Muslim communities with imams and other community leaders serving as mediators or even informal arbitrators. Even though religious arbitrations of family disputes will no longer be legally binding in Ontario, the results of such arbitrations may be subsequently embodied in a separation agreement that is legally binding. As long as these informal channels are known and regularly relied upon within the community, couples will opt out of the family law system and the statutory scheme.

Why do Couples Opt Out of State Family Law?

One of the reasons why Muslims are taking an active interest both in informal mediation, arbitration, and the secular court proceedings and in the intersections of these proceedings and principles is that many Muslims perceive that the secular state system would not correspond to their cultural values and religion. Indeed Alia Hogben, a retired social worker and President of the Canadian Council of Muslim Women, asked one man, who had approached the Islamic Centre for

23 Put another way, as one government policy lawyer stated, the new legislation brings 'family arbitrations' onto the same footing as mediated agreements under the act.

24 'Laila', Interview by author, 16 June 2005, Scarborough, Ontario.

25 *Ibid.*

26 Interviews with family mediators, November 2002.

mediation in Kingston, why he was not using the mediation services available at the Court. He responded, 'They would not understand our cultural differences'. Ms Hogben took this to mean that the court-annexed mediators would not understand the 'role of husband and wife in their Muslim home, the importance of family cohesiveness, the rights and responsibilities of the spouses and the group, and the fear of freedom given to children in Ontario (birth control for example).'[27] Arif Raza, a criminal lawyer who does family mediation pro bono in his Muslim Scarborough community, reiterates this point: people express a 'preference for the comfort of their own cultural framework'.[28]

A 1997 study of domestic violence in the Muslim community of Greater Toronto found that respondents thought women would approach parents, relatives or friends rather than talking to a doctor, teacher, social worker about abuse.[29] Of the Arab respondents, the results were most striking: 90 per cent said that when Muslim women do experience abuse in Canada they would *not* talk to a doctor, nurse, teacher or agency.[30] Indeed, results of questionnaires showed that an overwhelming majority (90.5 per cent) of service providers surveyed thought 'shame or embarrassment' would prevent women from approaching services in the Toronto area.[31]

Uzma Shakir, Director of the Council of Agencies Serving South Asians, reiterated this point when she, too, said people will go to a neighbour before going for counselling: 'People want advice not counselling … counselling model is too presumptuous, value laden, neo colonialism writ large.' By contrast, she asserted, a community-based model, not a professionalized model, is preferable. Ms Shakir noted that religious organizations are most direct method. Rather than the adversarial system in family courts, community-based mediation looks to reconciliation and crisis prevention.[32] Sangeeta, Executive Director of the South Asian Women's Centre, agreed.[33]

Another theme that arose in a focus group was the importance of religion for migrant Muslim woman in the diaspora. While in Somalia, India, or Egypt, women need not or may not organize around religion, in Canada religion becomes an important shared marker of identity. 'Halima' stated that we 'are becoming more faithful in the diaspora … restarting our identities in this country.'[34] Fazia reiterated that 'in diaspora we are getting closer to the religion because it is some

27 Interview by author, 16 July 2002, Kingston, Ontario.

28 Interview by author, June 2002, Scarborough, Ontario.

29 Muslim Community Services (Brampton Ontario) (1997), *Women Behind the Veil: A research Study of the issue of Women Abuse in the Muslim Community*, Brampton, MCS, 1997 at 68-69.

30 *Ibid.*

31 *Ibid.* at 72.

32 Interview by author, 9 September 2002, Toronto, Ontario.

33 Interview by author, 9 September 2002, Toronto, Ontario.

34 'Halima', Interview by author, 24 June 2005, Toronto, Ontario.

commonality.'[35] Since in Somalia, she added, 'everyone was Muslim ... culture was more important in many ways than the religion itself. But as we came out and they ask for [...] we are learning more about religion, we keep getting closer to religion because we have the opportunity now to see ourselves.'[36] Several of the women I interviewed demonstrated a complex gender consciousness encompassing a propensity to question dominant traditional interpretations of Islamic law, and a sense that at least some male proponents of Islamic law have a gender bias.[37]

Further, the 'space for mediation is needed because clients may not be able to pay', as Michael Abdul Rashid Taylor states.[38] Mr. Rashid Taylor works at a psychiatric facility in Toronto. He also counsels inmates in prisons and jail. Couples are referred to him by word of mouth. He was seeing a couple, a young couple, who felt a stigma attached to separation and divorce. Alia Hogben commented that some people have a 'fear of the system, lack of language facility and find the cost of lawyers' out of their reach. Boyd (2005, 103-4) also found in her consultations that 'many respondents to the Review perceived the availability of mediation and arbitration for family matters as an access to justice issue ... . Financial considerations can be a serious constraint to access to justice.'

On separation, many women in the Afghan community, Nillab[39] reported, are scared of going to court. Confidentiality is very important, as 'they don't want others in the community to know'. She noted that it is an issue of being 'comfortable' – language and culture. 'The worker needs to talk their language.' 'Talking their language' may also include understanding the cultural clues and context. Reem Abdul Kadur, a social worker of Arab descent, discussed the importance of a client being at ease and not needing to explain their cultural context.

Another reason for the interest in mediation by Muslim mediators is the importance of *Shari'a* law[40] to individuals and the community. Abdul Hai Patel would argue that there are potential conflicts between the provincial and federal laws and Islamic law. For example, there is the issue of enforcement of religious marriage contracts or *mahr* agreements. In marriage contracts, there may be a dower paid on the occasion of the bride's marriage and an agreed amount of money as 'deferred dower' or security should the parties divorce. If the wife initiates the divorce the contract may stipulate that she forfeit the *mahr*. Without going into the complexities of the *mahr*, suffice it to say that spouses may choose to mediate

35 Interview by author, 24 June 2005, Toronto, Ontario.

36 *Ibid.*

37 See Mahmood (2005).

38 Interview by author, 6 September 2002, Toronto, Ontario.

39 Nillab will be referred to by her first name only.

40 When discussing Islamic law, one has to be cautious not to over-generalize. And see Omar Saddiqui and Shahina Saddiqui's paper (2006) with interviews about the meaning of *Shari'a* in Muslims' lives.

the payment of *mahr* on divorce with a Muslim mediator rather than through the civil courts.[41]

In Canada, the matter has come before the courts with conflicting results. In British Columbia the contract was honoured and in Ontario the judge deferred to 'the religious authorities'. In the latter case *Kaddoura v. Hammoud* (1998), the payment of *mahr* was $30 000. While I am not going to comment on the merits of the case, the deference of 'Islamic law experts' is noteworthy. Two experts were called in the case: one the Imam of a mosque in Ottawa and a scholar in Islamic studies, the other an Imam in Ajax and Director of the Institute of Islamic Learning. The judge notes that both experts 'agreed that any such dispute was to be resolved according to religious authorities. Mufti Khan said he dealt with many Muslim communities in North America.'[42]

In the decision, the Judge found that the *mahr* is 'essentially and fundamentally an Islamic religious matter.'[43] 'Where, as seems to be the case here, the issue must be determined with reference to religious doctrine and principle, the civil court is least lacking in expertise and … constitutionally beyond its territory'.[44] Quoting a US Supreme Court decision (*Serbian East Orthodox Diocese*), Rutherford J. states: 'to determine what the rights and obligations of Sam and Manira are in relation to the undertaking of Mahr in their Islamic marriage ceremony would necessarily lead the Court into the 'religious thicket' a place that the courts cannot safely and should not go.'[45]

Interestingly, in the BC case, the court found the agreement concerning *mahr* to be an enforceable marriage agreement satisfying the requirements of section 61 of the *Family Relations Act*. (*Amlani v. Hirani* 2000)[46] The *mahr* was considered 'other property' in a marriage contract for the purposes of the Act. There were no references to expert witnesses, religious scholars or conflicting Islamic law; only the parties themselves testified.

Other issues of potential conflict between the statutory law and religious legal principles include religious upbringing, custody and access,[47] age at and consent to marriage, religious impediments to remarriage (*talaq* and *faskh*).[48] One lawyer I interviewed also listed 'bigamy, custody of the male child, succession, and fgm … hush hush issue'.[49] Thus, couples may choose to go to a family member, a respected member of their community, the mosque, or a community centre before

41 See Fournier (2006).

42 *Kaddoura v. Hammoud* [1998] O.J. 5054 at para 14.

43 *Ibid.* at para 25.

44 *Ibid.* at para 26.

45 *Ibid.* at para 28.

46 *Amlani v. Hirani* [2000] B.C.J. No. 2357.

47 *Langille v. Dossa* [1994] N.S.J. No. 640.

48 See the Council of Imams (Canada's web page) on the terms of *faskh*: http://www.islamcan.com/websites/imamcouncil/faskh.shtml [accessed July 31, 2002].

49 'DT', Interview by author, 11 September 2002, Toronto, Ontario.

going to the courts for a wide variety of reasons. Whether for cultural comfort or Islamic legal expertise, individuals may seek advice and counselling before and during legal proceedings.

Mediators on contract with the Ontario courts must have a minimum of sixty hours of family mediation training. To be a member of the Ontario Association of Family Mediators, mediators must have 40 hours of training; to gain Accredited Family Mediator status, they must have taken 40 hours of basic mediation training, 20 hours of skills development, 14 hours of domestic violence sensitivity, and have completed 5 mediations. Mediators must carry at least $1,000,000 of mediator professional liability insurance.[50]

Training for mediators may or may not include training on issues of racism, immigration experience, cross-cultural bias, religious practices or alternative norms in family law. Indeed, the family mediators in Ontario are not required to be 'culturally competent' in order to receive their professional certification. Family Mediation Canada's Practice Guidelines include that mediators 'be sensitive to the participants' cultural needs and understandings of fairness'[51]. Further, 'self awareness, including an awareness of one's own inter-personal communication style, its effect on others, and one's own culture, values and biases'.[52]

Feminist scholars and others have criticized family mediation for failing to address the power imbalances between the bargaining parties. Tina Grillo's (1991) article discusses the 'process dangers for women' and is often cited in this area.[53] In particular, there is a significant body of criticism of mediation for women who have experienced violence in their intimate relationship.[54] In my research, violence in domestic relationships was an important factor for counsellors and mediators. The presence of violence in a relationship, however, was not taken as a bar to mediated settlements for couples. Indeed, many of the mediators discussed police racism, the stress of immigration, stereotyping by mainstream service providers, and poverty when talking about domestic violence. Mediation was seen by a number of my research participants as an alternative to both criminal proceedings and family court even in the presence of allegations of violence. Uzma and Sangeeta said mediation ought to be 'crisis prevention' and 'prior to criminalization'.

It is difficult to glean from the reported cases whether mediation is taking place. Raza noted that the alternative community-based mediation of separation/divorce matters occur 'constantly' at the same time as court cases and even family court mediation. He went so far as to say 'higher than 75 per cent of cases' were

---

50 http://www.oafm.on.ca/mediators/AccFM%20Criteria.html [accessed 4 January 2008].

51 http://www.fmc.ca/ See 'certification' [accessed 4 January 2008].

52 http://www.fmc.ca/ [accessed 4 January 2008].

53 It should be noted that Grillo is criticizing the California model of family mediation which is mandatory mediation.

54 See for example, Goundry *et al.* (1998) and Landau (1993).

in mediation at the same time as court based proceedings.[55] At first glance it seems that it may have more to do with cultural, linguistic and economic factors than with religious factors but this is an element of my research that remains to be explored. One reason why it may be more cultural than religious is that women may choose to avoid a mediator from the mosque (Imams generally do not do the mediations but a well respected member of the Board or the President of the Mosque does). Further, Raza noted that the benefits of mediation have less to do with religion.

In *Wedatalla v. Tawfik* (1996) the reported decision indicates that both court mediation and mediation in the Muslim community were unsuccessful: 'Evidence was given by members of the Muslim community who have given an exceptional amount of support to this family, Dr. Mohammed Coouadia and Dr. Mesbah. They supervised Dr. Tawfik's access and were available for advice. They did their best to mediate the dispute but were unsuccessful.'[56] In *Husika v. Husika*, a custody case, it is clear that the mother of the child would not consent to a mediator from the mosque where her husband attended prayers and was an active member – indeed he was the President of the Mosque at the time of trial – because she was more secular in her personal views and this was an issue between the parties.[57]

In another Muslim family case described by a court-based mediator in southern Ontario, an uncle was involved with the couple. He also took an active part in the dealings with the mediator. For example, the uncle told the mediator that the parties were not to have close contact and therefore the mediation model was inappropriate. In this case the mediator can shuttle between the parties and not have the two together around a table. As well, the mediator indicated that he was going to incorporate the uncle into his mediation process.[58] People opt in and out of the family law scheme for a variety of reasons be they for cultural reasons, due to financial constraints, the importance of religious law, a fear of the courts, or lack of available culturally sensitive mediation services. These complex factors need to be assessed to appreciate family law's legal pluralism. We will now turn to the South African case.

Multijuralism in Family Law in South Africa

When writing about legal pluralism, community courts and traditional authority in Mozambique, Boaventura de Sousa Santos (2006, 60) observes that 'this is a field of intense hybridization between religious law and traditional law. All this vibrant legal life occurs outside the official legal field, mobilizing legal and political cultures that have very little to do with the legal and political cultures underlying the official legal system. Legal polycentrism merges here with multiculturalism

55 Arif Raza, Interview by author, June 2002, Scarborough, Ontario.

56 *Wedatalla v. Tawfik*, [1996] N.J. No 56 at para 16.

57 *Husika v. Husika*, [1994] O.J. No. 1808.

58 Interview by author, November 2002, Toronto, Ontario.

and, thus, with multicultural legal plurality.' De Sousa Santos's observation of community courts in Mozambique may well apply to dispute resolution in Muslim communities and traditional law in South Africa. More surprisingly, his argument can apply to dispute resolution and multicultural legal plurality outside of the African context. For very different reasons, his analysis offers a useful way to understand contemporary legal pluralism in Canada as well as South Africa. In the African context, the existence and complexity of non-state dispute resolution in family matters has to do with both the strength of religious and indigenous institutions and the weakness of the state to regulate social life – the state's 'loss of centrality' (De Sousa Santos, 2006, 44). In the Canadian context, multijuralism also exists because of the state's loss of centrality but in this case due to privatization of family law dispute resolution alongside alternative religious and cultural norms within various communities.

De Sousa Santos goes on to argue that, 'today, the recovery of the traditional in Africa, far from being a non-modern alternative to Western modernity, is the expression of a claim to an alternative modernity. Because it is occurring throughout Africa and indeed throughout the global South, it is a form of globalization that presents itself as resistance to globalization' (De Sousa Santos, 2006, 61). Similarly in the global North, communities reconstituting 'traditional' methods of dispute resolution in places like Canada do so in opposition to secular democracy or perceived Christian [Western] legality. They too are making a claim to an 'alternative modernity'. Thus, in both South Africa and Canada, some Muslim couples opt out of the state family law systems when negotiating separation agreements.

Unlike in Ontario[59] (and all other Canadian jurisdictions) Muslim religious marriages are not recognized in South Africa because of their potentially polygamous character. Polygamy is criminalized in South Africa. While Canada's *Criminal Code* also makes it an offence to have more than one spouse, this has not been a barrier to the legal recognition of Muslim (monogamous) marriages. Further, and again in contrast to the South African case, Muslim clerics applied to be marriage commissioners and have been empowered to perform civil and religious marriage rites at the same time. Imams in Canada did not see the criminalization of polygamy as a lightning rod of cultural politics. Of course they were not empowered to perform second marriages when one spouse was already legally married or to perform a marriage when one spouse was not legally capable to consent for reasons of age or otherwise. These and many other reasons make the comparison between Ontario's religious arbitration debate and South Africa's Muslim marriage recognition debate very interesting.

Waheeda Amien (2006, 733) writes;

---

59 See for example *Ayoub v. Osman*, [2006] O.J. No. 1176 (ON S.C.) concerning the validity of a Muslim marriage conducted by an Imam without a marriage licence.

> Contemporary South Africa inherited the legacies of colonialism and Apartheid, which refused to recognize Muslim marriage as legally valid. This was based on the assumption that a relationship could only be regarded as a 'civilized' marriage if it conformed to the Christian [and common law] requisite of monogamy. Anything other than a strictly monogamous union was considered 'anathema'.

As a number of scholars, including Amien and the Women's Rights Commission in South Africa, have pointed out, the burden of the lack of legal recognition for Muslim marriages has been borne by women. Because the property in a marriage and the matrimonial home is most often in the husband's name, should the couple separate, the wife does not have a legal claim on any property. Further, claims for community property have failed in the courts as recently as in the *Du Toit* case in the Constitutional Court of South Africa:[60]

> The applicant and the respondent were married to each other in 1974 in terms of Muslim personal law. At no stage was a civil marriage recognized by the common law of South Africa concluded. The marriage subsisted until 2002, when the respondent issued the applicant with what is termed an 'irrevocable talaq', an act or deed that confirms divorce in Muslim personal law. The High Court held that she had not established that a tacit universal partnership had existed during the marriage [...] [61]

Secondly, since there are rarely written records of marriages or marriage contracts in most communities in South Africa, women's rights at the dissolution of marriage are not set out according to Muslim law. In some cases, one wife does not know about the existence of another wife and they may be left unsupported by the husband.[62] Thirdly, religious divorces may be withheld by disgruntled husbands but women do not have any formal recourse in the state courts. As Waheeda Amien argues;

> women are often simply informed that their husbands have issued talaq against them, and members of the 'ulama tend to confirm the talaqs without consulting the wives. This is reinforcement of the traditional approach to Muslim divorces that regards talaq as the exclusive preserve of the husband, which does not require the wife's consent. On the contrary, a wife needs the 'ulama's permission to obtain a faskh to release her from the marriage. However, it appears that few

---

60 *Du Toit v. Seria*, Constitutional Court of South Africa, 23 May 2006, CCT 18/06.

61 *Ibid.* at para 2-3.

62 Polygamy seems to be practiced secretly in contemporary South Africa quite in contrast to other parts of subSaharan Africa.

> women apply for faskh because the process can be time consuming, difficult, expensive, and sometimes humiliating.[63]

While the Muslim Judicial Council – about which I will speak about more below – does adjudicate annulments of marriages that are brought by women, these cases may not be successful. In the British context, Bustami Mohamed Khir (2006, 303) calls this the case of 'limping marriages'. He goes on to explain that these are marriages 'recognized in some jurisdictions as having been validly dissolved, but in other jurisdictions are still subsisting'.

The South African case differs from both the British and the Canadian in that it begins with the lack of recognition of the marriage and proceeds to the lack of access to legal and religious divorce processes. While today Imams can apply to be marriage commissioners in South Africa and can perform the religious and civil ceremonies, it is still relatively rare. As well, the vast majority of Muslim couples continue to marry only according to religious rites.[64]

In the legal vacuum, then, are the religious and community bodies that oversee religious marriage and divorce matters, along with other matters such as *halal* decrees. As in all other locations, there are a variety of mosques and organizations representing a spectrum of religious affiliations and schools of law – whether Sunni or Shiite, Maliki or Hanafi, Indian or Malay. And as in Toronto, certain mosques are known to be more liberal, certain Imams are known to be more supportive of women who have experienced violence, and certain community centres are affiliated with ethnic or national groups in the area.[65]

The largest Muslim body of Islamic scholars is the Muslim Judicial Council (MJC) in Cape Town. The (MJC) has 150 mosques affiliated with it. With a long history of work in the Muslim community in and around Cape Town, the MJC has had a social welfare department for 50 years. For the past 21 years, the head of department has been Imam Abdul Mou'tie Saban. According to Saban, the mandate of the social welfare department is to 'adjudicate, reconcile and give divorce' including *faskh* applications from women.[66] Working with a priority to reconcile the couple, the MJC does have a *Shari'a* court 'every Thursday … on set procedure but treat each case separately and the offer a judgment'.[67] In spite of an increase number of cases in 2005 (from 2004), MJC saw a decrease in the divorce rate by 12 per cent and annulment rate decreased as well.[68] In part, Imam Mou'tie

63 Amien (2006) at 732.

64 Interview with lawyer Fatima Essop, Cape Town, South Africa, May 2006; and interview with Imam Abdul Mou'tie Saban, Cape Town, South Africa, 17 May 2006.

65 Interview by author with Professor Shahied Mathee, University of Cape Town, 9 May 2006.

66 Interview by author with Imam Abdul Mou'tie Saban, Cape Town, South Africa, 17 May 2006.

67 *Ibid.*

68 Muslim Judicial Council in house statistics, on file with author.

Saban credits his marriage classes in 'helping to stabilize the community' with course content about the 'typical Muslim home'[69]

In addition to the services offered by the MJC, mediation of marriage disputes was offered through the Islamic Social Welfare Association (ISWA). A social worker there, Zanab Baker, described their work as more 'marriage counseling ... working on psychological dimensions as well as the religious and legal issues in the marriage'.[70] Ms Baker explained that they had an ongoing caseload of approximately 38 cases per month with approximately 11 new cases per month. Another very experienced social worker who had worked with both the MJC and the ISWA, Nurunihaar Mintin, told me that her private practice includes drawing up agreements between 'husband and wife concerning the needs in a marriage', tries to reconcile couples who are separating, and assists women in their dealing with clergy and the MJC.[71]

Nurunihaar Minta argues that the MJC has been failing women who need religious divorces and other assistance. Suraya Williams, a lawyer with the Commission on Gender Equality, concurs: 'the religious system is failing women. Women go to dissolve their marriage to the MJC but go to the civil system for support'.[72] Echoing some of the concerns expressed about the Ontario family law system and the potential pitfalls in religious arbitration, Williams argues that the system is very inaccessible. Due to the non-recognition of Muslim marriages, the courts and the family law system in the Western Cape province have also been failing Muslim women who are married under religious rites and not according to civil law. Even though potentially polygamous marriages under South African customary law are now recognized, the 'recognition of Muslim marriage [some argue] is unconstitutional because of the separation of state and religion'[73] in South Africa.

Rashida Manjoo (2004, 272) asks 'Is Muslim Person Law compatible with the entrenched right of substantive equality as found in the South African Constitution?' and 'How does the *Draft Muslim Marriages Bill* relate to the challenges and lived realities faced by Muslim women in a secular constitutional democracy?'. The amended draft Bill was released in July 2003 after three years of discussions and debate convened by a project Committee of the South African Law Commission. The Bill currently sits with the Minister of Justice but was not tabled in Parliament in 2006. Manjoo (2004, 281) argues that the *Islamic Marriages Bill* will be a

69 Interview Imam Mou'tie Saban. I attended a marriage class on the topic of 'spying' or lack of trust in relationships. The class was attended by approximately 100 men and women. (22 May 2006)

70 Interview by author, Zanab Baker, Cape Town, 30 May 2006.

71 Interview by author, Mrs. Nurunihaar Mintin, Zeekoeivlei, Cape Town, 29 May 2006.

72 Interview by author, Suraya Williams, Commission on Gender Equality, Cape Town, 26 April 2006.

73 *Ibid.*

step to ameliorate historical hardship and discrimination but she cautions that some provisions, such as the sanction of polygyny and limited definition of *faskh* (women's application for divorce/*khul*), may conflict with the constitutional protection of gender equality or access to justice respectively.

Williams also acknowledges that the *marriage bill* – itself an example of multijuralism in family law – was a compromise document but one that would go some way in addressing the needs of members of the Muslim community. Given that the community is not homogeneous and there are different schools of thought, it was impossible to reach consensus on points such as the regulation of polygamy suggested in the Bill and the qualifications for Muslim judges. In Professor Shahied Mathee's words, 'legislation, recognition is important ... a lot takes place in the community. You see how innovative they can be. But for all intents and purposes, it is left to the community and women are suffering. I think legislation would help.'[74]

The multijuralism in family law in South Africa is the product of a history of non-recognition of Muslim marriage due to the potentially polygamous character of some Muslim marriages. Many critics argued that, in the interests of gender equality, religious marriage rites and divorce ought to be recognized by statute. Women's interests during marriage and at separation would be better protected with the regulation of religious marriage. There is significant disagreement within Muslim communities and other interested groups in civil society, however, and these conflicts have, in part, stalled the passage of the Bill in South Africa. Thus should a Muslim couple marry only according to Islamic law, they will have no recourse to the courts to enforce their marriage contract or division of property at divorce. As in Canada, should they negotiate a separation agreement according to Islamic legal principles, it will not be enforceable by the courts. And, should a Muslim couple decide to marry according to both civil law and religious law, they will have remedies for division of marital property through the civil law process at divorce and for religious legal obligations through an Imam.

Conclusions

The proponents of religious family arbitration articulated their claim in terms of freedom of religion while the critics expressed concern over 'vulnerable Muslim women' and women's rights. And while the provincial government publicly heralded its new law as 'one law for all' in Ontario, I have shown that the law allows for plurality in practice. And indeed the practice does not necessarily better protect Muslim women's interests. I also argued that the particular history and social context of any jurisdiction does matter for the mediation of these contests. This is readily apparent with my short comparison with religious marriage and divorce in South Africa.

74 Interview by author, Shahied Mathee, University of Cape Town, 9 May 2006.

In both Ontario and the Western Cape there is space for legal pluralism but for very different reasons and with different consequences. The role of the state and, in particular, family law regulation has been one of exclusion in South Africa thereby failing to protect Muslim women on the breakdown of their relationships. Only middle class women who are financially independent seem to benefit from the legal vacuum since they can cut ties with their spouse without concern about dividing matrimonial property.[75] Indeed they can also control access to any children they may have had together because it is relatively complicated to prove paternity in South African law.

The role of family law in Ontario is to provide a mechanism whereby couples can organize the division of property and spousal support according to religious or other principles with the default position being clearly articulated in legislation. According to the new legislation, the law does not empower arbitration tribunals in cultural or religious communities with decision-making authority. Paradoxically of course, arbitration and mediation providers do hold such power in the South African context. Another key finding of my research is that there is a general *lack* of empirical research about how women and men are negotiating their separation agreements and on what grounds they are coming to decisions. It is in the most private of matters – how to organize your affairs after marriage breakdown – that negotiations over rights take place. As one woman stated, Muslim women negotiate their rights and responsibilities to their families, religion and so on, 'women are constantly dealing with it'.[76]

Family law's legal pluralism in Canada and South Africa is a complex set of interacting norms. Some religious domestic contracts, marriage or separation agreements, are enforceable by the courts and others are not. Most commentators argue that enforcement is important for stability and predictability in this area. On the other hand, arbitrated separation and divorce decisions from Rabbinical courts and other religious bodies are rarely judicially reviewed, and therefore, rarely enforced through the courts. Professor Shahied Mathee argued in favour of legislation recognizing Muslim marriages and of enforcement of religious divorce decrees in the South African context while sounding a cautionary note: 'The state should not be allowed secular fundamentalism that would want to impose itself.'[77]

References

Amien, Waheeda (2006). 'Overcoming the Conflict between the Right to Freedom of Religion and Women's Rights to Equality: A South African Case Study of Muslim Marriages', *Human Rights Quarterly*, **28**(3): 729–754.

75 Interview by author, Fatime Essop, Cape Town, May 2006.

76 Interview by author, 'Sunita', Scarborough, Ontario, 16 June 2005.

77 Interview by author, Shahied Mathee, University of Cape Town, 9 May 2006.

Beck, Connie J.A. and Bruce D. Sales (2001). *Family Mediation: Facts, Myths, and Future Prospects*, Washington, D.C.: American Psychological Association.

Bernstein, Lisa (1992). 'Opting Out of the Legal System: Extralegal Contractual Relations in the Diamond Industry', *Journal of Legal Studies*, **21**(1): 115–157.

Bernstein, Lisa (1998). 'Private Commercial Law', in Peter Newman (ed.), *The New Palgrave Dictionary of Economics and the Law*, London and New York: Macmillan Reference and Stockton Press, Vol. 3, 108-114.

Boyd, Marion (2005). *Dispute Resolution in Family Law: Protecting Choice, Promoting Inclusion*, Toronto: Ministry of the Attorney General, Queen's Printer for Ontario. Available online: Ontario Ministry of the Attorney General http://www.attorneygeneral.jus.gov.on.ca/english/about/pubs/boyd/.

Brown, Katherine (2006). 'Realising Muslim Women's Rights: The Role of Islamic Identity among British Muslim Women', *Women's Studies International Forum*, **29**: 417–430.

De Sousa Santos, Boaventura (2006). 'The Heterogeneous State and Legal Pluralism in Mozambique', *Law and Society Review*, **40**(1): 39–75.

Drummond, Susan (2005). *Mapping Marriage Law in Spanish Gitano Communities*, Vancouver: University of British Columbia Press.

Engle Merry, Sally (1990). *Getting Justice and Getting Even: Legal Consciousness among Working-class Americans*, Chicago: University of Chicago Press.

Fournier, Pascale (2006). 'In the (Canadian) Shadow of Islamic Law: Translating *Mahr* into a Private Bargaining Endowment', *Osgoode Hall Law Journal*, **44**(4): 649–677.

Goundry, Sandra A. *et al.*, (1998). *Family Mediation in Canada: Implications for Women's Equality*, Status of Women Canada: Ottawa.

Griffiths, John (1986). 'What is Legal Pluralism?', 4 *Journal of Legal Pluralism*, **24**: 1–56.

Grillo, Trina (1991). 'The Mediation Alternative: Process Dangers for Women', *Yale Law Journal*, **100**(6): 1545–1610.

Khir, Bustami Mohamed (2006). 'The Right of Women to No-Fault Divorce in Islam and its Application by British Muslims', *Islam and Christian-Muslim Relations*, **17**(3): 295–306.

Kruk, Edward (1998). 'Practice Issues, Strategies, and Models: The Current State of the Art of Family Mediation', *Family and Conciliation Courts Review*, **36**(2): 195–215.

Landau, Barbara (1993). *Report from Toronto Forum on Woman Abuse and Mediation*, Waterloo, Ontario: Fund for Dispute Resolution.

Mahmood, Saba (2005). *Politics of Piety: The Islamic Revival and the Feminist Subject*, Princeton: Princeton University Press.

Manjoo, Rashida (2004). 'Legislative Recognition of Muslim Marriages in South Africa', *International Journal of Legal Information*, **32**(2): 271–282.

Mnookin, Robert H. and Lewis Kornhauser (1979). 'Bargaining in the Shadow of the Law: The Case of Divorce', *Yale Law Journal*, **88**(5): 950–997.

Muslim Community Services (Brampton Ontario) (1997). *Women Behind the Veil: A Research Study of the issue of Women Abuse in the Muslim Community*, Brampton, Ontario: MCS.
Qaisi, Ghada G. (2000). 'Religious Marriage Contracts: Judicial Enforcement of *Mahr* Agreements in American Courts', *Journal of Law and Religion*, **15**(1/2): 67–81.
Siddiqui, Shahina and Omar Siddiqui (2006). '"Imagining the Real": Legal Pluralism, Shariah, and a Just Society', *Focus Justice: Magazine of the McGill Legal Information Clinic*, **2**(1).
South African Law Reform Commission (2002). *Draft Bill: Islamic Marriages Act... of 20...*, Discussion Paper 101 on Islamic Marriages and Related Matters (Project 59). Available online: www.doj.gov.za/salrc/dpapers/dp101_prj59/dp101_prj59_2002.pdf.
von Benda-Beckmann, Franz (2002). 'Who's afraid of legal pluralism?', *Journal of Legal Pluralism and Unofficial Law*, **47**: 37–82.

Legal Cases

Canadian cases

Husika v. Husika, [1994] O.J. No. 1808
Langille v. Dossa, [1994] N.S.J. No. 640
Wedatalla v. Tawfik, [1996] N.J. No. 56
Kaddoura v. Hammond, [1998] O.J. No. 5054
Amlani v. Hirani, [2000] B.C.J. No. 2357
Ayoub v. Osman, [2006] O.J. No. 1176

American cases

Serbian Eastern Orthodox Diocese for the United States of America and Canada et al. v. Milivojevich et al., 426 U.S. 696 (1976)

South African cases

Du Toit v. Seria, Constitutional Court of South Africa, 23 May 2006, CCT 18/06

Legislation

Family Law Act, R.S.O. 1990, c. F.3
Bill 27, *Family Statute Law Amendment Act*, 2005 (now the *Family Statute Law Amendment Act*, 2006, S.O. 2006, c. 1)

Chapter 4
Regulatory and Sanctioning Powers of Independent Administrative Authorities in French Law

Alice Pezard

Introduction

In France, with the proliferation in the last thirty years of regulatory authorities – Independent Administrative Authorities (IAA), – one may wonder if we have witnessed the birth of a new national or even transnational jurisdictional order, running in parallel with positive domestic law against a backdrop of European harmonization. These IAAs have traditionally operated in highly technical fields, but recently also in more general activity sectors (for example the High Authority Against Discrimination and for Equality, known as the 'HALDE'). The emergence of a new law of IAAs raises the following questions: how is this new law positioned relative to supranational (European) and national law? What is the influence of the new law of IAAs on domestic law? Can a parallel be drawn with the relationship between federal law and provincial or state law in federations?[1]

To answer these questions, it is useful to start with a brief description of some of the approximately 40 IAAs in existence today. These descriptions are found in the second section. In addition to the HALDE, we have examined these five IAAs:

- the Financial Markets Authority (AMF);
- the Council on Competition;
- the Postal Services and Electronic Communications Regulatory Authority (ARCEP),
- the Energy Regulation Commission (CRE),
- the latest addition, the Regulatory Authority for Technical Measures (ARMT).

---

1 On the emergence of a new law of IAAs, see also Lombard (2005), Pistor and Xu (2006), Traoré (2004), and 'Rapport du 20 juin 2006 de l'Office Parlementaire d'Evaluation de la Législation' (OPEL) (2 tomes: Assemblée Nationale no. 3166 and Sénat no. 404) and 'Rapports du Conseil d'Etat' from 2001 to 2006.

Regulatory authorities are not always institutions that are separate from the government, but the six IAAs selected are. Based partly on this description, the third section presents a brief summary of the various powers exerted by IAAs. The fourth section covers the reasons that led to their creation, including the key role played by the European Union in the creation process of most IAAs. The fifth section discusses the way in which the law and, more generally, the action of IAAs fit into the national legal system. A comparison with Canada is sketched out in the sixth section.

Description of the Six IAAs

The High Authority Against Discrimination and for Equality (HALDE)

The HALDE was created in 2004 to help fight discriminatory practices, a role not always fulfilled satisfactorily by the judicial authority. It has jurisdiction over all types of discrimination, direct or indirect, prohibited by law or by any international agreement to which France is a party. Its regulatory powers are mostly limited to the influence it has on the government through its opinions, which the government must seek, and recommendations which it may issue spontaneously. But this power and influence are no less real because of the credibility quickly gained by the High Authority.[2] Thus the HALDE takes a more or less direct, but always active, part in the development of standards for the fight against inequality and discrimination.

In the implementation of existing regulations, the HALDE has asserted itself – especially since the employment equity law of February 2006 – as a major player in the judicial process. This takes the form of an assisting role to the judicial authority, including in the hearing but also the settling of cases. In hearings, the HALDE makes a valuable contribution to the administration of proof which, according to HALDE President Louis Schweitzer, is 'the main hurdle for victims'. For this purpose, it has far-reaching investigative powers. As for the direction and settlement of cases, we note the following:

- the HALDE has referral powers from the judicial authority, enabling it to initiate certain judicial proceedings;
- as part of an ongoing judicial procedure, it can be asked by civil, criminal or administrative jurisdictions to present its observations for discussion by the parties;[3]

2 For example, the HALDE recommended the authorization of the right to vote for foreign craftsmen in the elections of the Chambre des Métiers, as was the case before a 2004 order. The Prime Minister announced that the order would be amended accordingly.

3 This power is valuable when the High Authority has handled the case, or because of the experience it has acquired in this field.

- it can settle cases, using transactions that can include the payment of a fine and damages to the victim for the prejudice suffered; however, these transactions must be ratified by the *Procureur de la République* (Public Prosecutor).

The Financial Markets Authority (AMF)

The AMF is the product of the merging in 2003 of the Securities Commission (COB), the Financial Markets Council (CMF) and the Financial Management Discipline Council (CDGF).[4] The goal of this merger was to reinforce the effectiveness and visibility of the regulation of France's financial community. The AMF's mission is to ensure the protection of the savings invested in financial instruments and other investments subject to public issue, the proper information of investors, and the smooth operation of financial markets. It also assists in regulating these markets at the European and international levels.

To carry out its mission, the AMF has sweeping regulatory, control and investigative powers. Investigators may request and receive copies of any document, on any type of media, including any data stored and processed by telecommunications providers. They may summon and hear anyone who may have information. They may access premises used for professional purposes. Professional secrecy cannot be invoked.

Based on audit and investigation reports, the AMF College may initiate sanctioning procedures, which will be heard by a rapporteur and ruled upon by the Sanctions Commission. If the case is urgent, the College may also, when initiating a sanctioning procedure, order the professionals concerned to suspend their activities. If the report identifies potential offences, the College forwards it to the *Procureur de la République*. The procedure before the Sanctions Commission is an adversarial procedure. The Commission may hand down sanctions, including barring the practise of the professional activity, as well as financial penalties. The AMF also has a mediation service to which parties can turn to settle disputes amicably and avoid legal proceedings.

The Council on Competition

The Council on Competition was created in 1986 to replace an institution that had more or less the same role. Since then, the Council has seen a broadening of its scope of action and a reinforcement of its means of action.[5] It is responsible for enforcing economic public order and, more specifically, intervenes to ensure compliance with national and Community legislation that guarantees freedom in

4 On the AMF see also Arsouze et Ledoux (2006), Daigre (2000), Ducouloux-Favard (2006), Godet (2002), Salomon (2000), Thomasset-Pierre (2002).

5 On the Council on Competition, see also Lesquins (2006), Nussenbaum (2005).

pricing, prohibits abusive behaviour detrimental to free competition and renders dominant agreements and positions illegal if they result in skewing the field.

An issue raised was whether the Council on Competition, essentially a repressive body, could also act as a regulator and market organizer. It turns out that it wields such powers through its consultative function. Combined with its recognized expertise, this function allows it to influence many decisional authorities, but it is the Council on Competition's dispute-settlement function that accounts for the bulk of its activity. This function deals with the repression of abusive agreements and dominant positions. Since 1996, it also rules in cases of excessively low prices and exemptions. Its many powers allowing it to put a stop to anti-competitive behaviour, including by handing down financial penalties, offer a substitute to legal action. The Council may self-refer or be referred to settle disputes by the Minister for Economic Affairs, companies, territorial communities, professional organizations and boards, union organizations and consumer groups.

The Council can draw on a number of actions, including *provisional measures*, *sanctions* and *commitments*. Provisional measures are limited to enjoining the companies concerned to suspend the practice under dispute, for instance to suspend or eliminate anti-competitive clauses from some of their contracts. The Council may issue injunctions against offenders to put a stop to fraudulent behaviour, and order the decision published in the papers. If the measures are not obeyed, the Council may impose fines of up to 10 per cent of the offender's worldwide sales before taxes for a company; the fine is €3,000,000 when the offender is not a company. And finally, the Council has an alternate dispute-settlement mechanism. It may accept commitment proposals from the individuals concerned by these proceedings. Here, persuasion and compromise are preferred over sanctions. If the Council feels that the commitments proposed will restore the market to its competitive situation, it may close the proceedings, and the commitments accepted become enforceable. If the commitments are not honoured, a financial penalty for breach of commitment may be ordered by the Council.

The Postal Services and Electronic Communications Regulatory Authority (ARCEP)

The Telecommunications Regulatory Authority (ART) was created in 1996 to oversee the deregulation of the telecommunications sector. This sector, which had been characterized by a legal monopoly and stiff access barriers, required complementary regulations to the ordinary law of competition to allow access to new players. In 2005, the legislator entrusted this authority with regulating postal service activities; thus the ART became the ARCEP.

In the area of telecommunications, the ARCEP enjoys numerous prerogatives that guarantee it a major role in the operation of this sector. It ensures that there is free competition in the 18 market segments identified by the Commission. To do so, it imposes various obligations on operators such as transparency, non-discrimination, publicity, account unbundling and prohibition of excessive or predatory pricing. Ever since the European statutes laid down the principle of freedom of creation and operation of a public network, the ARCEP no longer hears individual applications; operators need only provide a declaration. The ARCEP is also responsible for the allocation of scarce resources such as frequencies and numbers. It is responsible for universal service, including the principles that govern it and funding thereof, notably concerning operator contributions. Finally, because of its responsibilities regarding universal service and competition, the ARCEP has regulatory power over rates.

Regarding postal service, the ARCEP regulates the sorting, collection, routing and distribution of mail.[6] Its mission is to reconcile the existence and viability of the universal service and the gradual introduction of competition. To do so, it has numerous means at its disposal. It issues market access authorizations and implements the rights and obligations related thereto. It also controls the postal service's universal service mission, including service quality. It oversees the accounting and rate-setting functions of the universal service provider. It helps prepare the French position in European and international negotiations and working groups, and is consulted on draft statutes and regulations regarding the postal sector.

To fulfill its various missions, the ARCEP has dispute-settlement and sanctioning powers. In the field of telecommunications, it is responsible for settling disputes between operators in three areas: interconnection and the network access conditions, restrictions to the provision of telecommunications services on cable networks, and conditions governing the shared use of existing installations. In terms of sanctions against operators that do not fulfill their obligations, the ARCEP may impose various sanctions, including withdrawing frequencies or numbers. In the postal sector, the ARCEP settles disputes pertaining to agreements that go against the terms of universal service or those facilitating the practice of postal activities held by the postal service, making sure in both cases that the technical and rate conditions offered are not discriminatory. It also has sanctioning powers, but this only applies to universal service obligations within the postal activity.

The Energy Regulation Commission (CRE)

The CRE was created in 2000 to regulate the energy sector (natural gas and electricity), which was about to be opened up to competition and was characterized by the presence of public operators. It manages market deregulation – including access by new electricity operators – by working to reconcile the introduction of competition and the fulfilment of public service missions. It guarantees access to, operation of, and development of public grids and the independence of system operators.

The CRE has the power to propose rates for the use of public systems, the amount of refunds that operators with public service responsibilities receive,

---

6 The distribution of bulk advertising, courier services and express transport are therefore excluded.

and the protective measures needed to ensure the security, safety and quality of public electricity grids. Its opinion is automatically sought on many draft orders or decisions. Regarding investments in electricity production, it organizes calls for tenders, examines the results, and formulates opinions on the tenders to be selected. In the area of electricity, it makes decisions, based on legislative and regulatory standards, regarding the missions of system operators, connection rules, conditions of access and use of systems, and so on.

Like some of the other IAAs examined here, the CRE has dispute-settlement and sanctioning powers. It may be applied to by the parties concerned regarding any dispute relating to access to public electricity or gas systems and transport or distribution facilities. The procedure is adversarial and the CRE has very broad rights of access to information held by natural gas and electricity market stakeholders and administrations. It may also initiate inquiries. With its sanctioning powers, it can convict individuals of violations to legislative or regulatory rules or resulting from its decisions. It may hand down two types of sanctions, that is, prohibition of access to systems or facilities for a maximum of one year, and financial penalties.

The Regulatory Authority for Technical Measures (ARMT)

The ARMT was created under a 2006 law 'on copyright and related rights in the information society' and was implemented in 2007. It has a general oversight mission in the areas of technical measures for the protection and identification of works and objects protected by these rights. More specifically, it ensures that technical measures do not result, due to mutual incompatibility or inability to interoperate, in creating limitations to the use of works that are unwished for by the holders of the rights.

The ARMT has dispute-settlement powers in the areas of private copy and interoperability. Any software publisher, technical system manufacturer and service provider may, if refused access to information essential to interoperability, ask the ARMT to guarantee interoperability between existing systems and services. They can also obtain the information essential to such interoperability from the holder of the rights on the technical measure.[7] Failing an agreement between the parties, the ARMT may issue orders detailing the conditions under which claimants may seek access to the information essential to interoperability. Its sanctioning powers take the form of ordering and defining penalties or, in the event of non-compliance with its order or the commitments it has accepted, imposing very heavy financial sanctions.

7 The term 'information essential for interoperability' means the technical documentation and the programming interfaces necessary for a technical device to legitimately access a work or object protected by a technical measure.

Recapitulation of IAA Powers

Some independent authorities exercise what are sometimes called 'regulatory' powers. However, this term encompasses very different prerogatives.[8] Thus to regulate a given sector, some IAAs have the option of organizing the sector or organization *ex ante*, which can be done generally by regulating, or more specifically by granting access rights to an activity, either for the benefit of individuals (certification, authorization) or for the benefit of goods or activities (certification, accreditation).[9] Without going back in detail over the powers described in the previous section, these can be briefly summarized by establishing a basic distinction between regulating *per se*, that is, producing regulations, and implementing existing regulations, including through the use of sanctions (we leave aside the special or individual decisions organizing a sector *ex ante*). Due to lingering reservations, IAAs have traditionally been granted regulatory powers, but not sanctioning powers. Today, these reservations have been partially lifted. In fact, the ability to sanction is often considered an essential prerogative by the authorities, including those responsible for economic regulation. Thus the Council on Competition considers 'the power to sanction to be the most important'.[10] The National Commission on Computers and Freedom (CNIL) also feels that the granting of such powers can have a profound impact on its action, as the possibility of sanctioning can become a determining factor.

All IAAs have influence over regulations, but only a few have been granted actual regulatory powers allowing them to enact general and abstract rules of law. These authorities are usually responsible for regulating an economic sector or for protecting fundamental liberties in an area where special techniques are used. In the previous section we saw that the AMF, the ARCEP and the CRE have such regulatory powers. Among the IAAs not covered in the previous section, the National Commission on Computers and Freedom (CNIL) and the Survey Commission also have this power.

We have seen how IAAs that have no regulatory powers, such the HALDE, the Council on Competition and the ARMT, can still exert considerable influence on regulations, and more fundamentally on the emergence of new legal standards, due to the consultative powers they have been granted (which IAAs with regulatory powers also have, of course). These powers include recommendations and notices that are issued, usually according to very specific procedures, for the benefit of the Government, Parliament or other IAAs. In addition, because they are often

8 On the power of IAAs, see Frison-Roche (2002), Godet (2002), Lafortune (2001), Pralus-Dupuis (2003), Prétot (2002), Quilichini (2006), Schwartz and Ribs (2000).

9 This regulatory power can shift and sometimes turn into an *ex post* power, including in the area of confidentiality.

10 Sénat français, 'Les autorités administratives indépendantes: evaluation d'un objet juridique non identifié (Tome 2: Annexes)', online: http://www.senat.fr/rap/r05-404-2/r05-404-219.html, note 22.

required to represent France on specialized international bodies, or because of their consultative powers with the Government or national Parliament, most IAAs have influence – direct or indirect, but usually major – on the evolution of standards at that level as well.

All IAAs are involved in the implementation of existing regulations and can therefore be considered key players in the judicial process. As we have seen, they play a major role in the hearing of cases because of, among other things, their control and investigative powers. In terms of case settlement, their powers vary. Some can apply sanctions independently (not only orders but also financial penalties, closing down activities, prohibiting access, and so on). Such is the case of the ARCEP, the ARMT and the CRE. Others (for example, the HALDE) can only do so in conjunction with the judicial authority. The use of alternative modes of settlement (transactions, commitments, and so on) usually comes under the control of the *Procureur de la République.* Some IAAs, especially the CRE, the ARCEP, and the Audiovisual Council (CSA), also have dispute-settlement powers. This feature brings them closer to the jurisdictions. The AMF has an actual mediation service.

Reasons for Creating IAAs

The reasons for the rise of IAAs are found in the nature of the functions and powers granted to them, as described in the six examples in the second section. But these reasons are also inextricably tied to the processes involved in European integration.

Let us begin with what could be called the intrinsic reasons. First, in many cases there is the technical nature of the standards to be instituted and enforced, and the need to constantly adapt them to follow scientific and economic progress. This consideration is found in most countries. For instance, it underpins the development of the authority and means granted to the financial regulator, in this case the AMF. Then there is the need to organize, impartially and independently from the public administration, the opening to competition, followed by the regulation, of certain sectors that used to be public monopolies (telecommunications, postal service, electricity, gas, rail and air transport, television, and so on). We will come back to the European aspect of this deregulation process.

For now, let us examine the internal logic. Privatization, at least complete privatization, is not required, even in practice, by the extension of the rules of market competition to public services. The result is that public companies often remain key providers of the services in question (postal services, for example). But these public companies – which in general inherited former public monopolies or even simple government departments – must not be given any privilege over competing French or foreign companies. At the same time, the government is responsible for setting up, then regulating this competition and must do it impartially, including by not, as the saying goes, 'appointing itself judge and jury'. And this objective must be pursued while ensuring the necessary maintenance of public service missions, which operate outside market logic. The use of independent regulatory agencies then becomes the natural and sometimes only way to reconcile these different requirements. Thus to allow competition in the telecommunications sector, a double obstacle had to be overcome, that is, the existence of a legal monopoly and strong barriers to access. The ordinary law of competition was not sufficient, which is why it was felt, in 1996, that it had to be supplemented by the creation of the ART.

A third consideration in the creation of IAAs is the feeling that the usual regulation tools proved ineffective. Thus the HALDE was created in 2004 to fight discriminatory practices because it had become clear that the judicial authority could not perform this task satisfactorily. In the words of the first President of the Paris Court of Appeal, Renaud Chazal de Mauriac, the HALDE was born of 'judicial failure'.

To a large extent, these factors would probably have led to the creation of IAAs anyway, but the process was accelerated and amplified by the impetus of European integration, which is also responsible for some of the traits this process acquired. The logic (already expressed in the Treaty of Rome and reaffirmed in the Single Act) behind the objectives to deepen the internal market, including services, and to eliminate all distortions to competition was the determining cause of the general policy to deregulate public monopolies; this opening in turn played a decisive role in the creation of many IAAs. Still, the Community policy has taken forms and has had impacts that are far more direct. In the area of financial law, competition law and telecommunications law, for instance, the effort by the European Union to become a credible interlocutor for North America and Asia has prompted it to flesh out considerably the corpus of rules applicable to its 25 Member States. In these areas and many others, through the adoption of Community regulations and the transposition of directives into the law of Member States, a real set of common references and principles for action has grown within the single internal market, despite diversified legal systems.[11]

Some IAAs are a direct result of European regulations. Such is the case of the ART, the result of European directives dating back to the early 1990s, the CRE, born of Directive 98/30/CE of 22 June 1998; and (in an area further from the economic objectives of the Union) the HALDE, which was created following

11 On the European dimension of IAA creation, see also AMF (2006a, 2006b), Argentieri (2005), Enfert (2005), Frison-Roche (2005), Georgopoulos (2005), Germain (2005), Heuzé (2005), Institut Montaigne (2002, 2004), Jappont (2005), Muller (1997), Rapp (2006), Rodrigues (2004), Sales (2005), Vogel (2002), and the Recommendation from the Commission No. 2005/309/CE of 12 July 2004 on the transposition into national law of directives relating to the internal market (*Official Journal of the European Union,* No. L 98 16 April 2005) and the acts of the seminar 'La commission européenne et le droit: dynamique institutionnelle et régulation de la concurrence dans une communauté de droit', held 1 December 2005 by AJE and CREDA of the CCP under the chairmanship of Guy Canivet (Gazette du Palais, June 25/27 2006, No. 176 to 178).

Directive 2000/43/CE of 29 June 2000. Even more significantly, the general authority granted to the Commission under article 211 of the Treaty of Amsterdam empowers the Commission to exercise real oversight powers over national regulatory regimes, which translates into a general obligation for IAAs to keep the Commission informed. This obligation results in a fairly marked increase in the Commission's powers, its significance being evaluated in the context of the obligation for national authorities to pursue the objective of deepening the internal market. Based on the information it receives, the Commission can therefore oppose the measures considered by an IAA if it deems them contrary to the interests of a single market.

Through their cooperation at the European level, the regulatory authorities of the different countries play a key role in the construction of the single market. Under the impetus of the Commission, national IAAs create more and more discussion forums to facilitate exchanges between them and reach common positions. This is the case with IAAs in the telecommunications sectors, which have created a forum and whose common positions have a broader prescriptive impact since they are taken into account by the European Commission. Likewise, the 'Florence forum' (for electricity) and the 'Madrid forum' (for gas) allow not only national IAAs to meet regularly, but also include other 'interested parties' (companies, administrations, professors, experts, and so on). The CRE, for its part, is a member of the Council of European Energy Regulators. The Council on Competition is automatically a member of the European Competition Network. The ARCEP belongs to the Communications Committee (COCOM), which assists the Commission. The HALDE also cooperates with its European counterparts within the network of European Union Specialized Authorities on Discrimination.

In the area of financial law, the necessity for convergence at the European and international levels is especially felt, as financial security cannot be achieved through national action only. This is why the *Financial Security Act*[12] entrusts the AMF with a mission of international financial cooperation, which it places at the heart of its activities. Article 2 of the law states that the AMF [Tr.] '*lends its support to the regulation of (financial instrument) market(s) at the European and international levels*'.[13] The AMF's structure, which includes a regulatory and international affairs branch, is evidence of this authority's vocation to act beyond the national level. In fact, the AMF and the institutions that preceded it (COB, CMF) have long been fully involved in the creation of a framework conducive to a Europe-wide regulatory process. This cooperation takes place within the Committee of European Securities Regulators (CESR), whose work consists largely in drafting opinions for the European Commission.

While these authorities are being thus organized into networks, certain European texts are explicitly beginning to take this Europe-wide regulation

12 *Loi nº 2003-706 du 1 août 2003 de sécurité financière* (1), J.O., 2 August 2003.

13 *Ibid.*

requirement into account. Thus the directives of the 'Telecom Paquet' of March 2002[14] kicked off the debate on the adequate level of regulation and the role of regulating authorities in the deepening of the internal market. Although in these directives, in accordance with the principle of subsidiarity, the Commission asserts the competence of national regulating authorities, it is organizing a measured decentralization of this regulatory activity. Thus the transfer of responsibilities to the benefit of national authorities is done within a uniform legal framework, specified by provisions that include those of article 8 of the 'Framework Directive'. This article lists a number of general objectives that must underpin the action of national regulators, particularly the development of a European internal market for electronic communication networks and services.

The cooperation of IAAs within the framework of the European Union must be analyzed in light of a public debate in which some suggest more in-depth integration, instituting true regulatory authorities on a European scale. Already in 2003, a report entitled *Vers une régulation européenne des réseaux* (Towards a European regulation of networks), edited by Christian Stoffaës at the request of the Minister of Foreign Affairs, expressed a preference for the creation of specialized European authorities. The idea was simple. Inasmuch as the ambition of a European market is already supported by European instruments and agencies, would it not be better served by a European regulatory authority? In the energy sector, for instance, given the need to ensure interconnection in transport, is the absence of European regulations *per se* not a handicap to building a unified European market, which was the purpose of the liberalization process initiated in 1996? More recently, the Institut Montaigne, a French think tank, advocated that [Tr.] 'where markets are fully integrated, regulation should be transferred from the national to the European level'[15] and 'where such integration is only partial, the European Commission should be entrusted with a mission to coordinate national authorities and audit their actions'.[16]

However, the creation of real European administrative authorities is unlikely to be deemed necessary for the moment. Certainly there are a few European agencies, such as the European Network and Information Security Agency, that wield power over technical standardization and network security. But many obstacles to the creation of European regulatory agencies remain. The current weakness of European institutions, which do not seem to be able to extend their powers to the national realm, is an obvious one. But the proximity imperative that governs the action of IAAs, including when they play a public liberties advocacy role, represents an ever more basic hurdle. It would therefore be both

14 European Parliament and the Council of the European Union, *Directive 2002/19/CE*, 7 March 2002, *Directive 2002/20/CE*, 7 March 2002, *Directive 2002/21/CE*, 7 March 2002, and *Directive 2002/22/CE*, 7 March 2002.

15 Institut Montaigne (2004), at p.3.

16 *Ibid.*

unrealistic and incorrect to consider Europe as the optimum regulatory level in all cases.

Integration in the National Legal System

Five aspects of this integration are noteworthy.

IAAs can only be created by legislative power. Although article 34 of the Constitution states that the law sets the rules concerning the creation of public establishment categories, there is no provision to the effect that the creation of independent authority categories rests exclusively with the legislator. Yet, Parliament has imposed its exclusive authority to create IAAs. In fact, other constitutional provisions impose this jurisdiction, namely when:

- the mission of the IAA concerns a matter that comes under the law, defined in article 34 of the Constitution, such as the fundamental guarantees granted to citizens to exercise their public liberties;
- the IAA is given a regulatory power, such delegation coming against the authority conferred upon the Prime Minister under article 21 of the Constitution to direct the actions of the Government;
- the authority is given sanctioning powers; therefore, the principle of legality of crimes and punishments, defined in article 8 of the 1789 *Declaration of the Rights of Man and of the Citizen*, require that the sanctions be defined by the law.

In other words, since IAAs work mainly in the areas of regulation and the defence of public liberties through broad regulatory and sanctioning powers, the creation of such authorities by the executive authority would carry a high risk of unconstitutionality. In addition, even outside any constitutional requirement, the independence required of IAAs seems to justify their creation being restricted to the legislator, as only Parliament can create authorities that do not come under the control of the executive branch. Indeed how independent could IAAs be from the administration if they were created by the executive?[17]

The Constitutional Council has circumscribed the regulatory powers granted, as we have seen, to certain IAAs. In fact it has a subordinate, secondary power. In a decision dated 18 September 1986,[18] the Constitutional Council set the conditions for exercising this power. It allowed that [Tr.] 'the provisions of section 21 of

17 On the delegation of powers by the legislator and the government, see also Boy (2001), Lombard (2005), Traoré (2004).

18 Cons. Constitutionnel, 18 September 1986, *Loi relative à la liberté des communications*, Rec. 1986. 141, 86-217 DC.

the Constitution do not prevent the legislator from entrusting an authority other than the Prime Minister with the setting of (…) standards to implement a law, as long as is it in a specific field and within the framework defined in the laws and regulations'.[19] Thus it rejects any exclusivity for IAAs to implement the law in their activity sector. The constitutional judge added that the ability conferred by law to certain Independent Administrative Authorities to exercise regulatory jurisdiction should concern [Tr.] 'measures that are limited in scope both by their field of application and by their content'.[20]

The conditions under which IAAs can be given sanctioning powers have also been specified by the Constitutional Council. The granting of sanctioning powers to IAAs was not without its legal hurdles, due among other things to the constitutional requirement regarding separation of powers under article 16 of the 1789 Declaration of the Rights of Man and of the Citizen.[21] The Constitutional Council had to rule for the first time on the sanctioning powers granted to the CSA. In a decision issued on 17 January 1989, the Constitutional Council ruled that the granting of sanctioning powers to an IAA does not go against the principle of separation of powers under certain conditions. It further specified its argument in a decision on 28 July 1989, allowing that the legislator could grant sanctioning powers to any administrative authority [Tr.] 'as long as, on the one hand, the sanction likely to be imposed is free of any restriction on freedom and, on the other hand, the law combines the exercise of the sanctioning power with measures to safeguard the rights and freedoms guaranteed under the Constitution'.[22]

The constitutional judge makes this power subject to fundamental principles such as the non-retroactivity of penal sanctions and the necessity or proportionality of penalties. In fact in his decision of 17 January 1989, he had considered that the overall principles concerning penal sanctions were applicable [Tr.] 'to any sanctions of a punitive nature, even if the legislator allowed a non-judicial authority to pronounce it'.[23] By this precedent, the Constitutional Council strengthened the fair trial requirement already included in article 6 of the European Council's Convention for the Protection of Human Rights and Fundamental Freedoms[24] (see below).[25]

---

19 Cons. Constitutionnel, 17 January 1989, *Loi modifiant la loi nº 86-1067 du 30 septembre 1986 relative à la liberté de communication*, Rec. 1986. 18, 88-248 DC, at para. 15.

20 *Ibid.* Despite this framework, the president of the National Assembly recently expressed concern about a 'decline in parliamentary authority' to the benefit of IAAs.

21 See also Quilichini (2004).

22 Cons. Constitutionnel, 28 July 1989, *Loi relative à la sécurité et à la transparence du marché financier* , Rec. 1989. 71, 89-260 DC, at para. 6.

23 Cons. Constitutionnel, *supra* note 18, at para. 36.

24 4 November 1950, 213 U.N.T.S. 221, ETS 5.

25 Next to this *sensu stricto* sanctioning power, IAAs are similar to jurisdictions in that they have another power, that of adjudicating disputes. We have seen that some IAAs wield such power. Although for now this power is essentially given to authorities

Should the sanctioning powers granted to IAAs be seen as a challenge to the courts on the part of the legislator? The answer is probably negative, although it is true that tribunals tend to be reactive, rather than proactive like IAAs. In addition, there was a time, unlike today, when IAAs were less subject to procedural requirements than courts.

To apply the obligation of fair trial to IAAs, one can refer to article 6 of the European Council's Convention for the Protection of Human Rights and Fundamental Freedoms (CPHRFF). By its procedural implications, the CPHRFF (open for signature in 1950) imposed common rules on IAAs that apply to all disputes. Therefore it intervenes as a truly federative element.

Article 6 of the CPHRFF, which bases the notion of 'fair trial' within the meaning of the European Council, states:

> In the determination of his civil rights and obligations or of any criminal charge against him, everyone is entitled to a fair and public hearing within a reasonable time by an independent and impartial tribunal established by law.[26]

Given that IAAs are empowered to adjudicate disputes and hand out sanctions, including fines, it is fair to question their adherence to this article. For the European Court of Human Rights based in Strasbourg, a tribunal is defined in the substantive sense of the term by its judicial function, that is to say 'determining matters within its competence on the basis of rules of law and after proceedings conducted in a prescribed manner'.[27] The Court of Cassation drew conclusions from this comprehensive notion of the judicial function by allowing, in *COB v. Oury* on 5 February 1999,[28] that the Securities and Exchange Commission, although not a jurisdiction within the French jurisdictional order, was governed by article 6 of the CPHRFF and the rules of fair trial.

In the *Didier* decision of 3 December 1999,[29] the Council of State adopted a similar principle regarding the Financial Markets Council, ruling that when informed of actions that could lead to financial penalties, is should be [Tr.] 'seen as ruling on the legitimacy of accusations in penal matters'[30] within the meaning of article 6 of the CPHRFF. Thus in this decision, the administrative judge, while stating that the Financial Markets Council sitting in a disciplinary hearing was

---

responsible for operator access to an infrastructure necessary to the practice of the activity, such as a telecommunications or energy grid, this power seems an interesting alternative to sanctioning powers and could be extended to other IAAs.

26 *Supra*, note 23.

27 This principle was laid down by the Court in *Demicoli v. Malta* (1991) 14 EHRR 47, at para. 39.

28 Cass., Ass. Plén., 5 Feburary 1999, *COB c. Oury*, Bull. Ass. Plén., n° 1, p. 1.

29 Cons. d'État, 3 December 1999, *Didier*, Rec. 1999.

30 *Ibid.*

not a jurisdiction under domestic law, still allowed that the means drawn from the violation of a principle under article 6 could [Tr.] 'regarding the nature, makeup and powers granted to this organization, be usefully invoked in support of a recourse before the Council of State against its decision'.[31] Thus when civil or penal matters are at stake, it is as tribunals in the European sense that IAAs must work out the guarantees related to fair trial and the impartiality of the jurisdiction.

The case law emanating from the Court of Cassation and the Council of State indicates that litigation has focused mainly on the participation in deliberations by the rapporteur who conducted the inquiry upstream. For the Court of Cassation, the rapporteur's participation in deliberations, if the inquiries needed have been conducted in the investigation of the facts, goes against article 6.[32] In a *KPMG* decision dated 7 March 2000,[33] the Paris Court of Appeal condemned the entire procedure followed before the COB, although the rapporteur had not participated in deliberations, because the functions of prosecution, investigation and decision had been combined; the COB bodies responsible for these offices were identically composed.

This jurisprudence has had an impact on the regulating and operating of IAAs. Thus the law of 1 August 2003, which created the AMF to replace the COB, has completely changed the procedure in order to make it compatible with article 6. Similarly, at the CSA, the rapporteur from the Council of State was eliminated, as was the rapporteur's participation in deliberations for the Council on Competition. It should be noted however that the Council of State used a more restrictive interpretation of article 6 in *Crédit Agricole* on 22 November 2000. It considered that if rapporteurs do not have prosecution powers in the drafting of grievances and the adoption of restrictive measures at the Financial Markets Council, their participation in deliberations does not go against the principle of impartiality.

To conclude on this matter, it has become clear that the legislator, when giving an IAA the power to impose financial penalties, must make sure that this prerogative is used in accordance with the conditions of the right to a fair trial as defined in article 6 of the CPHRFF.

In this regard the AMF seems to have the most protective sanctioning procedure possible. Its structure makes a clear distinction between the functions of prosecution and sanction, within the authority's collegial body and a sanctions commission, which is a collegial body in its own right.[34]

---

31 *Ibid.*

32 This solution was submitted in the aforementioned *COB c. Oury supra* note 28.

33 CA, Paris, 7 March 2000, *KPMG*, 1ère chambre, section H, n° 1999/15862.

34 The sanctioning procedure involves three stages:

- opening of sanctioning procedure by the AMF college, which notifies the respondent of the grievances and apprises the commission of this notification,
- investigation of sanctioning procedure, conducted by a rapporteur who is a member of the sanctions commission,
- sanction pronounced by the ruling sanctions commission, without the rapporteur.

The control over IAAs by national jurisdictions can come under either order of jurisdiction.[35] Before elaborating on this point, we note the important role played by tribunals as horizontal governance organizations for regulators, especially when it comes to harmonizing their jurisprudence. Actually it is not only a matter of exerting control, namely because not all IAAs are habilitated to adjudicate disputes or order sanctions. In some cases IAAs can refer cases to competent jurisdictions, thereby acting more as an aid or stimulant to legal action. In all cases, the intensity and quality of exchanges between IAAs and jurisdictions are essential.[36]

For a long time IAAs came under the control of the Council of State, a logical extension of their administrative nature. This solution had the advantage of being simple and avoided having conflicting case law. But since 1987, the legislator has tended to turn control over to the Paris Court of Appeal. This occurred notably with the Council on Competition and the financial markets regulator (today the AMF). The complexity resulting from the integration in two orders of jurisdiction, administrative on one side, civil and criminal on the other, also comes from the criteria that determine the allocation between the two. Depending on the type of power exerted by the Authority, the recourse will be referred either to the Paris Court of Appeal or to the Council of State. For authorities exercising only one type of power – such as the Council on Competition, which applies sanctions against anti-competitive behaviour but does not have regulatory or certification powers –, the allocation is easy. The Paris Court of Appeal always has jurisdiction, on a national basis, with the possibility of going before the Court of Cassation. But where powers are diversified, the exercise of regulatory powers will come under the Council of State and the power to settle disputes under the Paris Court of Appeal.

The issue of sanctioning powers creates specific difficulties, depending on whether it is the repressive type, leading to the judicial judge, or the disciplinary type, leading to the administrative judge. Thus the dispute tribunal (*Tribunal des Conflits*) often has to rule on the jurisdiction of this or that order, whether dealing with financial or energy matters (an example being the *Powernext* decision of 26 April 2004).[37]

A solution to this could be the creation by Parliament of a completely autonomous jurisdiction, that is, which would belong neither to the administrative nor to the judicial order. However, this solution appears rather shaky from a legal standpoint and does not seem to be the route of choice, especially since IAAs do not consider this difficulty to be a major problem. Thus Paul Champsaur, President of ARCEP,

---

Thus all functions are strictly separated and the principles outlined under article 6.1 are adhered to.

35 See also Costes (2006), Delvové (2001), Legros (2006), Simon (2004).

36 A citizens' right to participate and oversee could also be considered.

37 Trib.con., 26 April 2004, *Powernext*, n° C3379.

declared that this system [Tr.] 'works without any problems'.[38] In addition, the companies concerned by IAA actions are more interested in guarantees of technical competence and effective processual rights than the enacting of an *ad hoc* recourse jurisdiction.

An interesting question of principle regards the intervention or presence of IAAs in appeals. A problem was encountered concerning jurisdictional control over the action of IAAs by the Council of State, the Paris Court of Appeal and the Court of Cassation. Can IAAs be present when appeals of their decisions are being heard? If they are considered true jurisdictions, it seems the answer should be negative. But their presence is often justified by their expertise, unlike jurisdictions that do not consist of specialists on the topics concerned. Their assistance can therefore be useful in the decision-making process. This right to be present has been granted explicitly in instruments to some authorities on a case-by-case basis, including to the AMF, the ARCEP, the CRE and the Council on Competition. However, the Court of Cassation, in a decision of its commercial chamber on 22 February 2005, gave a restrictive interpretation to the right to comment thus granted to these authorities, attesting to the issues that can be raised by this right. It should be noted that on this occasion the power of the appeals judge is a power to cancel and/or reverse a decision, and that in this case the French judge is probably more of a lawmaker at this stage than his 'Anglo-Saxon' counterpart.[39]

A Few Elements of Comparison with Canadian Law

The development of an IAA model in Canada started well before it did in France, in the second half of the nineteenth century, with the creation of Statutory Regulatory Agencies, or SRAs. This movement was to support the development of Canada, in the particular context of a country requiring control over a vast territory.[40] As early as 1851, a Board of Railway Committee of the Privy Council was given regulatory powers by the *Railway Act*. However, it is at the beginning of the twentieth century when the true Canadian model of Independent Administrative Authorities started taking shape, with the reform of the Board of Railway Committee. After World

38 Sénat français, 'Les autorités administratives indépendantes: évaluation d'un objet juridique non identifié (Tome 2: Annexes)', online: http://www.senat.fr/rap/r05-404-2/r05-404-228.html, note 306.

39 Canadian judges rule as part of a judicial review procedure (reasonable or patently unreasonable decision).

40 Thus in his study on Canadian IAAs, Guy Scoffoni (*Les autorités administratives indépendantes: évaluation d'un objet juridique non identifié*; http://www.senat.fr'rap/R05-404-2/r05-404-216.html) explains [Tr.] 'the construction of a large modern railway system, the relations between the various population groups, the general administration of land or the economic relations between provinces, created the need for new administrative structures'.

War I the expansion of the federal government's scope of action led to the creation of new agencies, a movement which was accelerated by the Great Depression and the Canadian 'New Deal' of 1935. Thus regulatory agencies proliferated throughout the twentieth century.

The structure and mode of action of SRAs share several characteristics. As in France, regulatory bodies are created by the legislator, and their role and status are determined by their enabling instruments. Like French IAAs, these agencies also enjoy sweeping regulatory powers such as price, product or service regulation, enforcement of competitive rules, the definition of product quality standards and consumer protection. They also regulate the field of transport and communications through regulatory or quasi-jurisdictional powers. One of the features of these bodies is of course the independent nature of their action, which is distinct from the traditional areas of the executive, as ministers do not have direct control over SRAs.

However, the independence of these authorities seems less assured and less essential to their nature than in France.[41] In many cases the departments themselves did not completely transfer powers to these regulatory agencies and continue to exercise similar parallel functions of direction and control. The departments in charge of a given sector retain some powers of control. There are many ways in which departments can influence the work of regulatory agencies, including through the use of 'hierarchical' appeals (allowing the minister to substitute his decision to that of the regulatory body), as well as directives or directions adopted in Council. The governmental appeal mechanism is complemented by a jurisdictional control procedure allowing the agencies' decisions to be appealed before the courts. Finally, administrative and financial control is exercised over these agencies, with each agency's budget being part of the budget of the department to which it is attached. SRAs are therefore controlled on three levels.

Although there are similarities between the French and Canadian systems in the creation of these agencies and the powers they are granted, the two systems differ most in the way they are attached to a department – a characteristic of the Canadian system that is absent in France. These differences have historical origins. Canadian agencies were developed to improve social and territorial cohesion, notably by the construction of railway systems. They are closely tied to the action of the government. The development of French IAAs, on the contrary, results from a moving back or disengagement from the classic state administration.

Conclusion

IAAs have represented a powerful means of developing multijuralism in national legal systems, in a way not only compatible with the integration of these systems

41 In fact it is interesting to note that the term 'independent' is not part of the name of these Statutory Regulatory Agencies.

within the European Union, but in fact eminently favourable to their integration. Under the impetus of the Brussels authorities, but also due to the common character of evolutions related to technical progress and globalization, the process was about the same in France as in other European Union Member States such as Great Britain, Belgium, Germany, Italy and Spain. Community law and the implications of pursuing the deepening of the internal market have probably been the main drive behind the creation of a true law of IAAs under the control of the national judge, both in innovative fields such as new technologies, and in more traditional sectors such as competition. The fact that this process has been the same in a common law system, when the law applies, and in civilist systems, is worthy of note. However, this increase in the powers and responsibilities of the European judge should be compared with the reinforcement of autonomy of regulatory agencies in the United States.

References

AMF (2006a). 'Unified Arab Economic Report: 2006', League of Arab State, Arab Monetary Fund for Economic and Social Development and AOPEC, September 2006, UAE.

AMF (2006b). 'AMDB Quarterly Bulletin No. 48', Arab Monetary Fund, UAE

Argentieri, Laurent (2005). 'L'émergence d'un modèle européen de contrôle financier', *Les Petites Affiches*, 22 November, 232, 6 ff.

Arsouze, Charles and Patrick Ledoux (2006). 'Indemnisation des victimes d'infractions boursières', *Bulletin Joly Bourse*, July-August, 399 ff.

Boy, Laurence (2001). 'Réflexion sur le droit de la régulation', *Dalloz*, 37, 3031 ff.

Costes, Lionel (2006). 'L'heure est à l'autorégulation', *Lamy Droit de l'immatériel*, June, 17, 3 ff.

Daigre, Jean-Jacques (2000). 'La nouvelle procédure de sanction de la COB: une réforme en clair-obscur', *JCP Entreprises et Affaires*, 12 October, 41, 1602 ff.

Delvové, Pierre (2001). 'Le pouvoir de sanction et le contrôle du juge', *Les Petites Affiches*, 17 September, 185, 18 ff.

Ducouloux-Favard, Claude (2006). 'En matière de contentieux boursier, rien ne va plus: à propos de la décision de l'AMF du 16 décembre 2005', *Les Petites Affiches*, 10 March, 50, 3 ff.

Enfert, Carole (2005). 'Rapport d'information No. 3239 déposé le 4 juillet 2006 par la délégation de l'Assemblée Nationale pour l'Union Européenne sur la transposition des directives européennes', *RTDE*, July-September, 671 ff.

Frison-Roche, Marie-France (2001). 'Le droit de la régulation', *Dalloz*, 610 ff.

Frison-Roche, Marie-France (2002). 'La régulation, objet d'une branche du droit?', *Les Petites Affiches*, 3 June, 110, 85 ff.

Georgopoulos, Théodore (2005). 'Le Conseil Constitutionnel face à la directive communautaire: trois destinataires pour un message ambivalent', *Les Petites Affiches*, 15 November, 227, 3 ff.
Germain, Michel (2005). 'La régulation de la concurrence au sein de la directive du 21 avril 2004 concernant les marchés d'instruments financiers', *Les Petites Affiches*, 26 December, 256, 5 ff.
Godet, Romain (2002). 'La participation des AAI au règlement des litiges juridictionnels de droit commun: l'exemple des autorités de marché', *RFDA*, September-October, 957 ff.
Heuzé, Vincent (2005). 'L'Europe désenchantée', *JCP*, 27 July, 30, 1439 ff.
Institut Montaigne (2002). 'L'articulation recherché-innovation', Paris: Institut Montaigne.
Institut Montaigne (2004). 'Les oubliés de l'égalité des chances', Paris: Institut Montaigne.
Institut Montaigne (2004). 'Régulation: Ce que Bruxelles doit vraiment faire', Paris: Institut Montaigne.
Jappont, Frédéric (2005). 'L'encadrement juridique de la coopération entre les autorités de régulation', *Dalloz*, 13, 893 ff.
Lafortune, Maurice Antoine (2001). 'Les autorités indépendantes de régulation à l'épreuve des principes processuels fondamentaux dans l'exercice de leur pouvoir de sanction des manquements aux règlements du marché économique, financier et boursier', *Gazette du Palais*, September-October, 1449 ff.
Legros, Bertrand (2006). 'Le Conseil d'Etat, juge de la suspension des sanctions de l'AMF', *Les Petites Affiches*, 31 July, 151, 56 ff.
Lesquins, Jean-Louis (2006). 'Concurrence : les juridictions se spécialisent', *Échos*, 28 September, 16 ff.
Lombard, Martine (2005). 'Brèves remarques sur la personnalité morale des institutions de régulation', *RJEP/CJEG*, April, 619, 127 ff.
Muller, Isabelle (1977). 'Les organismes communautaires décentralisés', *Les Petites Affiches*, 22 January, 10, 23 ff.
Nussenbaum, Maurice (2005). 'Les difficultés de l'expertise en matière de pratiques anticoncurrentielles', *Les Petites Affiches*, 20 January, 14, 37 ff.
Pistor, Katharina and Chenggang Xu (2006). 'The Challenge of Incomplete Law and How Different Legal Systems Respond', in Albert Breton and Michael Trebilcock (eds.), *Bijuralism: An Economic Approach*, Aldershot: Ashgate Publishing, 71-108.
Pralus-Dupuis, Joëlle (2003). 'Réflexions sur le pouvoir de sanction disciplinaire reconnu à certaines autorités administratives indépendantes', *RFDA*, May-June, 554 ff.
Prétot, Xavier (2002). 'La CEDH?', *Revue de Droit Public*, 6.
Quilichini, Paule (2004). 'Réguler n'est pas juger: réflexions sur la nature du pouvoir de sanction des autorités de régulation économique', *AJDA*, 24 May.
Quilichini, Paule (2006). 'Réguler n'est pas juger: réflexion sur le pouvoir de régulation des autorités de régulation économique', *AJDA*, 24 May, 1060 ff.

Rapp, Lucien (2006). 'L'avenir de la régulation: réflexions libres autour d'un concept clé', *Lamy Droit de l'immatériel*, June, 17, 51 ff.
Rodrigues, Stéphane (2004). 'Quelques considérations en faveur d'un statut pérenne des autorités européennes de régulation', *AJDA*, 14 June, 1179 ff.
Sales, Eric (2005). 'La transposition des directives communautaires, une exigence de valeur constitutionnelle sous réserve de constitutionnalité', *RTDE*, July-September, 597 ff.
Salomon, Renaud (2000). 'La réforme de la procédure de sanction de la COB par les décrets du 1er août 2000', *RDBF*, September-October, 312 ff.
Schwartz, Rémy and Jacques Ribs (2000). 'L'actualité des sanctions administratives infligées par les autorités administratives indépendants', *Gazette du Palais*, 28 July.
Sénat français. 'Les autorités administratives indépendantes: évaluation d'un objet juridique non identifié (Tome 2: Annexes)', online: http://www.senat.fr/rap/r05-404-2/r05-404-219.html.
Sénat français. 'Les autorités administratives indépendantes: évaluation d'un objet juridique non identifié (Tome 2: Annexes)', online: http://www.senat.fr/rap/r05-404-2/r05-404-228.html.
Simon, François Luc (2004). 'Le Juge et les autorités du marché boursier', Paris: LGDJ, tome 427.
Thomasset-Pierre, Sylvie (2002). 'L'autorité de régulation boursière face aux garanties processuelles fondamentales', Paris: LGDJ.
Traoré, Seydou (2004). 'Les autorités administratives indépendantes dotées de la personnalité morale: vers une réintégration institutionnelle de la catégorie juridique?', *Revue mensuelle de droit administratif*, August-September, 16 ff.
Vogel, Laurent, (2002). 'Long on ideas, short on means', *TUTB Newsletter No 18*, March 2002, 3-6.
Vogel, Laurent, (2002). 'Framework Directive up before ECJ', *TUTB Newsletter No 18*, March 2002, 7.
Vogel, Laurent, (2002). 'ECJ rulings on compulsory membership of a statutory work accident insurance body', *TUTB Newsletter No 18*, March 2002, 8-9.

Legal cases

CA, Paris, 7 March 2000, *KPMG*, 1ère chambre, section H, n° 1999/15862
Cass., Ass. Plén., 5 Feburary 1999, *COB c. Oury*, Bull. Ass. Plén., n° 1, p. 1
Cons. Constitutionnel, 18 September 1986, *Loi relative à la liberté des communications*, Rec. 1986. 11294, 86-217 DC
Cons. Constitutionnel, 17 January 1989, *Loi modifiant la loi n° 86-1067 du30 septembre 1986 relative à la liberté de communication*, Rec. 1986. 754, 88-248 DC
Cons. Constitutionnel, 28 July 1989, *Loi relative à la sécurité et à la transparence du marché financier*, Rec. 1989. 71, 89-260 DC

Cons. d'État, 3 December 1999, *Didier*, Rec. 1999
Demicoli v. Malta (1991) 14 EHRR 47
Trib. con., 26 April 2004, *Powernext*, n° C3379

Legislation and Directives

European Parliament and the Council of the European Union, *Directive 2002/19/CE*, 7 March 2002.
European Parliament and the Council of the European Union, *Directive 2002/20/CE*, 7 March 2002.
European Parliament and the Council of the European Union, *Directive 2002/21/CE*, 7 March 2002.
European Parliament and the Council of the European Union, *Directive 2002/22/CE*, 7 March 2002.
Loi n° 2003-706 du 1 août 2003 de sécurité financière (1), J.O., 2 August 2003.

International documents

Convention for the Protection of Human Rights and Fundamental Freedoms, 4 November 1950, 213 U.N.T.S. 221, ETS 5

Chapter 5
European Contract Law: Towards an Optional Instrument?

Bénédicte Fauvarque-Cosson

Introduction

At first glance, the most fundamental controversies surrounding the construction of Europe do not revolve around the issue of the development of European Contract Law or even European private law. This subject appears much less sensitive and politicized than others, such as the development of the European Constitution. Yet contract law alone is a major issue, both from a practical and a political perspective.[1] Contract law is at the heart of private law, which itself is at the heart of economic relations between citizens.

Most European countries codified their civil law in the nineteenth century or at the beginning of the twentieth century. Recently some countries, including the Netherlands, completely revised their civil code whereas others, such as Germany, have re-codified- their contract law. These modern laws could serve as a reference for Europe. In France, when the Civil Code celebrated its bicentenary, the issue of a European civil code, or a European Contract Law at the very least, was on everyone's mind. In fact, though the issue is certainly primarily legal and economic in nature, it is also, for French lawyers, deeply cultural and political. Hence it underlies a passionate and impassioned debate, probably one of the greatest legal debates of this century in Europe as it raises innumerable questions and controversies.[2]

---

1 There is often a tendency to put the debate in the context of a political opposition between the advocates of a Europe of nations, sworn enemy of any project to unify European contract law, and, on a broader scale, a potential European civil code, and the supporters of a federal Europe, who are supposed to defend the European civil code project which is considered the real cement of legal unity in Europe. However this is a misinterpretation given that federalism is precisely the concept which carries and defines subsidiarity. Consequently, federalism does not imply unity of civil law; on the contrary, the federalist approach retains contract law within the realm of Member States, while transforming it in part through directives and, as needed, by adding consistent conflict of law rules.

2 The short bibliography reproduced here, though by no means exhaustive, illustrates the diverse range of opinions on the subject: Basedow (1998); Basedow, in Bergé and

Should European Contract Law be unified? Do systems that have one market and one currency call for one contract law? Is the diversity of rights an obstacle to commercial transactions and the development of an internal market or, on the contrary, is it a source of energy and evolution? Does consistency really encourage trade? Would it not, conversely, result in cultural impoverishment and a certain glaciation of contract law? Does legal security really require consistency? Is it necessary, in the name of legal security, to develop European rules that will even govern the internal relations of each Member State? Does not private international law offer ways of knowing with certainty the applicable law, especially when rules regarding conflict of laws are unified, such as in contract matters?

Although many today think that conflict of law rules are no longer an appropriate instrument for a largely integrated internal market and that a uniform instrument needs to be developed, others, on the contrary, are firmly opposed to this unification, for reasons that are not only cultural or political, but also economic.[3]

In reality, these debates involve several technical issues, related to the various ongoing projects, which are and to this day remain uncertain:

1. What area of law would be subject to a unified European law: contract law, law of obligations, the whole of patrimonial law (including securities, property, and so on[4]) or even the whole of civil law including human rights and family law?

Niboyet (eds) (2003); Cornu (2002); Fauvarque-Cosson (2002); Heuzé (2002); Huet (2002); Jamin in de Vareilles-Sommières (ed.) (1998); Legrand (1996); Lequette (2002); Lequette (2003); Malaurie (2002); Malinvaud (2002); Mazeaud, in Société de législation comparée (2005); Prieto, in Prieto (ed.) (2003); Prieto (2004); Racine (2003); Rampelberg (2005); Tallon, in Editions du JurisClasseur Collection (1993); Terré and Outin-Adam (2004); Witz (2000); Witz (2003); Fauvarque-Cosson and Mazeaud (eds) (2003). The list, already long, is incomplete and more ample references can be found, including in the very complete article by Denis Mazeaud (2005).

3 Is the diversity of rights really an obstacle to intra-community exchanges? The opponents argue that standardizing contract law at the European level would favour non-European companies, especially American or Canadian companies, by allowing them to deal with only one law to penetrate the common market, whereas European companies would continue to be confronted with a multiplicity of legal regimes in the United States and Canada.

4 It is easy to understand why it might be a good idea to harmonize contract law, especially that which is used in European internal trade (sale of goods and services, distribution networks, and so on) as well as the law of securities which could be used to guarantee the execution of such contracts (including personal securities such as bonds). Should it be extended to property law? The question merits examination. In a first approach, one could observe that a distinction can be made between movable and immovable property. For the former, it may be ideal that they be governed by common principles, at least insofar as the goods in question belong to international trade. For the latter, which are not part of cross-border trade (except when held by real estate companies, in which case they are represented by shares, that is, movable property), it does not appear necessary, or

2. What type of instrument should be used: a directive, an optional regulation, a Code or a simple Common Frame of Reference?
3. What should the main directions be? With regards to contractual relationships, should the traditional dogma of freedom of contract and free will win out over the domineering concerns of contractual balance, solidarity, social justice and the protection of the weakest?

Traditionally, the argument justifying intervention by Europe in the area of private law, which was economic in nature, is tied to the objective of creating an Internal Market and more specifically, to the idea – supported by the Commission – that the diversity of laws constitutes an obstacle to the development of an internal market, given that it increases the cost of cross-border transactions and therefore deters consumers and small businesses. This argument, as valid as it may be in economic law, cannot alone justify harmonizing the whole of private law. That is especially true since the construction of a European private law, extending to individuals and families, could result in tearing down national legal orders, to the detriment of cultural and legal pluralism and of the values proclaimed (pluralism in culture, language, philosophy and law).[5] Even when it comes to economic matters, where culture weighs less heavily, the whole issue is to advance the construction of European law – keenly wished for by the businesses themselves, as recently shown by a major survey of European businesses[6] – still without tearing down the national legal orders in this area.

---

even useful, to unify the regime, especially since their geographical ties necessarily entail numerous formalities that depend on where the immovable is located (publication of rights, local taxation, intervention needed by law experts, and so on). At the very most could it be suggested that, as was done for 'multi-property' or 'time-share property', a directive could be adopted to protect consumers in real estate matters that would ensure individual buyers or lessors of immovable property of having an equal level of protection in all European Union countries.

5 Family law is carried within the soul of the people. In this area, it would be a serious error to ignore this cultural dimension, which is a major factor involved in the rejection of laws originating elsewhere and imposed in a top-down manner. In addition, at first glance human rights and, even more so, family law only have a very indirect impact on the development of Community exchanges. Consequently, even if the European project now goes well beyond the internal market, conventional wisdom would demand that we let standards of behaviour evolve before launching an undertaking that might strike such sensitivities. While in human rights the reference to the 'soul of the citizens', their cultural references, and so on facilitates the defence of domestic law over European law and even makes it laudable, the defence in a commercial and financial context is, in my opinion, a wager lost in advance. In this area France has never carried the influence it has in constitutional matters or human rights. A fight on this basis is doomed to failure and other walls of the structure will fall with it.

6 This survey is a joint undertaking with between the law firm of Clifford Chance and the Oxford Institute of European and Comparative Law. As the university advisors

What are the best methods for this? In these times marked by legal pluralism, the use of an optional law could well be the best route.

Community institutions have long preferred the issuing of directives, which Member States had to transpose into their own legal systems. Inasmuch as these guidelines only imposed minimum standards – at least when it came to consumer protection, on which the Community legislator on contracts tended to focus – Member States remained free to distance themselves from the Community text, in order in particular to further reinforce consumer protection. Nowadays, the traditional route of directives agreed upon for transposition and directly applicable rules has shown its limitations. The *acquis communautaire* is, in contract law, only an aggregate of disparate texts that cover very diverse areas and disrupt the legal systems of Member States. In France as in other Member States, European directives are often seen as foreign matter, purely technocratic in origin, and difficult to fit into a pre-existing internal structure.[7] For all that, in a Communication dated 12 February 2003, entitled 'A more coherent European Contract Law – An action plan',[8] the European Commission itself denounced the many drawbacks of the sectoral harmonization of contract law. It first noted the difficulties inherent to Community law: a mosaic of texts that do not all use the same principles of resolution, so that identical situations are sometimes treated differently, there are inconsistencies within a given directive, or even conflicts between directives and some international covenants. Then it noted the difficulty of transposing these directives within Member States: the absence of real unification of the law because of the *a minima* transposition principle, the use of abstract terms that are not defined in directives, which can result in different interpretations by national judges and the risk of 'fragmentation of national contract law'.[9] It is not surprising therefore that for Member States, some delay – even a failure – is observed in

for this survey, Stefan Vogenauer and Stephen Weatherill published in several European magazines, including the *European Review of Contract Law*, their 'empirical analysis' of the results of this survey and its consequences on the first question asked, regarding the jurisdiction of the European Community to legislate in contractual matters. See Vogenauer and Weatherill (2005).

7 van Gerven's Introductory Report in Jamin and Mazeaud (eds) (2001); Rémy in Rémy-Corlay and Fenouillet (eds) (2003) writes (p. 3, note 11): [Tr.] 'Each introduction of directives, in French obligations law, creates a small psychodrama: there has been one regarding abusive clauses, product liability, consumer goods sales warranty; the theme seems to be the will to transpose 'French style' (*more gallico, alla francese)*, which then produces some cutting condemning, either for late or incorrect transposition. (see CJCE Apr. 25, 2002, Commission des Communautés c/ France)'.

8 See Commission of the European Communities, COM (2003) 68 final.

9 *Ibid.*, No. 22. When transposing directives, several avenues are possible:
a) transpose the directive, amending domestic law only when it becomes strictly necessary;
b) transpose the directive and take the opportunity to undertake an in-depth overall reform of domestic law.

the transposition of directives.[10] Nor it is surprising that Community institutions would seek alternatives.

The solution considered by the Commission would consist of relinquishing the sectoral approach for a general revision of contract law which could take the shape either of a European code of contracts, or, a more minimalistic option, a 'Common Frame of Reference' that could be paired with an 'optional instrument'.[11]

The methodical codification of European contract law today appears to be a priority compared to the development of a European civil code that can only be done while respecting the diversity and richness of the various national traditions. The development of a European Contract Law, even optional in nature, is a significant step towards building a common identity in Europe.[12] But even concerning contract law alone, we have to move progressively and test out various options.

Over the last few years, the Commission has launched a widespread debate on the development of a European Contract Law, which led to the amendment of its initial projects. The main stages of this debate and the development of European projects will be covered in the next section. The subsequent section will take a close look at the project selected, that is, the Common Frame of Reference, and more specifically its mode of development and the ways in which parties to a contract will be able to adopt it through opt-in or opt-out mechanisms that will be implemented to this effect.

The Commission's Projects in European Contract Law

In Europe, the respective roles of the three European institutions (Commission, Parliament, Council) are schematically as follows: the European Commission proposes, the Parliament deliberates and legislates, and the Council decides. Though the European Parliament for its part had already published several resolutions (1989, 1994, 2001) calling for harmonization of certain areas of the

For an example, see the various transpositions of the Directive 1999/44/EC of the European Parliament and of the Council of 25 May 1999 on certain aspects of the sale of consumer goods and associated guarantees (OJEC, 7 July 1999, at p. 12) and compare with France (narrow transposition after long debates) and Germany (where the directive was a factor that triggered a vast obligations law reform project).

10 On the delicate issue of transposition delay, or even 'failure', see Colonna, Minister Delegate for European Affairs, (2006); and Philip (2006). See also, A. Astaix, *Communication ministérielle sur la transposition des directives communautaires*, D. 2006.1910.

11 On this ambitious project, see Commission to the European Communities (2004).

12 For a more in-depth analysis, see Prieto, in Prieto (ed.) (2003) and Prieto (2004) The author aptly states 'the realism of the European Commission in its double self-limitation (limitation to contract law, limitation by eliminating the term 'code'). We have to proceed in steps and by trial and error'.

private law of the States,[13] the European Commission is the one to have revived the debate.[14] To this effect, it published three successive Communications that can be briefly summarized here.[15]

In July 2001, the European Commission, in a Communication to the European Council and Parliament concerning European Contract Law, launched a public consultation regarding the potential of establishing a European Contract Law in order to eliminate potential obstacles to market operations. The Commission would seek advice from the legal community on four possible options:

1. change nothing and therefore no Community action. Actually, this is not really an option: it simply translates into a *laissez-faire* market approach.
2. promote common principles, as well as strengthen research and cooperation in the area of comparative law.
3. improve the quality of current legislation, that is, simplify the directives (and the Commission refers to the SLIM initiative); adapt old texts instead of adopting new ones.
4. adopt a complete legislation at the Community level, concerning both general contract theory and special contracts.

The response deadline was very short: 15 October 2001. Many responses were submitted after the deadline, such as the one published in September 2002 by Philippe Malinvaud, on behalf of Association H. Capitant (Malinvaud, 2002). The great majority of responses (whether from government, businesses, consumer associations, lawyers or academics) favoured options 2 and 3 and rejected the fourth option. On 25 March 2002, the Commission issued a summary of the 'reactions' to its Communication, or at least what feedback it had received before 31 January 2002.

The responses from Parliament and the Council require special attention in that they reflected, at the time, a real political will to proceed. On 15 November 2001, the European Parliament, in a resolution 'concerning the reconciliation of civil law and commercial law of Member States', criticized the Commission's Communication for limiting its scope to contract law, going as far as proposing a very tight timeline to develop a 'single European code of private law' that would include property law and extra-contractual liability law). Although this timeline, to this day, still draws smiles, it should be revisited to illustrate the gap between the aspirations of some people in this area and the reality, which moves more slowly: developing common concepts and solutions for Member States by the end of 2004 and being able to consult, in all the EC languages, a vast data bank

---

13 In its Communication, the Commission makes sure to refer to these resolutions.

14 In reality, in many areas, the Commission holds major regulatory powers. As stressed by J. Prieur, the Commission has actually assumed the power to regulate. It decides in several economic, legal, fiscal, accounting areas (pressure from lobbies and Anglo-Saxon firms).

15 See also Vogenauer and Weatherill (2005), especially pp. 1218 and following.

on domestic legislation and jurisprudence in contract law; publishing, by the end of 2005, a comparative analysis of common legal concepts and solutions, applied by EU institutions and taught in law faculties; evaluating this legislation in 2008 and, around 2010, adopting regulations regarding contract law (which would be optional and legally based on article 95 of the Treaty).

On 16 November 2001, the Council for its part published a 'Report on the need to approximate Member States' legislation in civil matters', insisting on the central role played by contract law and also mentioning family law as a topic for discussion on the approximation of domestic private law. It also expressed the desired objective that a study be conducted in the areas of non-contractual liability and property law.[16]

On 12 February 2003, the Commission published a Communication entitled 'A more coherent European Contract Law – An action plan'. This was in reaction to the ambitious demands by Parliament and Council and the reserved responses of governments, businesses, consumer associations, jurists of all types, and so on. This action plan lists the obstacles of concluding cross-border transactions – tied to the diversity of current legislations. It revisits the European Contract Law unification project, which includes the law on special contracts, liability, property, sureties.

The text begins by listing the many drawbacks of the sectoral approach: incoherence (similar situations treated differently), contradictions (directives conflicting with each other but also conflicting provisions within a directive), the difficulties of integrating European law in Member States, different interpretations, the limits of harmonization given the minimum harmonization principle (which is beginning to be questioned). The Commission then proposed three sets of measures to improve the EC *acquis*.

1. create a 'Common Frame of Reference' (CFR) by, among other things, consulting groups of researchers;
2. promote the development of standard contract clauses applicable throughout the Union;
3. adopt an optional instrument in the area of European Contract Law (a measure announced cautiously and combined with the following important question: to opt in or to opt out?).

A second consultation procedure was then launched. Parliament and the Council expressed their opinions, which were favourable, inviting the Commission to continue thinking about an optional instrument and stressing the need to engage all interested parties in the process and, in particular, in the development of the CFR.[17]

16 This study was entrusted to Professors von Bar and Drobnig.

17 Still, at that time, voluntarism and optimism prevailed: a European Parliament Resolution on the Communication from the Commission to the European Parliament and

On 11 October 2004, the Commission published a new Communication entitled: 'European Contract Law and the Revision of the Acquis: The Way Forward'. This way, we are to discover, is first that of the CFR, possibly followed by an optional instrument, and the Commission takes care to specify that it is not its 'intention to propose a European Civil Code which would harmonize contract laws of Member States'.[18]

What does the CFR project entail? It is presented as a 'toolbox' with three parts. The first would set out 'common fundamental principles of European Contract Law, including guidelines for cases when exceptions to such fundamental principles would be required'.[19] The second would contain definitions of key abstract legal concepts (for example, contract, damages). The third, probably the most voluminous part, would complete the other two with model rules. It would form the 'core of the CFR' and contain detailed rules that could form the basis of the optional instrument. The rules regarding contracts among businesses or among individuals would be separate from those applicable to contracts between businesses and consumers.

What are the objectives of this Common Frame of Reference project? To inspire legislators. The Common Frame of Reference would constitute a reference to help European and national authorities in their law unification effort. The European legislator first:

> It would also be desirable that the Council and the European Parliament use the CFR when tabling amendments to Commission proposals. Such use of the CFR would be consistent with the shared goal of achieving high quality EU legislation[20] and the commitment of the European institutions to promote simplicity, clarity and consistency of the EU legislation.[21]

Then, national legislators could use the CFR not only to transpose European Directives related to contract law, but also to legislate in sectors of this branch of law that are not regulated by the Union. Even arbitrators are targeted by the Commission: in this instrument they could 'find unbiased and balanced solutions to resolve conflicts arising between contractual parties.'[22] The Commission also

---

the Council: A more coherent European Contract Law – An action plan, 2 September 2003, asked that the Common Frame of Reference be completed by the end of 2006 and introduced quickly ... A Resolution by Council on a More Coherent European Contract Law, 17 September 2003, encouraged Member States to get actively involved and asked the Commission to report regularly on the progress of the work.

18 Commission of the European Communities, *European Contract Law and the revision of the acquis: the way forward*, Brussels, 11 October, COM (2004), 651 final, p. 8.

19 See Commission of the European Communities, COM (2004) 651 final, p. 11.

20 Commission of the European Communities (2002).

21 Commission of the European Communities, COM (2004) 651 final, p. 5.

22 *Ibid.*

announced that it could use the CFR in its own contracts and that it would encourage other institutions and bodies to use the CFR when entering into contracts with third parties. Finally, it states that the Court of Justice could take the CFR into consideration.

Since then, probably due to the eurosclerosis caused by the failure of the Constitution, the Commission appeared to be backtracking again with a Communication dated 23 September 2005, entitled 'First Annual Progress Report on European Contract Law and the Acquis Review'.[23] Thus the idea of promoting development in the private sector of EU-wide standard terms and conditions (STCs), in particular by hosting a website on which Market participants could exchange useful information, was abandoned; it was the second measure in the 2003 action plan, and had encountered strong resistance.[24] Concerning the development of an optional instrument, which could be adopted in the form of an optional regulation, the Commission only gives it a short paragraph eloquently entitled 'Opportuneness of an optional instrument in SCL ('26th regime')', in which it refers to the 'Green Paper on Financial Services Policy (2005-2010)'.[25] This Green Paper develops the idea of a legislative instrument which completes but does not replace national regimes. This 26th regime, proposed as an option to the parties, would not change anything to the 25 sets of domestic regulations. As for the 'new priorities', they have to do first with a revision of the acquis as indicated by the title of the Communication: 'First Annual Progress Report on European Contract Law and the Acquis Review'. The CFR should focus on this objective and the results obtained during its development (definitions, standard rules, and so on) will be 'tested in the field of consumer protection, in the context of the review of the consumer acquis'.[26] In contractual matters, the EC acquis is mainly concerned with consumer protection. Before undertaking the acquis review phase itself, the Commission would like to develop a diagnostic phase which involves an

23 Commission of the European Communities (2005), about which see Bergé, Marais and Debet (2006).

24 The Commission abandons this idea for the following reasons. To be enforceable in all legal systems, standard terms and conditions (STCs) would need to comply with the most restrictive rules of national law. STCs are typically drafted for a given sector and it is hard to see how such contractual clauses could be of use to other sectors of the economy. The increased speed of legislative change requires STCs to be constantly updated. STCs posted on a Commission website would therefore quickly outlive their usefulness. The complexity and need for constant review mean that keeping STCs up to date comes at a great cost in terms of legal fees. The Commission doubts that parties that invest vast amounts to develop and update STCs will be eager to share the final result at no cost with their competitors. If STCs posted on the website are not checked as to whether they are valid and enforceable in all EU jurisdictions or compatible with EC law, this would greatly reduce the value of such exchange. Finally, the costs involved in the measure should not be overlooked.

25 Commission of the European Communities (2005), p. 11.

26 *Ibid.* p.4

analysis of the transposition and application of the consumer protection directives by the Member States.[27]

This deceleration was necessary because, given the Commission's various Communications, the process had got carried away. However, though the rules must be practical, they must also be coherent. The EC *acquis* must rest on general contract law principles. For this reason, it is not useless to provide a general framework, even if optional, that will then allow the revision and development of directives. This seems especially necessary despite the cultural cataclysm created by France's and the Netherlands' 'No' to the referendum on the European Constitution project, which had its repercussions. Since then the European construction process will continue, barring a collapse of the European structure. It is in the very nature of institutions such as the European Commission and Parliament to want to push forward.

In any case, the European Parliament has just published a Resolution in which it declared that it is the most important private law codification undertaken and even considers that it could become a binding instrument. After recalling the debate and tracing the history of all relevant texts,[28] Parliament:

1. Reiterates its conviction that a uniform internal market cannot be fully functional without further steps towards the harmonization of civil law;
2. Reminds us that the initiative on European Contract Law is the most important initiative under way in the field of civil law;

27 To this effect, it asked a network of law researchers and practitioners to conduct a comparative legal study. In addition, the Commission reports on the work undertaken so far on four directives (Unit Pricing, Injunctions, Timeshare and Distance Selling) and announced its intention to ensure the proper enforcement of these directives 'including self regulatory measures'. In paragraph 3.3 on 'potential outcomes', the Commission announced that if, during the diagnostic phase, it finds evidence that 'the acquis needs to be revised or completed the Commission could theoretically choose between 2 options: a vertical approach consisting of the individual revision of existing directives [...] a more horizontal approach, adopting one or more framework instruments to regulate common features of the acquis. This framework instrument(s) would provide common definitions and regulate the main consumer contractual rights and remedies.' With this in mind, the Commission announced the potential development of a Directive on contracts of sale of goods from professionals to consumers (B2C contracts), it would regulate consistently the contractual aspects of sale, which are currently scattered across several directives (for example, Directives on the Sale of Consumer Goods, Unfair Contract terms, Distance Selling and Doorstep Selling). Very attached to the principle of freedom of contract, it feels that 'appropriate differentiation be made between B2B contracts (between professionals) and B2C contracts (between a professional and a consumer) and situations must be identified where specific consumer protection rules are necessary'.

28 Resolution by the European Parliament on European Contract Law, 7 September 2006, P6_TA(2006)0352.

3. Strongly supports an approach for a wider CFR on general contract law issues going beyond the realm of consumer protection;
4. Underlines that, besides the work being done on revision of the consumer acquis, the efforts toward a wider CFR should go on; calls on the Commission to proceed, in parallel with the work on revision of the consumer acquis, with the project for a wider CFR;
5. Underlines that – even though the final purpose and legal form of the CFR are not yet clearly established – the work on the project should be done well, by accounting for the fact that the final long-term outcome could be a binding instrument; all the various possible options for the purpose and legal form of a future instrument should be kept open.

In three years (2001-2004), three Communications from the European Commission have successively launched the debate and announced several measures. Two new concepts appeared: the Common Frame of Reference (substituting the concept of 'code', which was too symbolic) and the optional instrument (as opposed to mandatory instruments), which could become part of the Common Frame of Reference. The European Contract Law development process is now underway, through an ambitious project promoting pluralism and participative democracy. The European Parliament has just published a Resolution in which it even predicts that the final long-term result of this process would be a binding instrument. All options remain open, but for now, the priority is the development of a Common Frame of Reference.

The Common Frame of Reference Project

The Common Frame of Reference project is characterized by its real originality, both in its development process since jurists from the most diverse backgrounds are invited to take part (academics, practitioners, political authorities) and in its enforcement inasmuch as it should be optional for the parties as indeed for contracting States. This dual originality will be highlighted in this second part of the chapter, which will present the development process, followed by the Common Frame of Reference adoption process.

The Common Frame of Reference Development Process: Towards a New Form of Participative Democracy?

Status Report The development of the Common Frame of Reference calls on several groups of players, who have successive and distinct roles. The first phase, is led by researchers, working together as the 'Joint Network on European Private Law'.[29]

Actually, the mobilization of academics is not a new phenomenon. In the 1970s a group brought together under the initiative of Professor Ole Lando undertook to develop the 'Principles of European Contract Law' (PECL), which is today recognized as the foundation for the development of the Common Frame of Reference.[30] The 'Study Group for a European Civil Code', chaired by Professor von Bar,[31] then took over from the Lando Commission, yet retained many of its members. This group is currently made up of about a hundred law professors from EU Member States (as well as from countries that are not yet members) and continues the codification work on contract law (general theory and special contracts) as well as on civil liability, securities, trust, and property transfer. The objective is to produce a body of codified rules in obligations law and on certain points of property law. Within private law therefore, patrimonial law is the first target. This group, whose work is done in English, constantly relies on the work done by the Lando Commission (on PECLs).

The network of researchers funded by the Commission, under the 'Sixth Framework Programme for Research and Technological Development',[32] is also chaired by Professor Christian von Bar. It is made up of eight research groups (the main one being the above Study Group). Three are drafting groups: they are the Study Group for a European Civil Code, the Acquis Group and the Insurance Group. These groups work not only on the whole field of contract law (general theory, common law, consumer law, special contracts), but also on civil liability and quasi-contract law. The Study Group for a European Civil Code is currently reviewing the Principles of European Contract Law, drafted by the Lando Commission; it is

29 The project synopsis of the Joint Network (CoPECL) is outlined in greater detail in the European Commission publication *Social Sciences and Humanities in FP6: all calls 2002* (2007), at pp. 204-206.

30 Another group known as the *Academy of European Private Lawyers* was created in Pavia, in 1990, under the initiative of Professor Gandolfi. In 2001 this group published, in French, a European code of contracts project. The main model of this group was Book IV of the Italian Civil Code, but given that this book is about 'obligations', the group preferred to keep the notion of 'contracts', in order not to introduce a concept which has a different meaning in English law). A new work containing the second part, regarding special contracts, is in progress. Regarding the operation of this group, of which Andre Tunc was an especially authorized member, cf. Stein, Introduction, in Gandolfi (ed.) (2001), and Gridel (2003).

31 von Bar (2001).

32 See Decision No. 1513/2002/EC of the European Parliament and of the Council of 27 June 2002 concerning the sixth framework programme of the European Community for research, technological development and demonstration activities, contributing to the creation of the European Research Area and to innovation (2002-2006), at p. 1. See also the publication by the Academy of European Law (ERA) (2006), member of this joint network, 'Special issue on European Contract Law'.

the work of a sub-commission called the 'Compilation and Reduction Team'. Reworked texts will then be inserted in a larger set called CoPECL which could, in the end, serve as a first model for an eventual European contract code.

One of the other five groups, which are entrusted with various missions, was created by Association Henri Capitant and the *Société de législation comparée*. Its purpose concerns the first two and main aspects of the CFR: it has to identify the fundamental principles that will underpin European contract and liability law, by explaining their meaning and assessing their value and scope, in order to direct the work of the drafting groups.

Researchers in this network must hand in their work in 2007. The second phase, which is already underway, consists of submitting the researchers' work to a 'network of stakeholder experts' (CFR-net) and to experts from Member States. The first group of experts, 177 in number, was appointed by the Commission on the basis of four criteria, that is, variety of legal traditions, balance of economic interests (members chosen from employer organizations, representatives from liberal professions and consumer advocacy organizations), expertise and commitment. The members of the second group were appointed by the governments of the Member States.[33]

After academics and practitioners will be the turn of parliamentarians, both European and national. The third, more political phase, will bring them together. The Commission, as well as the European Parliament, the Council, the national parliaments, the group of experts from Member States, periodically briefed on the progress made, will bring their final touch to the CFR project. Once developed, the CFR will be released in the form of a White Paper, translated in all the official languages of the EU, that will launch a new consultation phase before the revised document is adopted by the Commission. In principle, this vast process should end in 2009 (when the Commission and the Parliament's mandates end), with the publication of the CFR in the *Official Journal of the European Union* and with its adoption by the Commission. There is already a site available to researchers, experts representing stakeholders and Member States, on which the Commission and the European Parliament posts relevant documents (research projects, comments from the CFR-net, Commission's reports on workshops, and so on).

Critical observations All the authors who have written on the issue of European Contract Law, or about a European civil code, whether for or against, have insisted on the need for pluralism in all its forms: pluralism of research groups and their

33 The first scenes from the second act have already been played out at the European Commission, in the form of workshops. Researchers have presented their work, sometimes going back a very long time, which created some tensions with the experts. The first meeting was held in December 2004. Since March 2005, the following workshops have been held: Services contracts; Franchise, Agency, Distribution; Personal Security Rights; Benevolent Intervention; Unjust Enrichment; Notion and Functions of Contract and Notion of Consumer and Professional. A much-awaited workshop was given at the end of 2005 on the CFR structure.

makeup, pluralism of languages, of themes, of political opinions (although the Commission has testified several times to its attachment to contractual freedom, others put forward the need for social justice), and of course, pluralism of sources of law because, beyond the texts, jurisprudence has a major role to play.

In this perspective, a vast consultation process of never-before-seen proportions has been launched by the Commission, first in its various Communications on European Contract Law, then with the Common Frame of Reference project. The obstacles are many. There have already been frictions between academics and stakeholders and the Commission is progressively realizing how workshops are difficult to organize, even as far as the choice of themes to review[34] and, in the end, not very productive. As for political institutions, faced with the current euroscepticism, they are proceeding with the greatest prudence.

Whereas academics were the first to be solicited, their involvement goes back, as we have seen, to well before the creation of the European research network by the Commission. Contrary to what some expert practitioners have deplored, academics are far from being all-powerful. No one is asking law professors to develop tomorrow's European law. Their work represents only the beginning of a long process, meant to be reviewed and corrected by practitioners, Members States and European authorities. Thus in the European conception, these academic groups are not so much perceived to be 'making' laws as much as being 'in the service' of the law and, through that service, 'in the service' of the community it represents, and 'in the service' of the Europe of tomorrow.

Certain contemporary philosophers have shown how, recently, the nature of democracy has changed: next to the traditional voting ballot, we have seen the development of a sort of democratic legitimization of the decisions taken beyond the state structure. Beyond participation and expression of will, what also counts is 'access by everyone to all deliberative processes'[35] so that the [Tr.] 'emphasis that used to be placed on sovereign will, embodied by individual and electoral acts, is now placed on procedural requirements regarding communication and decision-making processes'.[36] According to this philosophical conception, [Tr.] 'democracy

34 On this point, see Beale's article (2006) which was presented at the second discussion forum held in Vienna in May 2006. See in particular the themes proposed by the author: 'In the Autumn, I think that the Commission should hold a new series of stakeholder workshops dealing with the "obvious" topics of general contract law that have not yet been covered, or at best have been only touched upon without proper discussion (for example, they have been included in the material for an "acquis revision" workshop but were not discussed in any detail.) This should include: 1. General provisions (including the ever-controversial good faith clause) and Interpretation, 2. Formation of contracts, 3.Validity and Illegality, 4. Performance, 5. Remedies for non-performance (this might be sub-divided), 6. Prescription (this is of considerable practical importance for example, in consumer sales and product liability). Further topics could be agreed by the workshops as work progresses and as the scope of the revised acquis becomes clearer'.

35 Habermas (2000) p.122.

36 *Ibid.*

is itself a form of political integration rooted in law. It relies on a political culture shared by all citizens. This learning process can extend beyond national borders. A European society of citizens must be formed'.[37] Along the same idea, other authors add that the social expression of defiance will become a significant phenomenon of contemporary democratic life. And this defiance, which has a 'structuring role for democracies' will even take the form, according to P. Rosanvallon, of a 'counter-democracy'.[38] One must constantly watch, denounce and take note. Although amplified by modern technology, this phenomenon is not new. Already, in *Contrat social*, Jean-Jacques Rousseau held that the right to vote came with the right to opine, propose, divide and discuss. To the electing people, the traditional symbol of democracy, is added that of 'the vigilant people, the veto people, the judging people', new symbols of 'counter-democracy'.[39]

From this perspective, we should commend the Commission's recent efforts to create, through the Common Frame of Reference project, a vast network of jurists involved in the European Contract Law development process. This innovative use of participative democracy was already used in the development of the Charter of Fundamental Rights, with the creation of many working groups and a vast electronic consultation process. The undertaking is beneficial and should be encouraged, even though it slows down the process of formulating a contract law, and even if in the end decisions are made by the politicians. Even if this new form of democracy creates power struggles, frustrations and sudden backtracking, even if pluralism encourages the non-linear development of law, beyond these hesitations and prevarications, a common legal culture is currently developing. It becomes more and more obvious that the development of a European contract code will not happen in a few months or even in a few years. In addition, though the Common Frame of Reference will take life with its official adoption by EC authorities, it will only truly develop when the instrument is adopted – at least the part that should contain contract rules – by the contracting parties and the Member States. Coming on the heels of the Common Frame of Reference development process, the adoption process also holds real originality.

The European Contract Law Adoption Process

We have said that the Commission does not intend to propose a 'European civil code', or even a European contract code that would substitute the contract law regimes of Member States. The project is more modest in scope, but also more complex: the idea is, through the Common Frame of Reference, to propose model rules to the contracting parties and States, each remaining free to adopt them or not. Thus conceived, the law is no longer prescriptive; it is to be used as a model, both by the parties and by the legislator. For this to occur, however, several conditions are needed.

37 *Ibid.* p.147.
38 Rosanvallon (2006) p.8.
39 *Ibid.* p.17.

Adoption by the contracting parties The first question is this: is this an area where the parties are allowed to choose other rules than those applicable in domestic law? The field covered by the CFR, as large as it is, only deals with contract law (general theory and some special contracts). Apart from cases where contracts are concluded between a professional and a consumer, the rules concerned are, for the most part, supplementary or, in other words, non mandatory. Traditionally, this means that the parties could ignore them to the benefit of other rules, devised by themselves or borrowed from other laws and other models; this also means that the parties could integrate into the contract the rules of the CFR instead of State supplementary rules. But the parties could also, for any cross-border contract (therefore 'international' within the meaning of private international law), choose the set of rules represented by the CFR.[40]

This gives rise to a second question, of a technical nature but absolutely essential: how should the choice of the CFR be expressed? This question regarding the conditions of the parties' choice is crucial because it reveals the place given, in the legal order, to these European rules emanating from the CFR. In its 2003 Communication entitled 'A more coherent European Contract Law – An action plan', the Commission considered two possibilities, that is, opt in or opt out. The opt-out system would be the most integrationist. The absence of a specific choice on the part of the parties in favour of another body of contractual rules would result in the *de facto* application of the optional instrument. This is the system adopted in the UN (Vienna) Convention on Contracts of the International Sale of Goods (CISG).

One argument that could have been attempted in favour of the opt-out approach relates to the security it would provide, from a judicial practice perspective. In reality, this would only be true if an express agreement was required from the parties to exclude the application of the optional instrument. Without such a requirement, a major dispute could emerge regarding how the exclusion would be expressed by the parties of European Contract Law. An even more serious concern is that the judicial treatment of this issue by national judges could lead to very diverse practices. In this regard, the example of recent jurisprudence from the Court of Cassation, regarding the exclusion of the Vienna Convention, is very revealing. After too easily allowing the tacit exclusion of the Vienna Convention simply by not invoking this instrument before the French judge,[41] the first Civil Chamber has come back to a position which appears stricter and more consistent with the spirit of the Convention: [Tr.]

> The CISG, establishing a uniform law on international sales of goods, constitutes substantive French law on the matter; as such, it must be applied by the French

40 On the possibility of making this choice in lieu and stead of State law, see *infra*.

41 *Société Muller École et Bureau c. Société Federal Tait*, First Civil Chamber, 26 June 2001, *Journal du droit international*, vol. 128(4), at p. 1121, note A. Huet, Cl. Witz and H. Muir Watt, *Recueil Dalloz* (2001), Jurisprudence, No. 44, at pp. 3607-3614; and Jobard-Bachellier (2001).

> judge unless it is excluded, even tacitly, according to art. 6, given that the parties have chosen to be governed by a given law: in the present case, it is clear from the procedure and the decision attacked that, by invoking and discussing without reservations the warranty on the item sold as defined under articles 1641 and following of the Civil code, all the parties, being aware of the international nature of the sales they had concluded, have voluntarily chosen French domestic law governing sales as their dispute resolution regime.[42]

At this stage of the reflection, the opt-in mechanism appears not only more respectful of the will and expectations of the parties (there again as long as an express choice is required in favour of the optional instrument),[43] but also more protective of national sovereignties. To require an express designation of the optional instrument is to admit that this instrument is not substituted to domestic laws, since it can only apply if the parties expressly wish it. Thus the optional instrument would have a status close to those doctrinal codifications which are the Principles of Unidroit and the Principles of European Contract Law, the effective application of which depends first and foremost on the parties.

What the institutions were unable to do, for lack of a political will and the legal basis underlying this lack, the parties could do by designating a Community instrument which has value only as an optional model. It is easier to understand, therefore, that in parallel with this work on European Contract Law, Community institutions have wanted to soften the prohibition on contracts without law.

Under article 3, par. 2, of the Proposal for a Regulation of the European Parliament and of the Council on the law applicable to contractual obligations (Rome I),[44] dated 15 December 2005, *'The parties may also choose as the applicable law some principles and rules of the substantive law of contract recognised internationally or in the Community'*. The explanation on the motives clearly indicates that the purpose of the formula is to [Tr.]

> 'authorize the choice of the Principles of Unidroit, the Principles of European Contract Law or a potential future optional Community instrument, while banning the option of the lex mercatoria, which is insufficiently precise, or of

42 First Civil Chamber, 25 October 2005, observations of Deumier (2006), at p. 515. This decision is tougher than the previous ones in that before deciding to exclude the Vienna Convention, it notes that the parties have discussed without reservation about the warranty on the item sold and that they knew about the international nature of the sales.

43 This would also help avoid difficulties related to the competing application, in international sales of good, of the Vienna Convention of 11 April 1980. Indeed if the parties expressly designate the EC instrument, it is because they wished to exclude the Vienna Convention, which is possible under article 6 of this convention.

44 COM (2005) 650 final.

private codifications that would not be sufficiently recognized by the international community'.[45]

The formula chosen, that is, the 'potential future optional Community instrument' relates without a doubt to the current work on European Contract Law. On the other hand, one can ask under what criteria and what authority the principles or rules of substantive law will be 'sufficiently recognized by the international community'. Another question also arises: in order to respect the will of the parties, which it will interpret as being first and foremost that of avoiding the use of State law, could the judge substitute the optional Community instrument or the Principles of Unidroit or the European Principles to the lex mercatoria or to any form of private codification designated by the parties but insufficiently recognized by the international community?

One thing is to authorize the selection of the optional instrument; another is for the parties to actually make use of this freedom. If the perspective of a law developed at the European level could in fact appeal to the parties that have European or even international contractual relations,[46] it remains necessary to specify that by electing these Principles (or indeed the Principles of European Contract Law), they expose themselves to a double risk: on the one hand, the inability of these texts to resolve their dispute due to gaps and on the other, the insecurity related to the absence of jurisdiction of the European Community Court of Justice to guarantee a consistent interpretation. The two phenomena are linked. The strength of the optional European instrument compared to other codifications purely rooted in doctrine, could just be to ensure completeness due to a European corpus of principles and definitions contained in the Common Frame of Reference

---

45 In that it authorizes a contract without law, article 3, par. 2 constitutes a small revolution. Whereas the Rome Convention did not consider the choice of non-State choice as illicit, it did consider that it was not a choice of private international law, so that [Tr.] 'it was up to the objectively applicable law to define the place it would give to non-state rules chosen by the parties' Lagarde (2006). Now in Europe, state legal systems remain very reserved when it comes to allowing a contract without law. There are different reasons for this: avoiding the confinement of the application of non-state law to its subsidiary status compared to state law; mistrust regarding free will, especially in contract relations where power relationships are uneven; fear of practical difficulties related to the choice of a doctrinal codification (incompleteness, risk of unpredictability due to the existence of very general texts and the absence of standard interpretation, slowness of the text revision process, and so on), new hypotheses of private codification conflicts, some of which receive quasi-official sanction and others not, and so on

46 Report *Principes du droit européen du contrat*, *op. cit.*, at 55 and following. The comments in the first chapter specify that [Tr.] 'the use of the Principles is justified by the fact that they were prepared in a comparative manner and discussed internationally. To settle a dispute regarding an international contract, the Principles can provide a more appropriate basis than any national contract law'.

and, if jurisdiction were given to the ECCJ to interpret this text, to guarantee consistent interpretation to the parties.

Choosing the opt-in system, as we have seen, means that the parties must expressly designate European Contract Law by an *electio juris* agreement which theoretically presents itself as an agreement in principle prior to the dispute. But difficulties may still arise later. In particular, parties could change their minds and prefer another instrument or another law. Thus they could, in the course of the dispute, favour the law of the sitting judge under a procedural agreement. Could the simple fact of not having invoked the rules of the Common Frame of Reference serve as a procedural agreement between the parties in favour of this law? Such an agreement would then invalidate, for the dispute (and not for the entire contractual relation) the choice of optional instrument. Similar questions have emerged within private international law in cases where both parties, who had elected a foreign law, both (whether deliberately or not) omitted to invoke it before the judges. How this difficulty is handled will then depend on the conception cultivated by each legal system of the office of judge: will the judge, who must automatically apply the rule of conflict of laws, also have to remind the parties that they had initially chosen either a foreign law, either the same European Contract Law as contained in the Common Frame of Reference, which is originally simply an optional model but to which, by their agreement, the parties have actually made binding? Under what conditions can the parties then maintain their choice in favour of the law of the forum (or of another law) by invoking the pre-eminence of their ulterior agreement which was entered into in the course of the procedure on the choice of applicable law clause?[47]

The idea of a 28th regime, applicable only if the parties have expressly wished it, is currently in vogue. This does not mean that in the longer term we should overlook the fact that the wish of Community authorities, from their perspective of law unification, is that this European law will be substituted to the law of Member States. The 28th regime would then become the only regime, following a process which could either be authoritarian, and which would mean amending the founding text to give legislative jurisdiction to the EU – which is unlikely at the moment – or be voluntary. For this to occur Member States would have to accept substituting their respective national law with this European Contract Law.

Adoption by Member States The adoption of this European Contract Law by Member States could happen in several stages. First, this European Contract Law will not be forced on the States but, like the Principles of European Contract Law

47 On this 'procedural agreement' and its effects, see the founding article by Lequette (1989), and also Mayer (2001). For a general reflection on the procedural regime of the rule of conflict of laws, as remodelled by the criteria of free availability of laws, see Fauvarque-Cosson (1996); Bureau (1996); Bureau (1999); Muir Watt (1997); Muir Watt (1999); Jobard-Bachellier (2001); Fauvarque-Cosson (2004)

or the Principles of Unidroit, it can serve as a model law for them. This will be especially useful in the context of an enlargement of the European Union.

This first stage could be followed with a second one, which would consist in going from an optional law to a dispositive law. Integrated into the legal order of States, in parallel with internal law, the European law would be applicable to cross-border contracts (a notion which remains to be defined), unless the parties have expressly excluded it to the benefit of domestic law (opt out), in accordance with the model already provided by CISG.

The third step, that of a European Contract Law mandatory for all (Member States and parties, subject to supplementary provisions) may never happen; it will depend directly on political factors which are not yet known. But if it must take place, one thing is sure: it will take time and will happen in stages.

To summarize, we feel that the CFR could take the form of a model law which, as such, would not be immediately imposed on the States and which, in order to apply, would assume that the contracting parties have expressly decided to do so.[48] It is appropriate, at least at first, to add a European model to the national models and to leave the possibility of choice to the parties when their contracts are cross-border in nature. If things were to happen in this way, we would then see, for several years or even decades, a new phenomenon of coexistence of this new European law with domestic laws. This solution seems to be the best. There is no doubt that this new European Contract Law would be even better accepted if it has been chosen freely by the parties.[49] Let us therefore leave it up to the potential users of European Contract Law to decide whether it should be preferred and thus substituted by them to their own internal law. It is at this price that [Tr.] 'European Contract Law will appear [...] through the grace of time and the heat of action, the respectful heir of all European legal traditions'.[50]

Conclusion

No one can predict the future. We can only draw a few lessons from past experiences and sketch out, without providing any dates, an outline of a potential direction. Despite current political obstacles, it seems appropriate that the efforts to develop a standardized contract law be pursued in the form of a 28th regime. It is also imperative to allow time for a true European legal culture to emerge.

Therefore, the first lesson to be drawn from the experience of recent years and the sometimes heated debates that have taken place, Portalis had already taught us

48 In this regard, see Fauvarque-Cosson, *eod.loc.*, especially No. 39.

49 In a dubitative sense, see Heuzé, *eod.loc.*, spec. p. 1344. For the author experience shows that [Tr.] 'economic agents [...] are very reluctant to subject their relationships, when given the opportunity, to uniform rules of law'. But is it not better to run this risk than to automatically impose a European Contract Law?

50 Heuzé, *eod.loc.*, spec. p. 1344.

in 1804: 'The codes that govern peoples develop over time; in reality, we do not create them.' Indeed, the creation of a true European legal culture which will include a European doctrine and a judicial network, is an indispensable prerequisite to the development of a European law. This is true, even in contractual matters, which is not a highly emotionally-charged area. The CFR, which must first and foremost serve as a 'toolbox' for Community authorities, already plays an essential role in this regard. Researchers from every country are pursuing their doctrinal work; it is no longer utopic to hope that, progressively, the dissemination, critical analysis, university teaching and potential application of texts by judges based on the will of the parties, will lead to the propagation of this new, less nationalistic and more European, legal culture. In the same vein, some may have wished for the creation of a European Law Institute and a European Law Academy whose role would have been, among other things, to coordinate research projects and prepare common texts. In a way, the Commission hoped to meet these expectations by creating this vast network of researchers and launching 'discussion forums' on European Contract Law.

If one day the CFR were to give rise to the optional instrument that the Commission had very concretely considered in its Action Plan, an important step would have been completed in the development of a European Contract Law. Despite the caution currently shown by the Commission, which now seems to focus on the revision of the *acquis*, without looking any further in the development of an optional instrument, in reality the process has begun and is following its course, which is a good thing. Indeed, we need specific rules when it comes to consumer law, but we also need coherent rules, founded on common principles, apt to form the future basis of a European Contract Law.

One last comment in ending: the future of European Contract Law cannot happen without the judges. According to some authors, European Contract Law and the unification project would be nothing but a delusion if the consistent interpretation of the rules was not assured.[51] The only possible solution would then be either to entrust the Court of Justice of the European Communities with a vast mission of law interpretation and unification,[52] or to create new Community jurisdictions, for example a European Court of Civil Law, or even European courts that could be substituted to national jurisdictions: what a revolution! But is it really necessary, in order to guarantee consistent interpretation of this European Contract Law, that we strip national judges from the Member States of their jurisdiction to the benefit of so-called 'European' judges because they sit in Community jurisdictions? Could we not opt for another way, not only because it is much more respectful of national judicial traditions, but also because it is to be hoped that with the European legal culture being disseminated and the texts refined, the risk of diverging interpretation

51 In this regard, see among others Heuzé, *eod.loc.*, spec. p. 1343; Huet, *eod.loc.*, spec. No. 5; Malinvaud, *eod.loc.*, spec. p. 2547; Witz, *eod.loc.*, spec. p. 82.

52 In this regard, see Basedow, *eod.loc.*, spec. p. 258.

will gradually fade away?[53] In addition, within the European Union, the free circulation of legal decisions, which rests on the postulate of trust and the quality of national justices, should promote convergence. Just like a European community of researchers is in the process of being formed, national judges are increasingly aware of their belonging to a community of European judges. The construction of the judicial common space has created new needs; European networks of judicial education are being formed.[54]

New Developments since 2007

From 2007 to 2009, European institutions have concentrated their efforts on the revision of the consumer acquis and the publication of the Commission Proposal of 8 October 2008 for a 'Directive on Consumer Contractual Rights'. The Common Frame of Reference is now back on the political agenda for 2010. A Draft Common Frame of Reference (DCFR) has been elaborated by the Study group on a European Civil Code and the Acquis group. This work is enormous and goes far beyond contract law. It is currently being analyzed, sometimes very critically, all over Europe. In 2008, the group that was formed in France within the network in charge of the preparation of a CFR (see p. 133) produced an important work. Rather than primarily drafting model rules – as the DCFR does –, it also concentrated on terminology and principles. The entire work has been published in French; a major part of it is available in English. The work on terminology (key notions of contract law analyzed in a comparative context) is unique in the academic world. The work on the guiding principles and the model rules has a great political value; it conforms exactly to what the European institutions have asked the researchers to prepare for the final CFR and could help the Commission in the preparation of the final (or 'political' as opposed to 'academic') CFR.

References

Academy of European Law (2006). 'Special issue on European Contract Law', ERA-Forum, at: https://www2.era.int/cgi-bin/era_forum/eraForum.cgi?action=show_forum&forum_id=5_1988_2483.

Basedow, Jürgen (1998). 'Un droit commun des contrats pour le marché commun', *Revue internationale de droit comparé*, **50**(1): 7–28.

53 Witz, *eod.loc.*, spec. p. 82.

54 The Hague program, which seeks to promote a 'common judicial culture', calls for national continuing education programs systematically to include Community law and the development of magistrate exchange programs. On this point, see Sturlese (2005) spec. at p. 57, 'Vers un Erasmus des juges'.

Beale, Hugh (2006). 'The European Commission's Common Frame of Reference Project: A progress report', *European Review of Contract Law*, **2**(2): 303–314.

Bergé, Jean Sylvestre and Marie-Laure Niboyet (eds) (2003). *La réception du droit communautaire en droit privé des Etats membres*, Bruxelles: Bruylant.

Bergé, Jean-Sylvestre, Astrid Marais and Anne Debet (2006). 'Codification et simplification du droit à l'aune du droit européen des contrats: premier rapport annuel sur l'état d'avancement du droit européen des contrats et de la révision de l'acquis', *Revue des contrats*, No. 2: 523–528.

Bureau, Dominique (1996). 'L'accord procédural à l'épreuve', *Revue critique de droit international privé*, No. 4: 587–620.

Bureau, Dominique (1999). 'L'influence de la volonté individuelle sur les conflits de lois' in *L'avenir du droit : Mélanges en l'honneur de François Terré*, Paris: Dalloz, pp. 285–306.

Colonna, Catherine (2006). *Communication ministérielle sur la transposition des directives communautaires – Présentée en Conseil des ministres*, 19 July, at www.archives.premier-ministre.gouv.fr/villepin/acteurs/gouvernement/conseils_ministres_35/conseil_ministres_19_juillet_830/transposition_directives_europeennes_56508.html.

Commission of the European Communities (2002). *Communication from the Commission – Action plan 'Simplifying and improving the regulatory environment*, 5 June, Brussels, at: http://eur-lex.europa.eu/LexUriserv/LexUriserv.do?uri=COM:2002:0278:FIN:EN:PDF.

Commission of the European Communities (2003). *Communication from the Commission to the European Parliament and the Council: A more coherent European Contract Law – An action plan*, 12 February, Brussels, at: http://www.isda.org/c_and_a/pdf/com_2003_68_en.pdf.

Commission of the European Communitie (2004). *European Contract Law and the revision of the acquis: the way forward*, 11 October, Brussels, COM(2004), 651, at: http://ec.europa.eu/consumers/cons_int/safe_shop/fair_bus_pract/cont_law/com2004_en.pdf.

Commission of the European Communities (2005). *Report from the Commission: First Annual Progress Report on European Contract Law and the Acquis Review*, 23 September, Brussels, at: http://eur-lex.europa.eu/LexUriserv/LexUriserv.do?uri=COM:2005:0456:FIN:EN:PDF.

Cornu, Gérard (2002). 'Un code civil n'est pas un instrument communautaire', *Le Recueil Dalloz*, Chroniques, No. 4: 351–352.

Deumier, Pascale (2006). 'Exclusion tacite de la Convention de Vienne', *Revue des contrats*, No. 2: 515.

de Vareilles-Sommières, Pascal (ed.) (1998). *Le droit privé européen*, Paris: Economica.

Éditions du JurisClasseur Collection (1993). *Mélanges offerts à André Colomer*, preface by Bernard Teyssié, Paris: Litec.

European Commission, Director-General for Research (2007). *Social Sciences and Humanities in FP6: all calls 2002*, Luxembourg: Office for Official Publications

of the European Communities, at: ftp://ftp.cordis.europa.eu/pub/citizens/docs/synopses-all-calls-2006.pdf.
Fauvarque-Cosson, Bénédicte (1996). *Libre disponibilité des droits et conflits de lois*, volume 272, Paris: LGDJ, Bibliothèque de droit privé.
Fauvarque-Cosson, Bénédicte (2002). 'Faut-il un Code civil européen?', *Revue trimestrielle de droit civil*, No. 3: 463–480.
Fauvarque-Cosson, Bénédicte (2004). 'L'accord procédural à l'épreuve du temps', *in Mélanges en l'honneur de Paul Lagarde*, Paris: Dalloz, pp. 263–284.
Fauvarque-Cosson, Bénédicte and Denis Mazeaud (eds) (2003). *Pensée juridique française et harmonisation européenne du droit*, volume 1 of the 'Droit privé comparé et européen' collection, Paris: Société de législation comparée.
Gandolfi, Giuseppe (ed.) (2001). *Code européen des contrats*, Avant-projet, Book I, Milan: Giuffrè.
Gridel, Jean-Pierre (2003). 'Sur l'hypothèse d'un droit européen des contrats : les propositions de l'Académie des privatistes européens (Pavie)', *Gazette du Palais*, **123**(1): 240–278.
Habermas, Jürgen (2000). *Après l'Etat-nation :une nouvelle constellation politique*, Paris: Fayard.
Heuzé, Vincent (2002). 'A propos d'une initiative européenne en matière de droit des contrats', *J.C.P. – Édition générale*, **I**(152): 1341–1345.
Huet, Jean (2002). 'Nous faut-il un « euro » droit civil?', *Recueil Le Dalloz*, Chroniques, No. 34: 2611–2614.
Jamin, Christophe (1998). 'Un droit européen des contrats?' in de Vareilles-Sommières, Pascal (ed.), *Le droit privé européen*, Paris: Economica.
Jamin, Christophe and Denis Mazeaud (eds) (2001). *L'harmonisation du droit des contrats en Europe*, Paris: Economica.
Jobard-Bachellier, Marie-Noëlle (2001). 'De la distinction nécessaire entre l'accord procédural interne et l'accord procédural international, en présence même d'éléments d'extranéité', *Gazette du Palais*, No. 346-347: 13–21.
Lagarde, Paul (2006). 'Remarques sur la proposition de règlement de la Commission européenne sur la loi applicable aux obligations contractuelles (Rome I)', *Revue critique de droit international privé*, **95**(2): 331–359.
Legrand, Pierre (1996). 'Sens et non-sens d'un code civil européen', *Revue internationale de droit comparé*, **48**(4): 779–812.
Lequette, Yves (1989). 'L'abandon de la jurisprudence *Bisbal* (à propos des arrest de la Première chambre civile des 11 et 18 octobre 1988)', *Revue critique de droit international privé*, 277–339.
Lequette, Yves (2002). 'Quelques remarques à propos du projet de Code civil de Monsieur von Bar', *Le Recueil Dalloz*, Chroniques, No. 28: 2202–2214.
Lequette, Yves (2003). 'Vers un code civil européen?', *Pouvoirs*, No. 107: 97–126.
Malaurie, Philippe (2002). 'Le Code civil européen des obligations et des contrats, une question toujours ouverte', *J.C.P. – Édition générale*, **I**(110): 281–285.
Malinvaud, Philippe (2002). 'Réponse – hors délai – à la Commission', *Le Recueil Dalloz*, Chroniques, No. 33: 2542.

Mayer, Pierre (2001). 'Le juge et la loi étrangère', *Revue suisse de droit international et européen*, No. 4: 481–501.

Mazeaud, Denis (2005). 'Faut-il avoir peur d'un droit européen des contrats?' in Société de législation comparée, *De tous horizon – Mélanges Xavier Blanc-Jouvan*, Paris: Société de législation comparée.

Muir Watt, Horatia (1997). 'Sur l'actualité de la jurisprudence *Roho*: de la licéité de l'accord procédural en matière de conflit de lois', *Justices*, No. 6: 264–274.

Muir Watt, Horatia (1999). *Répertoire Dalloz*, Droit International, volume *Loi étrangère*, No. 59, Paris: Dalloz.

Philip, Christian (2006). *Rapport d'information déposé par la Délégation pour l'Union européenne sur la transposition des directives européennes*, 4 July, No. 3239, at: www.assemblee-nationale.fr/12/europe/rap-info/i3239.asp#TopOfPage.

Prieto, Catherine (ed.) (2003). *Regards croisés sur les Principes du droit européen du contrat et sur le droit français*, Institut de droit des affaires, Centre de droit économique, Aix-en-Provence: Presses Universitaires d'Aix-Marseille.

Prieto, Catherine (2004). 'Un code civil européen: de l'utopie à la prospective juridique', *Petites Affiches*, No. 92: 19–29.

Racine, Jean-Baptiste (2003). 'Pourquoi unifier le droit des contrats en Europe? Plaidoyer en faveur de l'unification', *Revue du Droit de l'Union européenne*, **2003**(2): 369–407.

Rampelberg, René-Marie (2005). *Repères romains pour le droit européen des contrats*, Paris: LGDJ.

Rémy-Corlay, Pauline and Dominique Fenouillet (eds) (2003). *Les concepts contractuels français à l'heure des Principes du droit européen des contrats*, Paris: Dalloz, 'Thèmes et Commentaires' collection.

Rosanvallon, Pierre (2006). *La contre-démocratie, La politique à l'âge de la défiance*, Paris: Seuil.

Société de législation comparée (2005). *De tous horizon – Mélanges Xavier Blanc-Jouvan*, Paris: Société de législation comparée.

Rosanvallon, Pierre (2008). *Counter-Democracy: Politics in an Age of Distrust*, trans. by Arthur Goldhammer, Cambridge: Cambridge University Press.

Sturlese, Bruno (2005). *L'Europe de la Justice et la Constitution européenne*, Paris: PUF, ' Droit et justice' collection.

Tallon, Denis (1993). 'Vers un droit européen des contrats', in Éditions du JurisClasseur Collection, *Mélanges offerts à André Colomer*, Paris: Litec.

Terré, François and Anne Outin-Adam (2004). 'Codification: L'année d'un bicentenaire', *Le Recueil Dalloz*, Chroniques, No.1: 12–16.

Vogenauer, Stefan and Stephen Weatherill (2005). 'The European Community's Competence for a Comprehensive Harmonisation of Contract Law', *European Law Review*, **30**(6): 821–837.

von Bar (2001), Christian (2001). 'Study Group for a European Civil Code', *Revue internationale de droit comparé*, **53**(1): 127–139.

Witz, Claude (2000). 'Plaidoyer pour un code européen des obligations', *Le Recueil Dalloz*, Chroniques, No. 5: 79–87.
Witz, Claude (2003). 'La longue gestation d'un code européen des contrats – Rappel de quelques initiatives oubliées', *Revue trimestrielle de droit civil*, No. 3: 447–454.

Directives

Directive 1999/44/EC of the European Parliament and of the Council of 25 May 1999 on certain aspects of the sale of consumer goods and associated guarantees, *Official Journal of the European Communities*, 7 July 1999, **L 171**: 12–16.

Proposals, Decisions and Resolutions

Decision No. 1513/2002/EC of the European Parliament and of the Council of 27 June 2002 concerning the sixth framework programme of the European Community for research, technological development and demonstration activities, contributing to the creation of the European Research Area and to innovation (2002-2006), *Official Journal of the European Communities*, 29 August 2002, **L 232**: 1–33, at: http://eur-lex.europa.eu/LexUriserv/LexUriserv.do?uri=OJ:L:2002:232:0001:0033:EN:PDF.
European Parliament Resolution on the *Communication from the Commission to the European Parliament and the Council: A more coherent European Contract Law – An action plan*, 2 September 2003, Strasbourg, P5_TA(2003)0355, at: www.europarl.europa.eu/sides/getDoc.do?pubRef=-//EP//NONSGML+TA+P5-TA-2003-0355+0+DOC+PDF+V0//EN.

Recent publications

Association H. Capitant et Société de législation comparée (eds) (2008). *Projet de cadre commun de référence. Terminologie contractuelle commune*, Paris : Collection Droit privé européen et comparé, vol. 6.
Association H. Capitant et Société de législation comparée (eds) (2008). *Projet de cadre commun de référence. Principes contractuels communs*, Paris: Collection Droit privé européen et comparé, vol. 7 (http://www.legiscompare.com).
Fauvarque-Cosson, Bénédicte and Denis Mazeaud (eds) (2008). *European Contract Law: Materials for a Common Frame of Reference. Terminology, Guiding Principles, Model Rules*, Sellier European Law Publishers.
Principles, Definitions and Model Rules of European Private Law. Draft Common Frame of Reference (DCFR) (2009). Sellier European Law Publishers.

Chapter 6
Comparative Reflection on the Transposition of European Directives: Unfair Terms

Elise Poillot

Introduction

'To be good is to be in harmony with oneself. Discord is to be forced to be in harmony with others'.[1] These words attributed to Oscar Wilde are relevant in many respects to a discussion on the harmonization of contract law within the context of the European Union (EU). Their primary merit is to draw attention to the meaning of the word 'harmonization' – one of the major issues raised alongside the approximation of law in Europe. The desired harmonization of laws permits the proper functioning of a single market. In this sense, the concept is synonymous with integration. However, as will be seen in the selected examples, once the European harmonization process was implemented, it did not necessarily lead to a consistent body of national laws. There is an abundant literature on this observation. The contribution offered herein refers to two specific examples rooted in the transposition of directives on unfair terms and consumer goods and associated guarantees.[2] These directives are interesting due to the generality of their provisions and the specificity to each country of the national transposition measures called for by such provisions. The use of comparative law seems to be particularly well suited to an analysis of transpositions in various legal contexts.

Before getting to the heart of the matter, we will make several general comments that are inspired by both the Wilde quotation and the specificities of the European structure. With regard to the former, the quote enables us to draw a distinction between external harmonization and internal harmony in each country, a distinction that corresponds to the basic analysis developed in the following lines. In reference to Wilde, one will observe that community harmonization generally does not lead to a forced harmony. Indeed, the process is driven by the

1 From *The Wit and Humor of Oscar Wilde*, edited by A. Redman, Dover Publications, at p. 112.

2 Council Directive 93/13/EEC of 5 April 1993 on unfair terms in consumer contracts, *Official Journal of the European Communities*, **L 95** of 21 April 1993, p. 29 *et seq.*; Directive 1999/44/EC of the European Parliament and of the Council of 25 May 1999 on certain aspects of the sale of consumer goods and associated guarantees, *Official Journal of the European Communities*, **L 171** of 7 July 1999, p. 12 *et seq.*

will of the States as expressed through their voluntary membership in the EU. Furthermore, in the area of contract law, the process does not seek to achieve harmony; it simply seeks an approximation between laws of Member States. This is very clear in that community authorities and treaties use both terms, even though a certain amount of confusion is apparent in Article 95 of the Treaty Establishing the European Community (EC),[3] among others. If harmonization is understood as an approximation, the pursuit of harmony among these laws or within the EU does not correspond to the prioritization of consistent laws across Member States. Harmony must be seen as referring to [TR] 'relationships between the parts of a whole that cause these parts to contribute to a same aggregate effect,' with the aggregate effect being the effective functioning of the single market.

The Wilde quotation, like the European context, refers to the idea of harmony with self. In community law, this ties into the relationship maintained between this law and that of the Member States. From this perspective, things are clear because community law takes precedence over national law, which is required to conform.[4] Furthermore, the Court of Justice of the European Communities (CJEC) specified in 1964 that 'the EEC treaty has created its own legal system which, on the entry into force of the treaty, became an integral part of the legal systems of the member states and which their courts are bound to apply.'[5] From this perspective, the concept of interiority seems relevant. It justifies devoting some thought to the type of multijuralism to expect when contract law is harmonized for the purpose of serving the market.

---

3 Furthermore, on a more global level, Chapter 3 of the Treaty Establishing the European Community addresses the issue of the approximation of laws. Indeed, paragraph 1 refers specifically to the term 'approximation': 'By way of derogation from Article 94 and save where otherwise provided in this Treaty, the following provisions shall apply for the achievement of the objectives set out in Article 14. The Council shall, acting in accordance with the procedure referred to in Article 251 and after consulting the Economic and Social Committee, adopt the measures for the approximation of the provisions laid down by law, regulation or administrative action in Member States which have as their object the establishment and functioning of the internal market.' Paragraph 5 refers to harmonization, without specifying whether this is the same thing: 'Moreover, without prejudice to paragraph 4, if, after the adoption by the Council or by the Commission of a harmonisation measure, a Member State deems it necessary to introduce national provisions based on new scientific evidence relating to the protection of the environment or the working environment on grounds of a problem specific to that Member State arising after the adoption of the harmonisation measure, it shall notify the Commission of the envisaged provisions as well as the grounds for introducing them.'

4 This does not mean that there is no discussion of the scope to give the supremacy of community law, particularly in France; among other texts concerning this issue, refer to the perspective of a *Common Lawyer*, C. Richards (2006), 'The supremacy of Community law before the French Constitutional Court.' *European Law Review*, p. 499 *et seq*.

5 Judgment of the Court of Justice, 15 July 1964, Case 6/64 *Costa v. ENEL*, [1964] ECR 585 at p. 1141.

In the EU setting, for reasons closely linked to internal market developments, harmonization of contract law was not primarily addressed from the perspective of what can be referred to as civil contract law. It is mostly the law of consumer contracts (the consumer contract being, as it were, the driving force of the internal market), which has attracted the attention of community legislators. In fact, whether the EU has the authority to intervene in matters of contract law outside consumer relations is highly debated.[6] Consumers receive special protection in consumer law due to their economic weakness. Therefore, the scope of the rules pertaining to consumer contract law is not the same as the scope of contract law *tout court*, which, for the sake of convenience, will be referred to here as 'civil contract law.'

Thus, in large part, the issue of harmonizing contract law amounts to what national legislators have chosen as the scope for the transposition of directives. Here, two solutions can be considered. The transposition of directives can be limited to consumer relations. In this case, the natural scope of harmonization set out by the community legislator is respected. The aspiration must therefore be to achieve harmony between national consumer law and community consumer law. The issue raised by this choice concerns its implications regarding the degree of consistency or harmony within national law. If, under the influence of this consideration, the national legislator decides to expand the scope of directives beyond this natural domain, the result could be the harmonization of civil contract law across EU Member States through a process of alignment on consumer law. Harmonization limited to consumer contract law will first attract our attention before we consider the harmonization of civil contract law.

Harmonization Limited to Consumer Contract Law

This form of harmonization was chosen exclusively by the Member States in which consumer law is considered to be a special matter. This is the case of France, which

6 It is important to briefly specify here that in this area, the EU does not have authority in the strict sense of the word; however, the treaties contain a number of articles on which an action could be based. Among the most plausible bases, we may cite article 95 of the EC Treaty on the approximation of laws when the establishment and functioning of the internal market are at play, and article 308 of this Treaty, which says that 'If action by the Community should prove necessary to attain, in the course of the operation of the common market, one of the objectives of the Community and this Treaty has not provided the necessary powers, the Council shall, acting unanimously on a proposal from the Commission and after consulting the European Parliament, take the appropriate measures.' Concerning this point, see S. Vogenauer and S. Weatherill (2005), 'The European Community's Competence for a Comprehensive Harmonisation of Contract Law – An Empirical Analysis', p. 1218 *et seq.* *Adde* E. Poillot (2006), *Droit européen de la consommation et uniformisation du droit des contrats (European Consumer Law and Standardisation of the Law of Contract)*, preface by P. De Vareilles-Sommières, No. 1237 *et seq.*

adopted a Consumer Code in 1993, but also of the United Kingdom, wherein the place occupied by consumer law owes its specificity to the sources of this law (essentially legislative in nature – the weaknesses of the common law regarding consumer protection having been acknowledged[7]) and recently Italy, which adopted in October 2005 a Consumer Code based on the French 'separationist' model.[8] Within this context of integration limited to consumer law, two subtypes of transposition can be identified: harmonization resulting from faithful transposition and that resulting from interpretative transposition. As we shall see, these subtypes can generate paradoxical consequences that are worth noting.

Harmonization Resulting from the Faithful Transposition of Directives

This kind of transposition does not essentially change the content of the directive. The national wording reiterates the articles almost word for word. An example of a faithful transposition can be found in English law in the *Unfair Terms in Consumer Contract Regulations* (UTCCR) of 1994. That text, which will serve as a basis for our discussion, carefully transcribes the provisions of the directive on unfair terms.[9] Its status was that of 'lower' laws: that is, *regulations*, which English jurists believe 'will only interest specialists'.[10] It did not, however, go undetected inasmuch as it introduced the concept of 'good faith' into English law, pursuant to article 3 § 1 of the directive.

This introduction resulted in the following provision in the transposed text: 'a contractual term which has not been individually negotiated shall be regarded as unfair if, contrary to the requirement of good faith, it causes a significant imbalance in the parties' rights and obligations arising under the contract, to the detriment of the consumer'[11] – note that the passage uses the term obligations, which is unusual in common law.

---

7 On this point see, among other references, G. Howells and S. Weatherill (2005), *Consumer Protection Law*, spec. p. 18 *et seq*. In 1974, the United Kingdom will adopt specific consumer credit legislation: the *Consumer Credit Act*. Under the conservative legislatures of Ms. Thatcher and Mr. Major, the adopted consumer law legislation will correspond to the transposition of community directives, the State's interventions to regulate the market were considered to be negative; *supra*, p. 76 *et seq*.

8 See our thesis, *supra*, No. 806 *et seq*.

9 *Unfair Terms in Consumer Contract Regulations* of 1999 and 2001; both Regulations are available on the *Office of Public Sector Information* site: www.opsi.gov.uk. Amended in 1999 and 2001, this legislation nevertheless remained very faithful to the directive's provisions.

10 H. Beale (2006), 'La réforme du droit français des contrats et le 'droit européen des contrats': perspective de la *Law Commission* anglaise' [The reform of French contract law and European contract law: English Law Commission's perspective], p. 135 *et seq*., spec. p. 136.

11 Point 5 (1).

It is common knowledge that the Romano-Germanic concept of 'good faith' is foreign to common law since, in the words of a Canadian '*common lawyer*', it would involve 'an invitation to judges to abandon the duty of legally reasoned decisions and to produce an unanalytical incantation of personal values.'[12] Therefore, the question was how English law would absorb this notion. It was not a matter of whether 'continental' good faith would be received by English law – at this point, there would be much to say because the concept of good faith has different meanings in different national laws[13] – but of whether the concept translating the notion would be consistent with good faith as understood by the directive.

In fact, for the sake of clarification, particularly with regard to common law, the directive's 16th 'whereas' clause had made the concept more precise. In order to assess a party's good faith, '*particular regard shall be had to the strength of the bargaining positions of the parties, whether the consumer had an inducement to agree to the term and whether the goods or services were sold or supplied to the special order of the consumer*.' Thus, we are confronted with a subjective term, given that the judge is invited to review the circumstances surrounding the contract. As understood by the directive on unfair terms, good faith corresponds to a global assessment method of the various interests involved, based on a detailed factual assessment. Clearly, this legislation causes problems for common lawyers who are uncomfortable with subjective assessments.

The English transposition legislation opted for a literal terminological transposition: point five of the *Regulations* refers to 'good faith.' In fact, the *Regulations* reiterate the specifications of the concept provided in the directive.[14] It would seem that a subjective interpretation of the concept of good faith has prevailed.

When we turn to the way the concept has been understood by the Court of Appeal and by the House of Lords, however, we do not face the same concept! Both jurisdictions were confronted with the issue of assessing good faith when they had to rule on the unfair nature of a provision inserted into a consumer loan contract.[15] They interpreted the concept of good faith in an objective manner, that is as the requirement of a comprehensible and fair contract. The House of Lords' decision specifies that 'comprehensible' must be understood to mean that the [TR] 'terms should be expressed fully, clearly and legibly, containing no concealed

12 M. G. Bridge (1984), 'Does Anglo-Canadian Contract Law Need a Doctrine of Good Faith?', p. 412 *et seq*., spec. p. 426.

13 See E. Poillot, thesis, *supra*, No. 619 *et seq*.

14 See point 6, assessment of unfair terms.

15 With regard to the Court of Appeal: *Director General of Fair Trading v. First National Bank plc* [2000] 2 Weekly Law Reports 1353, see C. Twigg-Flesner (2000), 'A Good Faith Requirement for English Contract Law?'; with regard to the House of Lords: *Director General of Fair Trading v. First National Bank plc* [2000] I. Weekly Law Report 98.

pitfalls or traps.' 'Fair' dealing, likewise, requires that [TR] 'a supplier should not, whether deliberately or unconsciously, take advantage of the consumer's necessity, indigence, lack of experience, unfamiliarity with the subject matter of the contract, or weak bargaining position.' This is far from the UTCCR provisions, which reiterate the directive's provisions and, therefore, lead to a subjective assessment of good faith – that is, an assessment *in concreto*. In his *opinion*, Lord Steyn even went as far as to affirm that good faith is an 'objective criterion'.

This decision is not surprising. When the directive was transposed, most of the English doctrine had drawn parallels between the concept of good faith and the *fair and reasonable test* – which consists of asking how an average reasonable person would have reacted in the given set of conditions. In addition, it is important to specify that within a favourable context of merging different parts of legislation pertaining to protection against unfair terms (one part being of general application and the other involving consumer contracts), as recently approved in principle by the British government, the reference to good faith would be replaced with a reference to the 'fair and reasonable test'.

It is therefore possible to have doubts regarding the harmonization of English law with community law. The faithful transposition of a directive is not a pledge of faithfulness. What can then be said about interpretive transposition, presumably inclined to stray from the meaning of community law?

Harmonization Resulting from an Interpretive Transposition of Directives

Such harmonization allows Member States to use the freedom left by the directive, a text restrictive in terms of the result to be achieved, but much less so regarding the means of achieving it. Interpretive harmonization is in a way encouraged by community law, which recalls in most directives that the prescribed harmonization is 'minimal'. Directives impose a 'bottom-line' level of harmonization but allow legislators to adopt in the transposition rules that are more protective of consumers' rights. National legislatures favour this type of transposition which allows for a better adaptation of the text into national law. However, this technique risks betraying the community concept, and this is more likely the further it removes the transposition text from the directive's provisions. Yet interpretive transposition does not betray the community text when its spirit is respected. The way French law perceives the good faith principle in the context of legislation on unfair terms will prove this.

The French legislators, relying on 15 years of experience in dealing with unfair terms in consumer/professional relations, transposed the directive quite liberally. The transposition was an opportunity to enshrine the jurisprudence developed since the founding legislation.[16] It was thought that there was no

16 On this issue specifically, D. Mazeaud (1995), 'La loi du 1er février 1995 relative aux clauses abusives – véritable réforme ou simple réformette?', p. 42 *et seq.*

need to refer to the concept of good faith, already familiar in French law.[17] This absence of reference may be surprising since good faith, if not central to defining an unfair term criterion, is nonetheless an important concept under the directive. In French law, however, this lack of reference to good faith does not appear to have led to a betrayal of the spirit of the directive. The French interpretation of the concept is not far removed from that formulated in the community text. The subjective interpretation of the good faith concept is part of the French legal tradition.

Indeed, this subjectivism may also be found in French jurisprudence on unfair terms, in which the approach is one of casuistry – giving the priority to a circumstantiated appreciation of the facts of the case and contract.[18] Doctrine does not fail to highlight the difficulty of determining criteria for assessing an unfair provision.[19] Yet this legal blur meets the spirit of the directive, as pointed out by the CJEC in a 2004 ruling.[20]

Even German law, which adopts an objective interpretation of good faith,[21] took this course. It is true that the 1993 directive is largely inspired by the German law on general business conditions. That law already made reference to good faith, though without consequence. It had in fact been demonstrated that this reference was introduced to mask the difficulty of legally founding the legislation.[22] In any case it created no obstacle to a casuistic implementation of the law.

At this stage of the reflection, it therefore appears that the harmonization of contract law in the EU exists when the transposition texts are consistent with the spirit of the directives. It is not the transposition method that makes the harmonization. We can already say that common law regimes will likely betray the community texts more, insofar as the latter are very often dominated by a 'Romano-Germanic' approach to law.

Of course, there are counter-examples. One can think, for instance, of the directive on all-inclusive tours, largely inspired by the common law's vision of the bonds of contract. That directive adopts, in large part, the theory embodied in the *Sale of Goods Act* regarding non-compliant performance and it also introduces the

17 See in particular J. Ghestin and I. Marchessaux-Van Melle (1995), 'L'application en France de la directive visant à éliminer les clauses abusives après l'adoption de la loi n° 95-96 du 1er février 1995'.

18 X. Lagarde (2006), 'Qu'est-ce qu'une clause abusive?'.

19 *Ibid.*

20 Judgment of the Court of Justice, 1 April 2004, Case C-237/02 *Freiburger Kommunalbauten GmbH Baugesellschaft & Co. KG v. Ludger Hofstetter and Ulrike Hofstetter*, [2004] ECR I-3403, Gazette du Palais, 19 May 2005, No. 139, p. 32; Proceedings, July 2004, No. 139, obs. C. Nourissat; *Revue de jurisprudence commerciale* 2004, p. 264, obs. A. Raynouard.

21 See B. Jaluzot (2001), 'La bonne foi dans les contrats, Étude comparative de droit français, allemand et japonais', preface by F. Ferrand.

22 *Ibid.*, No. 1647 *et seq.*

notion of *anticipatory breach of contract* into continental law regimes.[23] However, inasmuch as the matter is about contractual techniques rather than principles, harmonization is not called into question as it is in the case of the transposition of the good faith concept. Transposition texts have little difficulty accepting contractual techniques, but when it comes to accepting the spirit of community law, the situation is no longer the same. The issue of harmonization extended to civil contract law will illustrate and confirm this observation.

Harmonization Extended to Civil Contract Law

The choice to extend harmonization to civil contract law necessarily entails an interpretive transposition because it goes beyond what is required under community law. It is a political choice that reflects a desire to extend the scope of consumer law. This desire is itself often inspired by the desire to maintain internal consistency in the national legal system that a newly added sectorial provision could disrupt. This policy to expand community law implementation is traditionally a responsibility of the legislature, which is a quasi-natural directive transposition body, but it may come from a judge.

Harmonization Resulting from an Expansionist Legislative Policy

The difference between Germany and France in the methods of transposition of directives on consumer goods is particularly revealing of the political choice underlying the issue of integrating directives into national laws. Before going further, a few words should be said about the origins of the community text. It is no mystery that the 1999 directive is heavily based on the Vienna Convention on the International Sale of Goods. Yet the purpose of the Convention was to develop international business, not consumer protection. Although the 1999 directive specifies that its scope concerns relations between professionals and consumers, it is nonetheless largely consistent with the provisions of the Vienna Convention. Unlike the Romano-Germanic system, it enshrines a monistic doctrine of compliance, ignoring the distinction between latent defects and the failure to

23 This is when the debtor states a wish to not perform the contract, whether by choice or because it is not possible to do so. In English law, if the creditor agrees to this breach of contract, he is freed from his obligations, recovers the amounts paid, which have become without cause, and collects instalments that were paid. This provision is clearly set out in article 4 § 5 of directive 1990/314/EEC, which stipulates that 'If the organizer finds that before the departure he is constrained to alter significantly any of the essential terms, such as the price, he shall notify the consumer as quickly as possible in order to enable him to take appropriate decisions and in particular: – either to withdraw from the contract without penalty, – or to accept a rider to the contract specifying the alterations made and their impact on the price.'

conform. Worthy of note here is that if community law is restricted to consumer/professional relations, it is probably only because the Treaties do not give the EU the authority to legislate in the domain of 'civil contract law'. For these reasons, a transposition of the directive outside the sphere of consumer law certainly seems conceivable, even consistent with the true spirit of the text. Indeed, the German legislators made this choice in the interest of modernizing the law.

A similar approach was briefly considered in France. However, it was set aside in favour of a transposition of a directive within the *Code de la consommation* [Consumer Code], which, let us note in passing, did not simplify French law, endowed henceforth with three compliance regimes. In this case, European harmonization did not lead to the harmony of French law!

The French refusal is stressed here to illustrate the degree to which the harmonization of contract law is related to the issue of the spirit of community law. The parallel with the way good faith was understood when received in English law is striking from this perspective. French legislators refused an expansionist transposition perceived as affecting an essential part of the French legal culture, the Code, in the same manner as a subjective conception of good faith was felt to undermine the legal culture of the *common lawyer*. The recent ceremonies that took place in France for the 200th anniversary of the *Code civil* show how attached the French still are to their Code and to its structure. The French debate on the Europeanization of contract law was essentially considered in terms of the Code's influence in Europe and not in terms of a need to modernize French law *vis-à-vis* European law.[24] Now, these assertions must be qualified somewhat, since judges sometimes undertake to do things that legislators refused to do.

Harmonization Resulting from an Expansionist Jurisprudence

This issue will again be illustrated by the directive on unfair terms. Its inspiration is clearly German but the 1976 German text[25] is a general text, unrelated to consumer law. The development by community law of a consumer-oriented legislation that differs from the German solution is probably again related to the question of the competencies of the EU.[26]

Although, in French law, the community text has been integrated into the *Code de la consommation* without any serious attempt to extend its scope, it is

---

24 The draft reform of prescription and contract law in France is not offered as a French answer to the Europeanization of law. See Poillot, thesis, *supra*, No. 2.

25 *Gesetz zur Regelung des Rechts der Allgemeinen Geschäftsbedingungen* (Act on General Terms and Conditions of Trade), 9 December 1976.

26 Incidentally, French doctrine has been reflecting for a long time on whether it would not be necessary to extend the protection offered to consumers to all the parties to contracts. For an overview of the discussion in France, refer, *inter alia*, to J. Ghestin (ed.) (1991).

interesting to note that the judge did what the legislator had refused to do, thereby in some measure restoring the spirit of the text.

The 1996 *Chronopost* ruling is a striking example of this. It was about a contract of the Chronopost courier company which promised delivery within 48 hours. The promise was not kept, and the unhappy customer, who had just lost the benefit of a government contract valued at more than €150,000, demanded compensation at the level of his missed opportunity. Chronopost invoked a clause limiting its responsibility to compensation capped at the cost of the service paid by consumers (that is, approximately €15). In that ruling, the *Cour de cassation* overruled the enforcement of the clause; it based its decision on article 1131 of the *Code Civil* relative to causes but also on the breach of its essential duty by Chronopost.[27] A wide-reaching doctrinal reaction followed, going from condemnation to praise. The Court had invoked consumer law outside its domain of application. To deem the limitation clause unwritten, it had used as a model the penalty for unfair terms specified under article L. 132-1 of the *Code de la consommation*, a provision itself coming from the transposition of community directive 93/13/EC on unfair terms in contracts entered into with consumers. In doing so, the Court's decision respects the spirit of the directive and its capacity to apply beyond consumer contracts as attests its Article 3 which addresses contracts that are not subject to negotiations. This jurisprudence has since made a number of rebounds but it has basically been confirmed by a recent ruling.[28]

---

27 Commercial, Economic and Financial Law Chamber, 22 October 1996, *Bulletin civil,* IV, No. 261. See the numerous comments on the decision, including: *Quotidien juridique*, 26 November 1996, observations of P. M.; *J.C.P. – Édition entreprise & affaires* (1997), II, No. 12 at pp. 49-51, note K. Adom; *Droit et patrimoine*, January 1997, No. 1552, observations of P. Chauvel; *J.C.P. – Édition générale* (1997), II, No. 28, note D. Cohen; Summary at p. 175, observations of Ph. Delebecque; *J.C.P. – Édition générale* (1997), I No. 1, observations of M. Fabre-Magnan; *J.C.P. – Édition générale* (1997), I, No. 17, observations of G. Viney; *Contrats concurrence consummation*, 1997, No. 24, observations of L. Leveneur; *Gazette du Palais*, 16 August 1997, No. 238 at p. 12, note R. Martin; *Revue trimestrielle de droit civil* (1997), at p. 418, observations of J. Mestre; *Défrenois* (1997), article 36516, No. 20, note D. Mazeaud; *Recueil Le Dalloz* (1997), Jurisprudence, at p. 121, note A. Seriaux. *Adde* Ch. Larroumet (1997), 'Obligation essentielle et clause limitative de responsabilité', *Recueil Le Dalloz*, Chroniques, No. 19, at p. 145; Ph. Delebecque (1997), 'Que reste-t-il du principe de validité des clauses limitatives de responsabilité', *Dalloz Affaires*, No. 8, at p. 235; Ch. Lavabre (1997), 'Éléments essentiels et obligation fondamentale du contrat', *Revue de jurisprudence de droit des affaires*, No. 4, at p. 291; J.-P. Chazal (1998), 'Théorie de la cause et justice contractuelle. A propos de l'arrêt *Chronopost*', *J.C.P. – Édition générale*, I, No. 29, at p. 1315; J.-M. Guéguen (1999), 'Le renouveau de la cause en tant qu'instrument de justice contractuelle', *Recueil Dalloz*, Chroniques, No. 33, at p. 352 *et seq*. The Chronopost jurisprudence was also confirmed by the commercial division of the *Cour de Cassation* in a ruling of July 17, 2001, see *J.C.P. – Éditions générale* (2002), I, No. 17, note G. Loiseau.

28 Commercial, Economic and Financial Law Chamber, 30 May 2006: the judicial decision enshrines the referral to article 1131 of the Civil Code to eradicate an unfair term

It would seem then that the trend to bring civil law and consumer contract law closer is one of the consequences of respecting the spirit of certain texts. Indeed, even some provisions of the draft reform of French prescription and contract law testify to this phenomenon: the draft contains articles meant to bring about an application to civil contracts of the provisions against unfair terms.[29] The English project to merge the two texts existing in this domain is also moving in this direction.

It is true that there is some resistance, as the adoption of an Italian consumer code could illustrate. Italian doctrine, however, does not view this as reflecting an obstacle to the phenomenon of reconciling contract laws.[30] The French example does seem to support that view. Though harmonization is checked with regard to content, it might experience a revival due to form, reflecting a convergence of laws. Harmonization may not be where it was expected.

Conclusion

In conclusion, two remarks should be made. Firstly, the illustrations herein are particularly striking examples of the culture shock that can exist between the common law and the Romano-Germanic system and certain laws of this system (German and French laws). One must bear in mind, however, that the harmonization of contract law does not really pose a problem if we stay within a very technical framework, as shown by the transposition of the directives relative to consumer credit, time sharing, all-inclusive tours and contracts *inter absentes*. There is thus a reasoned multijuralism of consumer contract law in Europe. Secondly, the harmonization of contract law up to this point has occurred through consumer law. Therefore, it is difficult to draw general conclusions on this issue at this time, unless we accept to get involved in the theoretical issue of European civil contract law, which, as we know, stirs passion and controversy. This, however, is another matter.

---

from a 'civil contract' where a French law on ground transportation, authorizing a limitation on responsibility, is deemed not applicable. See Mazeaud (2006), at p. 2288; E. Poillot, thesis, *supra*, No. 950 *et seq*.

29 Art. 1121 par. 3, 1122-2 and 1125 par. 2 of the draft prescription and contract law reform. See E. Poillot, thesis, *supra*, No. 873 *et seq*.

30 See G. Alpa, 'Presentazione al Codice del consumo', available through the *Ministero Della Guistizia* (Rome), at www.consiglionazionaleforense.it, spec. p. 1.

References

Beale, Hugh (2006). 'La réforme du droit français des contrats et le "droit européen des contrats": perspective de la *Law Commission* anglaise', *Revue des contrats*, **1**: 135–146.

Bridge, Michael G. (1984). 'Does Anglo-Canadian Contract Law Need a Doctrine of Good Faith?', *Canadian Business Law Journal*, **9**(4): 385–426.

Chazal, Jean-Pascal (1998). 'Théorie de la cause et justice contractuelle. A propos de l'arrêt *Chronopost*', *J.C.P. – Édition générale*, I, No. 29: 1315.

Delebecque, Philippe (1997). 'Que reste-t-il du principe de validité des clauses limitatives de responsabilité', *Dalloz Affaires*, No. 8: 235.

Ghestin, Jacques (ed.) (1991). *Les clauses abusives dans les contrats types en France et an Europe*, Paris: LGDJ.

Ghestin, Jacques and Isabelle Marchessaux-Van Melle (1995). 'L'application en France de la directive visant à éliminer les causes abusives après l'adoption de la loi n° 95-96 du 1er février 1995', *J.C.P. – Semaine Juridique*, **I**(3854): 275–282.

Guéguen, Jean-Marie (1999). 'Le renouveau de la cause en tant qu'instrument de justice contractuelle', *Recueil Le Dalloz*, Chroniques, No. 33: 352 –358.

Howells, Geraint and Stephen Weatherill (2005). *Consumer Protection Law*, 2nd edition, Aldershot: Ashgate.

Jaluzot, Béatrice (2001). *La bonne foi dans les contrats: Étude comparative de droit français, allemand et japonais*, Paris: Dalloz.

Lagarde, Xavier (2006). 'Qu'est-ce qu'une clause abusive?', *J.C.P. – Semaine Juridique – Édition générale*, **80**(6): 255–259.

Lavabre, Christian (1997). 'Éléments essentiels et obligation fondamentale du contrat', *Revue de jurisprudence de droit des affaires*, No. 4: 291.

Mazeaud, Denis (1995). 'La loi du 1er février 1995 relative aux clauses abusives – véritable réforme ou simple réformette?', *Droit et patrimoine*, **28**: 42.

Mazeaud, Denis (2006). '"Saga Chronopost": les maîtres du temps perdent une manche', *Recueil Le Dalloz*, **33**: 2288–2292.

Poillot, Elise (2006). *Droit européen de la consommation et uniformisation du droit des contrats*, Paris: LGDJ.

Redman, Alvin (1959). *The Wit and Humor of Oscar Wilde*, New York: Dover Publications.

Richards, Claudina (2006). 'The Supremacy of Community Law before the French Constitutional Court', *European Law Review*, **31**(4): 497–515.

Twigg-Flesner, Christian (2000). 'A Good Faith Requirement for English Contract Law?', *Nottingham Law Journal*, **9**(1): 80–84, at: www.ntu.ac.uk/nls/centreforlegalresearch/nlj_recent_editions/8371.pdf.

Vogenauer, Stefan and Stephen Weatherill (2005). 'The European Community's Competence for a Comprehensive Harmonisation of Contract Law – An Empirical Analysis', *European Law Review*, **30**(6): 821–937.

Legislation

The Unfair Terms in Consumer Contracts Regulations 1999 (UK), at: www.opsi.gov.uk/si/si1999/uksi_19992083_en.pdf.

The Unfair Terms in Consumer Contracts (Amendment) Regulations 2001 (UK), at www.opsi.gov.uk/si/si2001/uksi_20011186_en.pdf.

Gesetz zur Regelung des Rechts der Allgemeinen Geschäftsbedingungen (act relative to general business conditions) (Germany), 9 December 1976 [BGBl. I 3317].

Directives

Council Directive 90/314/EEC of 13 June 1990 on package travel, package holidays and package tours, *Official Journal of the European Communities*, 23 June 1990, **L 158**: 59–64.

Council Directive 93/13/EEC of 5 April 1993 on unfair terms in consumer contracts, *Official Journal of the European Communities*, 21 April 1993, **L 95**: 29–34.

Directive 1999/44/EC of the European Parliament and of the Council of 25 May 199 on certain aspects of the sale of consumer goods and associated guarantees, *Official Journal of the European Communities*, 7 July 1999, **L 171**: 12–16.

Legal Cases

Court of Justice of the European Communities

Case 6/64 *Costa v. ENEL*, [1964] ECR 585.

British cases

Director General of Fair Trading v. First National Bank plc [2000], Weekly Law Reports, **2**: 1353–1367.

French cases

Chronopost, Cour de cassation, Commercial, Economic and Financial Law Chamber, 22 October 1996, *Bulletin civil*, IV, No. 261.

Chapter 7
The Role of International Law Firms and Multijural Human Capital in the Harmonization of Legal Regimes

Gillian K. Hadfield

Introduction: Harmonization and Legal Human Capital

When multiple legal orders co-exist within a single legal regime – whether within a single country such as Canada, or a cross-country trading regime such as the EU – the potential exists for differences in legal rules to undermine the effort to engage in productive transactions and effective dispute resolution. If parties are completely free to choose the legal regime governing all aspects of their transaction or dispute – including a choice of law clause in a commercial contract or selecting an exclusive state of incorporation, for example – divergent or inconsistent sets of overlapping legal rules do not present much of a problem; indeed a diversity of choices may promote higher value transactions.[1] But in many settings, the rules of multiple legal regimes can attach to a transaction or dispute without regard to the parties' preferences. This generates a need for problem-solving by the parties: how to structure a transaction or a dispute resolution process that responds simultaneously to the environment in which the parties are operating and the multiple legal orders in which this environment is situated? And it generates a need for problem-solving by the legal regimes involved: what to do when presented with a transaction or dispute that has been structured, at least in part, in response to the legal rules from a different legal order and which may be simultaneously subject to the authority of those different legal rules? A legal regime that is uninterested in the impact of the resolution of this puzzle on the value of transactions and the efficiency of dispute resolution may find this an uninteresting problem, but a regime that recognizes that one of law's functions is to provide an environment in which transactions generate value and disputes are efficiently resolved will see in this a central challenge of its coexistence with other legal regimes.

For a regime that approaches the problem of overlapping legal orders with a view to generating value in transactions and dispute resolution, the problem of harmonization is thus, in part, a problem of knowledge. In particular, it is a

---

1 This is the hypothesis of the regulatory competition literature. For a discussion of the tradeoffs of harmonization and competition in regulation see Sykes (2000).

problem of knowing how differences in legal rules and environments affect the value of transactions and disputes. This is a more complex version of any legal design question: how will a change in the measure of contract damages affect the quality of deals struck and the likelihood of inefficient breach? Will compulsory licensing of computer software lead to more or less innovation? Will workers be better or worse off (legislative goals promoted or undermined) if safety legislation is interpreted to provide an exemption for small firms? These legal design questions are encountered by regulators and legislators when designing written legal rules *ex ante*, and they are encountered by adjudicators called upon to interpret and implement rules (statutory or common law) *ex post*. In both cases, the social welfare goals of law depend on the level of expertise about the relationships between legal rules, environments and outcomes available to the regulator, legislator or adjudicator. I call this expertise *legal human capital* (Hadfield 2007). When this expertise includes knowledge of the legal rules of overlapping legal regimes and the particular problems generated by multijuralism, I call this expertise *multijural human capital.*

In this chapter, I argue that understanding the nature and consequences of legal harmonization in multijural settings requires attention to the availability and quality of multijural human capital. How are regulators, legislators and adjudicators educated about multiple legal rules, how they interact with each other and with changing transactional and dispute environments, and the impact of various solutions to harmonization problems on the value and efficacy of transactions and disputes? In Hadfield (2007), I develop a model of the accumulation of legal human capital and its impact on the capacity of a regime for welfare-improving adaptation over time, premised on the idea that much of the knowledge necessary to generate effective legal rules, tailored appropriately to local and changing environments, is embedded. That is, it is known initially and at lowest cost to the parties involved in a particular transaction or dispute, the parties who 'live' in the environment and wrestle with the problem of adapting their transactions or dispute resolution processes to the legal rules around them. The problem of rule generation – through *ex ante* legislation or *ex post* interpretation – is then a problem of how embedded information is produced and transmitted so as to raise the level of multijural human capital available to courts, agencies and legislatures. Put differently, private parties need multijural human capital to design their multijural transactions and dispute processes, and public actors need this same multijural human capital to harmonize legal regimes to improve the economic value that private actors can generate.

In the second section of this chapter, I discuss the deeply local and contextual legal problem-solving that may be required when transactions or relationships cross jurisdictional boundaries using as an example a complex Russian securities offering studied by McBarnet (2002). In the third section, I then examine the market failures that may attend the production of the specialized legal human capital necessary to engage in cross-border problem-solving. These market failures arise because, as is the case for most information assets, multijural human capital is subject to externalities that lead, generally, to underinvestment in production and transmission. Section III therefore also looks at the role of multi-jurisdictional law firms in overcoming some of these failures. Section IV then examines the obstacles to the development of truly multi-jurisdictional law firms posed by the regulation of the legal profession globally. As I discuss here, globalization of trade in legal services lags far behind globalization more generally. This, I argue, poses a major challenge for the long-run production of multijural human capital by private actors and thus the availability of multijural human capital to courts, legislatures and regulators. Obstacles to the creation of multi-jurisdictional law firms thus pose a risk of undermining the integration of legal regimes in multijural settings.

Multi-jurisdictional Problem-Solving and the Role of Shared Legal Human Capital in Harmonization

In the 1995 film *Apollo 13*, depicting the near-fatal complications that developed during the American attempt at a third lunar landing, there is a scene in which NASA engineers are presented with a pile of miscellaneous odds and ends of equipment available to the astronauts on the spacecraft and told to come up with a way to convert those random materials into a highly specific fix for the damaged system that keeps the astronauts' level of carbon dioxide below toxic levels. Modern lawyers operating in a multijural environment are often in a similar, if decidedly less dramatic, situation. Their clients have specific legal needs and constraints and face a hodge-podge of alternative mechanisms available to satisfy those needs and constraints. Lawyers who serve their clients well are experts in evaluating the cost and efficacy of alternative solutions to both transactional and litigation challenges, and, if they are particularly effective, imaginative in their efforts to cobble together a structure that promotes the interests of their clients. Like the NASA engineers, in order to accomplish these tasks, lawyers need to be knowledgeable about the complex ways in which different pieces will fit together and the detailed specifics about the environment in which the solution will be deployed. And they need to know whether and how well the people who will actually implement the solution will be able to carry it out, possibly far away in another world. In the transactional context, Gilson (1984) dubbed lawyers 'transaction cost engineers.'

McBarnet (2002) provides a case study of the issuing of securities by a Russian company to foreign investors in the late 1990s that illustrates this phenomenon well in a regulated transactional setting. The securities offering faced several key legal problems in attracting investors. First, much of the regulatory environment that supports securities transactions in developed markets – the markets in which the Russian company hoped to find investors – was then absent in Russia. Under the existing legal framework, for example, ownership of company shares was evidenced exclusively by a list of shareholders maintained or controlled by the company itself; efforts to move to an independent registry system were still incomplete and the risk of having ownership rights simply struck off the books was both ongoing and complex to evaluate. As another example, there was no effective financial reporting regulation in place: there was limited public reporting and what public reporting might be forthcoming was subject to little or no oversight, and unreliable. Both problems were solved through contractual terms: the company undertook liability for the accuracy of shareholder information held by the registrar, and undertook to publish audited annual financial statements in accordance with US GAAP accounting rules.

A second major difficulty facing a successful securities offering by this Russian company (40 per cent still owned by the state) presented a classic harmonization problem: divergent regulatory treatment, specifically tax treatment, of the securities in question. The Eurobonds the company sought to issue were at the time attractive to foreign investors in part because they had been constructed in such a way as to avoid withholding tax in the issuing country. Competing for these investors was hampered by the fact that these securities were not exempt from withholding tax in Russia. To overcome this obstacle, lawyers for the Russian company put in place an elaborate structure, dubbed the 'passport deal,' to avoid Russian withholding: the company established an Irish subsidiary, which issued the shares (Ireland did not withhold tax); proceeds from the Irish offering were collected by the Luxembourg subsidiary of a German bank, which established a secondary market in the securities; the German bank was then able to (finally) route the money to the Russian company through a commercial loan, which did not attract Russian tax. As described by McBarnet who studied the transaction in detail: 'The whole structure involved a network of guarantees, pledges of indebtedness on two levels of priority, certificates of indebtedness, and of course the aforementioned loan agreement, each of these also transnational, between Russian company, Irish company, UK, US, German and Austrian underwriters, German bank and its Luxembourg subsidiary.'[2] (McBarnet notes the irony of a largely state-owned company going through elaborate procedures to avoid its own tax structure.)

McBarnet's focus is on the design of this transaction and she does not explore the enforcement of the contractual or tax obligations created and avoided by the deal. But it is easy to see the complicated multijuralism implied on the enforcement side. Suppose the Russian company fails to respect the independence of the share registration, in violation of the contract but not Russian law, or arguably fails to meet its financial disclosure obligations in accordance with US GAAP rules. How will Russian courts interpret the contract and the Russian company's conduct? How will they assess damages? Will they issue an injunctive order to correct the share registration? Will they order a restatement or other disclosure of otherwise private financial records? Are these obligations enforceable in foreign courts? An arbitral forum? Suppose the Russian Federation decided that the complicated structure was not effective in avoiding tax obligations. How would a Russian court interpret the structure and the implications of Russian tax law? Would courts in Germany or Luxembourg or Ireland cooperate in subpoenaing documents or individuals or attaching assets located in their jurisdictions? Would they provide enforcement of

2 McBarnet (2002) p.108.

the contractual obligations of registration oversight or disclosures? How would they interpret the deal's structure, Russian tax law, the state of Russian company registration and disclosure requirements, and the application of any relevant international treaties for enforcement of foreign court orders?

For the US, Canadian or UK investors (the primary purchasers of these securities) seeking to enforce or avoid enforcement of the various contractual and regulatory implications of this complicated arrangement, the problem of overlapping jurisdictions is heightened by the need to understand the operation of and possibly choose between court systems quite different from those that operate in common law jurisdictions. Modes of interpretation differ, rules of evidence differ, discovery and interim relief procedures differ, available remedies differ, the roles played by experts differ, the availability and relevance of legal materials differs, the relationship between the courts and the state differs, methods of enforcement for court orders differ, the availability of public enforcement tools such as contempt orders differs, and the list goes on. One can also imagine complex enforcement strategies involving actions in multiple jurisdictions. And control over which courts or forms will resolve even contractual matters can be elusive. Efforts to control which court manages a particular transaction or relationship, or to select an international court or arbitral forum, are themselves contractual agreements that one party to the transaction may seek to enforce or avoid in a domestic court.

For the parties to this particular transaction, making its complex design effective – and thus giving the Russian company access to an expanded capital market – requires substantial amounts of detailed, context specific legal expertise about multiple jurisdictions and their overlaps and interaction. More to the point, however, it requires the various courts and regulatory agencies that might play a role in its enforcement – or in its regulation to comport with state law – to have access to substantial expertise about the detailed nature of the transaction, its commercial and regulatory environment and the legal regimes of other jurisdictions. Will the Russian court, for example, be able to understand the intricacies of US GAAP accounting regulations? Allow testimony from US accounting experts? Recognize established precedents from other legal regimes interpreting and applying these obligations? Enforce private registration obligations that go beyond those required by Russian law? Recognize a difference between a commercial loan and intra-company transfer? As defined by Irish, Luxembourg or German law? Pierce the entire structure and impose tax withholding obligations on the company, leaving the Russian tax authority to enforce these obligations through the Irish, German or Luxembourg courts?

Without substantial multijural human capital on which to draw, the various courts that may play a role in the interpretation, enforcement or regulation of this multijural transaction are unlikely to implement 'the' substantive legal rules as designed by the parties to this transaction or the states that regulate the transaction. Nor are they likely to evolve over time to increasingly accurate interpretation and implementation of these legal rules. The private effort to harmonize the regulatory regimes is thus likely to be undermined.

This is still true even if in response to efforts such as this one there are public efforts at harmonization – international treaties about tax treatment for Eurobonds, for example, or the wholesale adoption of US-style accounting regulation by the Russian Federation. Even if legislation is implemented that attempts to direct the legal treatment of arrangements such as this, such legislation still needs interpretation (although perhaps less so) and the evidence, perhaps complex (what do US GAAP rules require? When does a passport deal cross over from legitimate structure to tax evasion?), still needs to be understood in relation to that legislation. As Johnson et al. (2000) document with respect to 'tunneling' (the removal of assets from a company by controlling shareholders at the expense of minority shareholders,) the development of effective legal rules to control behavior can require detailed knowledge of the myriad ways in which entities respond to the rules in different environments. The enactment of 'harmonized' rules by the state is only a first step, not necessarily even a required first step, toward the development of a harmonized multijural regime. The multijural human capital available to individual courts in those multiple jurisdictions is an important factor in the achievement of harmonization. This implies that the incentives facing private parties to produce and transmit multijural human capital play a significant role in the public process of harmonization.

Market Failures in the Production and Distribution of Legal Human Capital and the Role of the Law Firm

Legal human capital is costly. Identifying what knowledge is necessary to resolve a legal issue requires skill and experience, resources and effort; so too does actually producing knowledge to fill identified needs. My premise, in Hadfield (2007), is that although the ultimate public value of legal human capital is achieved when it reaches public bodies such as courts, this costly work is, primarily, done privately by lawyers and paid for by their clients. The Russian company and its investors described in the previous section both face (different) incentives to expend the considerable resources necessary to develop expertise in how the Russian shareholder registration system is working in practice, Irish securities and tax law, US GAAP rules and their interpretation and application in different settings, German banking law, and so on. These incentives come from the initial incentive to design and evaluate a mutually attractive transaction and from the later incentive to effectively pursue or defend a legal dispute about the transaction's implementation or regulation by the state.

The key observation is that the multijural human capital acquired to promote the private interests of the parties to a transaction or its regulators ultimately must make its way into the legal system as a whole – into courts and other enforcement agencies – in order to improve the quality of the interpretation, application and adaptation of legal rules. Individual legal human capital must become shared legal human capital. Hadfield (2007) looks at the institutional attributes that can affect the extent to which the sharing of individual legal human capital with courts and other legal professionals occurs. Here I want to focus on a more fundamental question: whether the initial individual incentives to invest in legal human capital are subject to market failures and thus likely to result in underproduction.

Market failures routinely characterize the production and distribution of information. Information is subject to well-know externalities; it is hard to package and price. It is difficult to exclude others from using information and thus difficult to ensure that all those who value the information pay for it and so are included in the demand that generates production and distribution incentives. Because of these problems, many markets for ideas are supplemented by intellectual property regimes such as patent and copyright law and by public production or subsidy of intellectual endeavours through grants, university funding, and so on. The highly specific nature of the legal knowledge that supports particular transactions, however, makes these methods of supporting the production and distribution of legal human capital inadequate. Although a portion of legal human capital clearly can be subsidized by public funding of legal education and law reform efforts, this kind of abstract knowledge takes a lawyer only so far in devising a structure that is adapted to the needs and legal environment in which a client resides. Patent and copyright protections are also ill-suited to the protection of investments in legal human capital at least in part because of the ineffability of much legal knowledge: much of what is valuable in legal work is the exercise of judgment and an appreciation for how multiple considerations work together to recommend a particular course of action or strategy. Some legal products can be encapsulated – in standard contract provisions or other documents, for example – but much of what can be learned is learned only through shared practice – learning-by-doing, together.

If legal human capital were *completely* specialized to a particular transaction, such that what was learned in one was not valuable to what was needed in another, the difficulties that attend markets in information would be largely inconsequential for legal design. Researching and analyzing a client's legal problem takes lawyers' time and other resources, which *can* be packaged and priced. If of no value to anyone else, the demand for the information and ideas produced by the lawyers who put together and evaluated the Russian securities offering described above would be completely captured by the demand for lawyers' time generated by the Russian company, the prospective investors, the German bank, and so on.

But much of what lawyers learn *in situ* in solving a particular client's problem is of value to others. This is evident in the phenomenon of specialization: I want a lawyer working on my transaction who has done others like it because I expect that the experienced lawyer will do a better job of anticipating the problems I face and know the terrain of possible solutions better. Moreover, information displays increasing returns to scope. The value of information about new Russian registration or German banking or EU tax laws, or court procedures, is higher to the lawyer who is already well-informed about the problems faced and solved in putting together the 'passport' deal or steeped in the practical realities of enforcing the deal in various courts.

Because of the accumulated nature of legal expertise, the production and distribution of legal human capital presents problems for legal design. We want lawyers to invest optimally in learning, not merely with a view to the value of that learning for a particular piece of work done for a particular client, but also with a view to the value of that knowledge for future clients, including state regulators. We want legal human capital to be shared among lawyers, and in multijural settings we want information shared across jurisdictional boundaries so that what one lawyer has learned from her experience in Irish courts can be shared with another who is working on designing a securities offering for a Russian company or contemplating a German challenge to a questionable tax-avoidance structure implemented with the cooperation of a German bank. This means we need to pay attention to the incentives lawyers face to gain and share multijural information with each other.

Beyond professional camaraderie and intellectual curiosity, the incentive for lawyers to invest in and share expertise about transactions is a function of the extent to which they can expect to capture some of the value of those efforts. In the absence of formal intellectual property protections which would allow lawyers to license their expertise in exchange for a royalty or other fee, lawyers need to ensure that they receive some of the fees generated by legal work that makes use of their expertise. They do this by working in collaborative settings: partnerships and firms. Within the confines of a firm, and with established rules about the sharing of income and opportunities that come into the firm, lawyers overcome many of the difficulties of transactions in intellectual work and ideas, particularly knowledge that is difficult to reduce to written form. In a smaller firm, knowledge is shared informally through conversation and feedback on strategies, documents, and so on. In a larger firm, more formal mechanisms for exchange also arise: databases of memoranda, model contracts, forms and other writings and established training sessions or even (in multi-locational firms) conferences and workshops for firm members. In many settings, large and small, overt mentoring relationships are established, with junior lawyers assigned to work with senior lawyers to learn both didactically and by osmosis from exposure to the daily practice of law. Rotation among different offices is often used to expose younger lawyers to the work of more senior lawyers in multiple locations. In all these settings, protection against the distribution of valuable information to those outside the firm is assisted by confidentiality obligations and access restrictions (only firm members can attend a firm luncheon or look through password-protected databases, for example) and by the sheer need to be in frequent and informal contact with experts in order to learn much of what they know.

The function of the law firm as a solution to problems of generating and sharing human capital has been studied by three important contributions. Gilson and Mnookin (1989) and Galanter and Palay (1991) both analyse the value of human capital transfers from experienced to novice practitioners and the role of the law firm in facilitating the sharing of senior lawyers' (partners') human capital with a number of junior lawyers (associates).[3] Galanter and Palay in particular emphasize the capacity to maximize the value of senior human capital by overcoming the limit that any individual can only work so many hours; the fact that human capital is non-rival (many can use it at once without reducing its value to any one of them) implies that the value of senior human capital can be expanded by sharing that knowledge with others with a fresh labor supply to exploit it. Gilson and Mnookin (1989) focus on the law firm's investment in the associates' training, paying them more than they are worth during the apprenticeship period. Gilson and Mnookin (1985) look to the sharing of law firm profits as a portfolio mechanism to reduce the risk associated with investment in specialized human capital through diversification.

All of these contributions are specifically interested in the growth of the large multi-specialty American law firm and the changing patterns of partnership decisions. In the global context, however, it is the basic formation of shared practices among lawyers (not necessarily large, multi-specialty or patterned on the American model) that, I argue, proves critical to understanding the role of international law firms in generating the multijural human capital needed to support the expansion of cross-border interaction and the generation of the shared legal human capital necessary for public bodies such as courts and regulators to harmonize law in multijural settings. Indeed, in the global context the creation of multi-jurisdictional legal practices and the facilitation of cross-border exchange of legal human capital is a fundamental legal design question, one that has by and large not been well understood in the ongoing efforts to develop the legal structures needed to support globalization and multijuralism.

The embedded, local and often ineffable knowledge necessary to design, evaluate and regulate transactions takes on dramatic proportions in the multijural context. The sheer volume of what must be known to effectively evaluate alternatives increases several-fold over what is required in the domestic context. What this implies for multijuralism is a substantial need for multijural human capital not only about the particular transaction or relationship at stake, but also about the law, norms and practices of the jurisdictions potentially relevant to the transaction or relationship. Some of this legal human capital – the practices of contract law and enforcement in Irish or Russian courts, for example – will be available to domestic lawyers practicing in particular jurisdictions. Accessing that expertise is possible through the retention of the services of domestic lawyers in the process of putting together the transaction. The very nature of the cross-border setting, however, suggests the need for lawyers from all relevant jurisdictions involved in the transaction. How are these services to be combined?

3 Gilson and Mnookin are more focused on the need to create an incentive for associates to invest in firm-specific human capital, given the risk of firm opportunism later in their careers, taking somewhat for granted that this human capital is provided in training by the senior lawyers in the firm. Galanter & Palay make this point more explicitly.

A simple answer would be to separately retain the services of attorneys possessing the requisite expertise. These services could be retained by each of the transacting parties, or by the primary attorneys responsible for the transaction. The difficulty here, however, is the one we have already explored, namely the economic difficulties of contracting over information. We are concerned not only with accomplishing a particular transaction or regulating a particular relationship, but also with the ongoing capacity of global legal systems to generate investments in multijural human capital, the value of which transcends the gains in a particular transaction. What incentive is there for the domestic Russian lawyer, for example, to invest in legal human capital about US accounting law and practices and how they interact with Russian law and practices beyond what is needed to carry out a specific transaction? To assist in devising a transactional structure that will reduce reliance on Russian legal mechanisms (and hence Russian legal advice), where this is cost-effective? What incentive is there to share expertise in Russian law or legal norms with foreign lawyers, such as those putting together similar deals in other emerging market economies lacking developed registration or disclosure regulation? What incentive do US, Canadian or UK lawyers have to share their expertise in evaluating these transactions for their investor clients with European lawyers seeking to advise their investor clients? If the legal relationships are limited to separate contracting arrangements, the problems of generating appropriate incentives for the production and distribution of appropriable information lead to underinvestment in trans-border legal expertise and inadequate sharing of global legal human capital.

To support and regulate the multijural transaction or relationship, then, it is important to have in place mechanisms that support the investment in and sharing of the legal human capital specific to such transactions and relationships. This brings us back to the importance of law firms. The law firm, as we have seen, is an organizational structure that helps to overcome the individual disincentive to invest in and share appropriable and generalizable legal human capital. When transactions move across jurisdictional boundaries and the expertise and legal innovation necessary to support them include issues unique to the multijural setting, then the law firm as a solution to the underinvestment problem must also transcend borders. The multi-jurisdictional law firm captures the returns to both generating expertise in multijural transactions and relationships and sharing legal human capital between lawyers situated in different jurisdictions. It is not necessary for a specific lawyer – Russian, Irish, German, or American in McBarnet's securities example – to anticipate repeat business of this type; it is now sufficient for the firm as a whole to anticipate repeat business to generate incentives for efforts to be made to learn more about the issues at stake and their more general characteristics, and to invest in mechanisms for transferring that information to other lawyers in the firm. If the Russian and US and European lawyers are in the same firm, jointly benefiting from future revenues, the incentive to hoard expertise in domestic legal knowledge is alleviated and the incentive to invest in sharing that information is generated.

The sharing of legal human capital across jurisdictions is particularly important in the multijural context because of the likelihood that lawyers, steeped in their domestic jurisdiction, will fail to appreciate the subtle ways in which legal and non-legal mechanisms operate in foreign environments. This is knowledge that it is difficult to access in the abstract. Indeed, like the proverbial fish that knows nothing of the sea in which it swims, it is likely that the domestic lawyer is oblivious to many of the features of the domestic jurisdiction that make particular transactional solutions or regulatory approaches effective. Yet such knowledge is essential to the ongoing effort to facilitate global interaction. Thus Russian, German, Irish, Luxembourg and American, British or Canadian lawyers are each likely to exercise poor judgment about transactional design or enforcement in the absence of being educated by the other, in an ongoing and embedded way, about the way in which different mechanisms are likely to function in the effort to integrate US accounting practices, common-law contract interpretation, Irish securities law, German and Luxembourg banking procedures and Russian tax and company laws with enforcement in any one (and probably many) of these individual jurisdictions.

In the absence of a truly multi-jurisdictional law firm in which lawyers from different countries share in firm profits, lawyers have an incentive to hoard information about their respective expertise in order to preserve the value of their services in future transactions. Lawyers also have a disincentive to devote effort to identifying transactional, regulatory or enforcement solutions that reduce reliance on the legal environment in which they are expert. Both actions increase their bargaining power in the distribution of the rents generated in any given transaction or litigation that requires their input. Relatedly, in the absence of future profit-sharing, individual lawyers in separate jurisdictions have little incentive to innovate costly solutions for cross-border transactions and relationships if they do not have reliable access to the other jurisdiction in the future. The truly multi-jurisdictional law firm, in which all members of the firm reliably share in the increased present and future value created by improved information-sharing and innovation, can help to alleviate these sub-optimal incentives.

As those who have studied the economic function of law firms have emphasized, however, in order for the sharing of future revenues to support current collaborative efforts such as information-sharing and transactional innovation, it is important for the law firms' 'hold' on the value of the information to persist. This means that the risk that lawyers in the firm will opportunistically defect in the future, taking with them the value created by their joint efforts, has to be effectively reduced in order for the firm to serve its function. Both Gilson and Mnookin (1989) and Galanter and Palay (1991) look at the risk that junior associates will abscond with the value of the mentorship and training they have received from senior partners or degrade the value of the investment by shirking; this risk, they argue, is managed by the partnership decision, which holds out a large partnership prize for the associate who remains loyal, hard-working and productive through a probationary period. Gilson and Mnookin (1985) look at the risk that the lawyers whose specialties turn out to be profitable will abandon the lawyers whose specialties turn out to be unprofitable, or threaten to leave if they are not given a greater share of firm revenues, thus undoing the value of diversification that they suggest motivates the creation of large multi-specialty firms. This risk, they claim, is reduced by the law firm's creation of a valuable set of clients who are bonded to the law firm rather than particular lawyers and the establishment of a firm-level reputation, reducing the value to a given lawyer of defecting.

In order for the multi-jurisdictional law firm to support the sharing of information and investments in innovative cross-border transactional solutions, then, it is important for the law firm to effectively share profits among lawyers from different jurisdictions (to prevent hoarding and shirking), and to be largely protected against hold-up and abandonment threats by lawyers from different jurisdictions.

Global Regulation of Legal Services and the Obstacles to Multi-jurisdictional Law Practice

The globalization of the legal services market lags substantially behind the globalization of other goods and services, with an arcane web of barriers to the creation and stability of the truly multi-jurisdictional law firm. Barriers to the sharing of law firm profits among a multi-jurisdictional set of lawyers abound in the form of restrictions on the formation of business relationships such as partnerships, or even employment relations, between lawyers from different jurisdictions. Restrictions on the creation of firm reputation, as a bonding mechanism for the firm, are widespread, particularly for multi-jurisdictional firms. And most critically, the legal profession in most countries, organized as a self-governing body often considered beyond the reach of state regulation, operates a tight cartel over access to the provision of legal services that either rely on the country's law or are provided to the country's residents. The hold-up threat created by these cartels effectively thwarts efforts to form an enduring commitment between lawyers from multiple jurisdictions to share the profits generated by sharing expertise and innovating new solutions for cross-border transactions and relationships.

In the domestic context, the capacity of bar associations (directly or through their influence on statutes regulating the legal professions) to restrict entry into the practice is well-documented. Restrictions adopted in different jurisdictions include numerical quotas (particularly with respect to notaries, who generally hold a territorial monopoly on the preparation of certain documents), control over bar exam passage rates and the accreditation of law schools, limits on advertising, ranging from complete bans on any form of advertising to prohibitions on the content, form or medium of advertising and price controls.[4] Moreover, most jurisdictions

4 Minimum fee schedules for lawyers persist in the EU, for example, in Germany, Italy and Austria. Notaries are subject to minimum and/or maximum fee schedules in

control the organizational form of law practice. In most countries, for example, law firms must operate as partnerships among lawyers; some jurisdictions now allow law practice to be organized as a limited liability corporation but continue to require that the corporation be owned exclusively by lawyers and limited to the provision of legal services (excluding combinations with other services providers such as management consultants and accountants).[5] In major European countries such as Germany (Paterson et al. 2003), as well as in Asian countries such as Japan (Kelemen and Sibbitt, 2002) and transition countries such as Slovakia,[6] law firms may not operate multiple offices. 'Almost everywhere' in the OECD countries, lawyers are subject to local presence requirements (OECD 2000), meaning that lawyers cannot provide legal services (electronically, by telephone, and so on) without setting up shop in the country. In the UK, lawyers with authority to appear in court (barristers) must work as self-employed solo practitioners and may not enter into practice arrangements with solicitors; in some countries such as Slovakia, lawyers may not be employed by other lawyers, limiting the potential for law firms to grow through the use of associates prior to partnership. In many jurisdictions throughout the world, lawyers are prohibited from presenting themselves to the market as specialists in particular areas of law. Many of these regulations are of dubious value to the welfare of domestic markets, although they are all generally defended as being necessary to protect the independence of the legal profession and protect the consumers of legal services. Of greatest concern for the development of multijural transactions and relationships, however, are the restrictions these domestic regulations place on foreign lawyers and the emergence of multi-jurisdictional law firms.

In most jurisdictions, conventional authorization to practice law in the country – being physically present in the country and providing legal services to foreign or domestic clients, or providing services to clients located within the country from outside the country – is limited to those who have been admitted to practice by that country. The requirements for admission to practice generally include completion of a law degree (often within the country itself), passing an examination (usually administered only in the language of the country), meeting various moral standing criteria (such as the absence of a criminal record and evidence of good moral character), and, in many places, completion of a period of apprenticeship with practicing lawyers in the country. Historically, there have been citizenship and residence requirements imposed on would-be practitioners; some countries (such as Greece) continue to impose this requirement. Effectively, these requirements

Austria, Belgium, France, Germany, Greece, Italy, Netherlands and Spain. (EC 2004).

5 The capacity of the legal profession to restrict the formation of multi-disciplinary partnerships – between lawyers and accountants, for example – was recently upheld by the European Court of Justice against an attack under the EU competition laws in the *Wouters* case (C-309/99.).

6 Parliamentary Act No. 132/90 Coll. On Advocacy.

make it very difficult for foreign lawyers to gain admission to practice in a jurisdiction other than their own.

In the European Union, various directives and court decisions have attempted to reduce the barriers to practice between Member States. Member States are not, for example, allowed to impose citizenship or residency requirements on lawyers seeking to gain admission to the bar in a given State. Member States are also obligated to recognize the law degrees offered by other Member States as fulfilling the education requirement, subject to the requirement that the prospective lawyer pass an aptitude test or undertake a period of adaptation to local practice. Most recently, the 1998 Lawyers' Establishment Directive has exempted applicants from the requirement of completing an aptitude test or an adaptation period if they have 'effectively and regularly pursued for a period of at least three years an activity in the host Member State in the law of that State, including Community law.' These provisions apply only to Member States, however: lawyers from non-Member States are generally subject to the much more stringent requirements of admission to practice described above.

Many countries allow some legal practice by foreign lawyers who do not gain admission to the local bar (often called foreign legal consultants), generally under the restriction that the practice is limited to advice on matters of the foreign law or international law, although some (such as Greece, Luxembourg, and Denmark (CCBE, 2006)) prohibit any practice by foreign lawyers. In China, foreign lawyers are restricted to providing advice exclusively on foreign law, prohibited from opening more than one office, or entering into any partnerships with domestic firms; in Japan, foreign lawyers are required to maintain residency in Japan, and in Korea, no foreign lawyer has ever been granted authority to engage in even the limited assistance to Korean lawyers allowed by statute. (Kim 2006) Other countries (such as Germany) require the foreign lawyer to work in collaboration with a lawyer admitted to practice in the host country (OECD 2000 [1996 data]); others, such as Japan, Mexico, France, and Turkey, prohibit foreign law firms from employing local lawyers (OECD 2000 [1996 data]; Kelemen and Sibbitt 2002). In some countries, such as Russia and Indonesia, foreign firms are prohibited from practicing under their home name and required instead 'to practice under the aegis of a local client, a local firm, or simply to list their resident foreign lawyers' (Abel 1994). In the United States, where the legal profession is regulated at the state level, only half the states recognize foreign legal consultants; requirements differ state-by-state but generally restrict foreign legal consultants to advising on matters of their home country's law; some also allow advice on international law or third-country law (Silver 2005). Some require the foreign legal consultant to practice alongside a local lawyer; some do not (Hill 2006). Most allow foreign legal consultants to be employed by or enter into partnership with lawyers in the host state; some (such as North Carolina) do not (Silver 2005).

The most liberal regime for foreign lawyers exists in the European Union, where lawyers from one Member State are permitted to practice law in another Member State under their home professional title, expressed in the language of their home country.[7] While such lawyers may give advice on the law of either their home country or the host country, they may be required by the host country to practice in conjunction with a lawyer in the host country for the purposes of representing a client before the host country's courts.[8] They may also be restricted from engaging in activities reserved to notaries (such as preparing deeds, administering estates, and conveyancing). Furthermore, lawyers from Member States are permitted to form partnerships with or be employed by lawyers in the host country, if these practice arrangements are available to lawyers admitted to practice in the host country.

Efforts to reduce barriers to cross-national legal services are apparent in the General Agreement on Trade in Services (GATS) governing WTO Member States, but it is clear that the impact of GATS is still slight. GATS requires Member States to engage in negotiations to reduce trade barriers in services, including legal services, and to establish disciplines governing the licensing of services with a view to ensuring that licensing requirements are based on objective criteria and not overly burdensome as a restriction on the supply of the service (Terry 2004). Lawyers, however, have had little trouble in the international context, as they have had little trouble in the domestic context, defending limitations on practice as justified by the independence of the profession and the need to protect the consumers of legal services. By and large, the impact of GATS is to require that Member States allow lawyers from other Member States to gain access to the legal profession on the same terms as their own citizens, that is, to satisfy the same requirements of legal education, training, language, form of practice, and so on, as their citizens must satisfy. Much deference to the local regulation of legal practice by lawyers therefore continues.

Both the OECD and the European Commission have recently devoted substantial attention to reviewing the control of the legal (and other professions) by self-governing bodies under competition law (OECD 2000, EC 2004); however little progress has been made in shifting the balance of regulation. The Council of Bars and Law Societies of Europe (CCBE) and the International Bar Association (IBA) both have adopted strong positions defending the bulk of self-governance of the legal profession, seeking to establish as a core principle the uniqueness of the legal profession and the need for deference to its special status among the professions.[9] The legal professions throughout the world largely share the view

7 The European Court of Justice recently held that registration with a member state could not be conditioned on a demonstration of proficiency in the language of the host country. *Commission of the European Communities v Grand Duchy of Luxembourg*, C-193/05 (19 Sept 2006).

8 Article 5(3) of Directive 98/5.

9 The International Bar Association, for example, has adopted a resolution on 'core values' in the legal profession that requires a recognition that the legal profession is different from other services, fulfilling a special function, and that no deregulation of the profession should occur which fails to observe the principle that 'preservation of an independent

that the legal professions and only the legal professions can determine appropriate regulation of the practice of law, and that, given its essential independence from the state, the legal profession falls outside the purview of government. As articulated by the Canadian Bar Association: 'Our view is that the legal profession should not have to prove the 'necessity' of rules which it is convinced are required to preserve its integrity and protect the public' (Paton 2003, p.399).

All told, the web of continuing regulation of individual country legal markets imposes tremendous barriers to the creation of multi-jurisdictional law firms, particularly expanding beyond the EU, and thus to the resolution of the disincentives facing lawyers to invest in the global legal human capital necessary to support globalized exchange and the development of multijuralism. Overt restrictions on the formation of partnerships and other business relationships clearly limit the growth of multi-jurisdictional law firms. Mere collaboration or networks of independent firms cannot substitute for the internalization of incentives that occurs with the creation of a business entity that shares profits among lawyers in multiple jurisdictions. Even where such profit-sharing arrangements are possible, by making it so difficult for out-of-country lawyers to provide legal services, the existing state of regulation undermines the capacity for multi-jurisdictional law firms to avoid the risk of hold-up that destabilizes cooperative agreements to share information and innovate cross-border transactional and regulatory solutions. The stability of a multi-jurisdictional law firm depends on the capacity of the firm to retain sufficient independent access to individual jurisdictions (and the clients resident there) in order to make the profits available from continuing in the firm greater than the profits available from defection for lawyers from the separate jurisdictions. Access to clients and business has to be a firm asset, not an individual lawyer asset, in order to stabilize the firm and thus generate the benefits of shared information and innovation. Much of the regulation of the global profession, however, prevents exactly this.

Surveys of international law practice confirm that the incentives for truly collaborative multi-jurisdictional practice are weak. Silver (2003) concludes that US law firms, which still dominate lists of multi-jurisdictional law firms, are increasingly 'going global by going local,' that is, by staffing foreign officers with lawyers who are foreign-trained and who practice the law of the host country. She sees in this strategy a segregation of US and foreign practice, and thus limited opportunities for shared practice and collaborative work. Abel (1994), documenting the number and nature of international law practices around the globe in the late 1980s, emphasizes that foreign firms face the risk that by expanding their services in a given country they will restrict the referrals they

legal profession is vital and indispensable for guaranteeing human rights, access to justice, the rule of law and a free and democratic society.' IBA, Resolution on Deregulating the Legal Profession, available at www.ibanet.org/aboutiba/resolutions.asp. The CCBE also emphasizes the uniqueness of the legal profession and advocates only minimal changes in the existing regime of self-governance. CCBE (1998).

receive from local lawyers. In light of the regulatory structure in most countries, which makes access to locally admitted lawyers essential for some of the services that a law firm might need to provide in a given transaction or litigated dispute, we can understand the limited extent to which local and foreign lawyers are likely to collaborate. The local monopoly gives the local bar substantial hold-up power to extract sunk investments in collaboration and innovative legal work, including the work to develop reputation and a network of client referrals.

Conclusion

Both private and public harmonization efforts depend ultimately on courts and other adjudication bodies. The legal rules that are written into statutes, treaties and guidelines are not static and self-effectuating; they are dynamic and in need of interpretation, application and adaptation to local and changing circumstances. Courts therefore need access to grounded problem-specific knowledge in order for harmonization to be effective across multiple jurisdictions. My claim is that the principal source of this multijural human capital – expertise about the interaction of legal rules and their impact on transactions and dispute resolution – is the legal human capital generated by lawyers for clients and shared with courts in the process of transactional design and dispute resolution. For courts and regulators to become expert, sufficiently so as to promote economic value in transactions by resolving the harmonization problems of overlapping legal orders – private parties and their lawyers must invest in generating this expertise and sharing it with public bodies.

The global markets in which lawyers' investments in multijural human capital take place are thus important not merely for how well they serve the interests of particular clients but, more fundamentally, for how well they work to generate the multijural human capital that ultimately feeds into the quality of the harmonization work of courts. These global legal markets, however, are characterized by both market failure and monopoly restrictions. Market failures arise because of the externalities that attend the production and distribution of information, externalities that in other settings are mitigated through the use of intellectual property protection, public subsidy and so on. Law firms are an important organizational form for overcoming legal human capital market failures. In the multijural setting, however, extensive jurisdiction-specific monopolies over the provision of legal services inhibit the development of truly multi-jurisdictional law firms. Reducing the barriers to multi-jurisdictional legal practice is thus an important policy step in the direction of promoting the harmonization of law in a multijural world.

References

Abel, Richard L. (1994). 'Transnational Law Practice', *Case Western Reserve Law Review*, **44**: 737–870.

Bonell, M.J. (1992). 'Unification of Law by Non-Legislative Means: The UNIDROIT Draft Principles for International Commercial Contracts', *American Journal of Comparative Law*, **40**: 617–633.

CCBE (1998). *Discussion Paper Presented at the Forum on Transnational Legal Practice*, Paris (available at www.ccbe.org/en/documents).

CCBE (2006). *Conditions for the Admission of Lawyers from non-EU Member States*, (available at www.ccbe.org/en/documents).

European Commission (2004). *Report on Competition in Professional Services* (available at www.ec.europa.eur).

Galanter, Marc S. and Thomas M. Palay (1990). 'Why the Big Get Bigger: The Promotion-to-Partner Tournament and the Growth of Large Law Firms', *Virginia Law Review*, **76**: 747–811.

Galanter, Marc S. and Thomas M. Palay (1991). *Tournament of Lawyers: The Transformation of the Big Law Firm*, Chicago: University of Chicago Press.

Gilson, Ronald J. (1984), 'Value Creation by Business Lawyers:, Legal Skills and Asset Pricing', *Yale Law Journal*, **94**: 239–313.

Gilson, Ronald J. and Robert H. Mnookin (1985). 'Sharing Among the Human Capitalists: An Economic Inquiry into the Corporate Law Firm and How Partners Split Profits', *Stanford Law Review*, **37**: 313–92.

Gilson, Ronald J. and Robert H. Mnookin (1989). 'Coming of Age in the Corporate Law Firm: The Economics of Associate Career Patterns', *Stanford Law Review*, **41**: 567–95.

Hadfield, Gillian K. (2000). 'The Price of Law: How the Market for Lawyers Distorts the Justice System', *Michigan Law Review*, **98**: 953–1006.

Hadfield, Gillian K. (2007). 'The Quality of Law: Judicial Incentives, Legal Human Capital and the Evolution of Law', Manuscript.

Hill, Louise L. (2006). 'Services as Objects of International Trade: Bartering the Legal Profession', *Vanderbilt Journal of Transnational Law*, **39**: 347–78.

Johnson, Simon, Rafael La Porta, Florencio Lopez-de-Silanes and Andrei Shleifer (2000). 'Tunneling', *American Economic Review*, **90**: 22–27.

Kelemen, Daniel R. and Eric C. Sibbitt (2002). 'The Americanization of Japanese Law', *University of Pennsylvania Journal of International Economic Law*, **23**: 269–323.

Kim, Hyung Tae (2006). 'Legal Market Liberalization in South Korea: Preparations for Change', *Pacific Rim Law and Policy Journal*, **15**: 199–231.

McBarnet, Doreen (2002). 'Transnational Transactions: Legal Work, Cross-Border Commerce and Global Regulation.' in M. Likosky (ed), *Transnational Legal Process*, Lexis Nexis: Butterworths.

OECD (2000). *Competition in Professional Services* (available at www.ssrn.com).

Paterson, Iain, Michael Fink, and Anthony Ogus (2003). *Economic Impact of Regulation in the Field of Liberal Professions in Different Member States: Regulation of Professional Services*, Vienna: Institute for Advanced Studies.

Paton, Paul D. (2003). 'Legal Services and the GATS: Norms as Barriers to Trade', *New England Journal of International and Comparative Law*, **9**: 361–416.

Silver, Carole (2003). 'Regulatory Mismatch in the International Market for Legal Services', *Northwestern Journal of International Law and Business*, **23**: 487–550.

Silver, Carole (2005). 'Regulating International Lawyers: The Foreign Legal Consultant Rules', *Houston International Law Journal*, **27**: 527–44.

Sykes, Alan O. (2000). 'Regulatory Competition or Regulatory Harmonization? A Silly Question?', *Journal of International Economic Law*, **3(2)**: 257–264.

Terry, Laurel S. (2004). 'Lawyers, GATS and the WTO Accountancy Disciplines: The History of the WTO's Consultation, the IBA GATS Forum and the September 2003 IBA Resolutions', *Penn State International Law Review*, **22**: 695–795.

Teubner, Gunther (ed.) (1997). *Global Law Without a State*, Aldershot, UK: Dartmouth.

Chapter 8
Standard Contracts In Financial Law: An Emerging New Legal Order

Marc Favero

Introduction

Current financial law is characterized by a widespread and growing use of two forms of contracts: 'standard' or 'framework' contracts and 'model' contracts.[1] For several reasons, this usage provides food for thought regarding the development of multijuralism. The fact that the law in question is far from crystallized makes it easier to examine the dynamic forces at play. As standard and model contracts are generally international in scope, the terms and conditions adopted in each case reflect answers to queries regarding the choice of the most effective law, the most competent court and the most appropriate language. As a consequence of the decisions made on these matters, using these contracts is likely to have an impact on power relationships between legal systems. This is at least one of the hypotheses we are looking to validate or invalidate.

This study is based on a qualitative survey addressed to decision-makers in law firms, banks and business firms based or operating in France. The third section provides some information on the method that was adopted. Before that discussion, the second section circumscribes what is of interest to us in the body of law referred to somewhat ambiguously as 'financial law' and characterized by the use of the aforementioned contracts. Given the open-endedness of the questions in the survey, the organization of the following sections cannot reflect a narrow distinction between the reporting of the answers collected and the comments/reflections they inspire. The empirical study will confirm that model and standard contracts have become primary references for practitioners, which raises the following questions: a) have not these contracts also become a source of autonomous law within international financial law? b) are they merely an instance of the possibilities offered by local law or are they in a league of their own, one which legal theory has not yet fully apprehended and which would signal the appearance of true multijuralism? The fourth section covers the use of standard and model contracts; the fifth section considers their relationship with national law

1 While there are sometimes nuances between these terms, we take the terms framework contracts (*contrats cadres*), standard contracts (*contrats standard*) and, depending on the context, market contracts (*contrats de place*) to be synonymous.

and their implications for multijuralism. A few concluding remarks are formulated in the final section.

Financial Law and Financial Contracts

Initially, 'financial law' more or less covered the laws of banking and of the recovery of financially distressed companies. It constituted, already then, a source of complications for the traditional legal categories.[2] With the end of fixed exchange rates *vis-à-vis* the dollar and the liberalization of foreign exchange markets, new financial instruments were developed, the primary objective of which was protecting holders against foreign exchange risks. This is where swaps with currency options came into play; it must be noted that these instruments were created by financiers, not by jurists. Soon, rate risk management turned into an issue as significant for financiers as exchange risks had become for business firms. Then interest-rate swaps, as well as *cap* and *floor* options (which make a *collar* when combined), became instruments highly traded on markets. Swaptions, combining swaps and options, logically followed.

Jurists were required to provide a legal framework for these products. Now, for a jurist seeking to find a legal framework for a product, it is not enough to understand what that product is used for and how it is used; it is also important to know under what legal category it can be classified.[3] Faced with contracts containing esoteric terminology, used for completely new and complex operations falling into no existing category, civil law lawyers found a way out by concluding that these contracts were *sui generis* – an obvious admission of helplessness.

It is in this context that two standard contracts appeared in 1992: that of the *Association Française des Banques* (AFB), which has since become the *Fédération Bancaire Française* (FBF), and that of the International Swap Dealers Association (ISDA), the term 'dealers' being subsequently abandoned for 'derivatives'. These contracts make up the core of financial law in the current sense of the word – that is, the law of financial instruments which now also deals with structured financing projects, securitization and other complex operations. From that basis,

2 In France, it became fashionable in the 1980s for jurists to have a double curriculum: law and business school. This was understandable since drafting a security for liabilities or presenting the recovery plan of a distressed company required that the jurists developing these instruments were able to understand the statements of accounts provided by the business firms involved.

3 I am discussing the matter from a civil law perspective. Common law jurists, although not really concerned with 'legal' categories, have to use a similar approach to find precedents to which they can link the novelty.

framework or standard contracts multiplied and gained considerable importance for practice.[4]

At the same time, law offices – followed by banks and more recently by business firms – adopted internal model contracts, which they create continuously on the basis of experience and which they attempt to impose during negotiations. The purpose of these contracts is to be a reference for a given operation, and therefore to save time by avoiding overly frequent legal validations. Model contracts may be derived from standard contracts and form their internal interpretation – as standard contracts always require some negotiation and need to be completed.

To explain the relationship between a standard contract and a model contract, it is helpful to describe how a standard contract is set up, using the ISDA framework contract as an example. This contract may only be used in English, American or Japanese law. It includes a 'master' contract whose length in the 1992 version was approximately 35 pages. A master contract is non-negotiable: it is simply selected and referred to. It is meant to be fully implemented, as are arbitration rulings once they are relied upon. On the other hand, there is an appended document – the 'schedule' – that contains choices that the parties must necessarily make. Negotiations therefore deal with certain key elements and fundamental choices only and not with the entirety of a contract, thereby saving time and energy. For example, parties must choose between two methods to be used in the event of an early contract termination: the so-called 'loss' method (allowing the request of all estimated losses) and the 'market quotation' method, under which one may seek to obtain the market value of the product on the termination date.[5]

In practice, it is not infrequent that negotiations between two ISDA schedule specialists last a year. The work usually consists in taking the full master contract, and singling out clauses that are unfavourable to one party or another (generally the business firm as these standards originate in the banks). Clause amendments that are not present in the model schedule will then be inserted into the schedule: for example, removal of 'potential event of default'. Through this kind of process, one often moves from a standard contract to an 'internal model' but internal models are not precluded from existing independently of standard contracts. In

4 ICMA (International Capital Market Association), replacing IPMA (International Primary Market Association), for the Euro Medium Term Notes programs; LMA (Loan Market Association) for loan contracts; AFEI (French Association of Investment Firms) for liquidity contracts related to listings; ISLA (International Securities Lending Association), GMRA (Global Master Repurchase Agreement), GMSLA (Global Master Securities Lending Agreement) and OSLA (Overseas Securities Lending Agreement) for loan contracts and sale/resale of securities contracts ('repo' contracts); IBMA (International Bullion Master Agreement), IFEMA (International Foreign Exchange Master Agreement), EFET (European Federation of Energy Traders), Incoterms, and Euromaster for derivative contracts; FBF for financial instruments and buy-back agreements, combination agreements, etc.; and, more recently, IETA (International Emissions Trading Association) for CO^2 contracts.

5 Since the *Peregrine* case in the U.S., the 2002 version of the ISDA contract offers a new 'close-out amount' option.

merger acquisitions, for instance, all major law offices have their own database of clauses which they go through to come up with an internal model legally sound and favourable to their client.

The Survey

With regard to negotiating financial contracts, three parties come into play: the business firms which are the clients, the banks which offer the products, and the lawyers who serve as intermediaries in the negotiation. It was essential that the survey include these practitioners (see the Appendix for the complete list). Fifteen law offices were selected from among the largest in Paris, which means that for the most part they are of American or British origin (Clifford Chance, Linklaters, Skadden Arps, Freshfields, Landwell, Latham & Watkins, Orrick, and so on), but the largest wholly French office, Gide Loyrette et Nouel, was also selected. The list of selected banks was more limited since three banks cover a large part of the French market as far as financial law is concerned. Thus, BNP Paribas, Société Générale and Crédit Agricole Indosuez were selected, but ABN Amro and CDC Ixis were added so as to enlarge the sample. For the business firms, the selection focused on large corporations equipped with a financial law department. The five business firms selected were: Total, France Telecom, Veolia, Chargeurs, EADS and PSA. Even with this limited number, approximately 40 per cent of the French financial law market was covered (France Telecom, which had recourse to a 'jumbo' credit of €30 billion, is France's largest issuer and borrower). Of 26 questionnaires that were sent, 22 responses were received.

The questionnaire included sixteen questions falling into four categories:

1. The first group dealt with the existence, or lack, of standard contracts and internal models, their origin, the number of models used, and the nature of the *contrats de place* (market contracts) used.
2. The second group dealt with the way these contracts are employed, the questions being: for what types of operations? In what cases are they referred to? Do they evolve? and if they do, is it in a local or in a global context?
3. The third group attempted to identify contract relations with the local legislation, in this case, French law: is this law adapted to deal with a new financial product? Do *contrats de place* aim at filling a regulatory gap?
4. The fourth group covered relationships with local institutions, courts and universities, for the purpose of comparing them to relations with associations issuing standard contracts.

Questions were indirect and open-ended so that respondents could express themselves with ease, and the groups of questions were not identified as such. We expected the answers to the first two sets of questions to support the importance of standard and model contracts, and we expected the answers to the last two groups of questions to be more varied.

In exploring the answers, it should be noted that the categories of respondents – law offices, banks and business firms – were treated as homogeneous. In reality, there are economic and competitive disparities within each category that have an impact on negotiations. However, banks are fairly homogeneous and financial centres are organized around them. The banks created the professional associations, mobilized the lawyers, and to date prepared all the models of contracts. Professional business associations such as AFTE (*Association Française des Trésoriers d'Entreprises*) and *Cercle Gödel* are trying to organize and federate business firms to re-establish a measure of equality in this respect.

The Use of Standard and Model Contracts

The main lesson drawn from the survey is one of confirmation. Standard contracts and model contracts occupy a truly central, inescapable role in the financial world. There is no business firm, bank or law office that can go without using standard and model contracts today. This phenomenon goes beyond financial law into real estate law (even though that law is so deeply rooted in the national soil), and into merger acquisition law.

Let us be a little more precise. All law firms have a large number of internal models. English firms appear to be best equipped from this perspective: one office belonging to an English firm has 300 French law models, while another, linked to an American firm, has over one hundred. In fact, most have between 20 and 50 models. Law offices are using fewer standard contracts (between two and eight) and they use them mainly for derivatives operations. The breakdown is different for banks: they use some 20 standard contracts, that is, almost all of the existing standard contracts, but few internal models, between one and two and mainly for matters regarding syndicated credit. Business firms only have four to five internal models in the best of cases. On the other hand, they make greater use of standard contracts, though still less frequently than do banks and law offices.

Prior to explaining these differences, we note another result of the survey, this one somewhat less expected. The practice of using model contracts has spread to all branches of law, and law offices use them in the broadest possible manner. For example, in one law firm these contracts are used '*for any type of transaction*'; in another for financing and '*capital market*' activities; and in another for transactions pertaining to acquisition (or M&A) as well as to financing or real estate. Even more remarkably, the practice of using model contracts also extends to the broader fields of corporate law, economic law and even intellectual property law. In an article published in *La Tribune* on 24 August 2006, the head of Knowledge Management at Clifford Chance (a law office position responsible for managing office doctrine and its base of models) explained that 'there is a very high demand for model contracts in real estate'.[6] To date this field seemed a stranger to the use of model contracts.

On the other hand, there is a consensus that standard contracts continue to be used primarily in financial law. The survey confirms their widespread use in this field. Should we fear that the choice of law offices, banks and business firms in the survey has had an impact on these two outcomes? Would the results have been different had smaller business firms, provincial law offices or more modest banks been selected? Regarding the use of standard contracts the answer is negative without hesitation. Even the smallest provincial business firms can be exposed to foreign exchange risk, and may therefore enter into swap contracts or use a syndicated credit contract or a security loan contract and therefore resort to the use of a standard contract in the end. In fact, as the rest of the survey shows, any transaction on a financial instrument, even when purely local, involves a standard contract. Additional confirmation is provided by the AFTE's 2002 study among its members on the use of the FBF standard contract. The association comprises more than one thousand French small- and medium-sized enterprises. The study showed that 80 per cent of the treasurers surveyed use this standard contract (which allows the use of French law) for swaps.

How can we explain this difference between the practice of law offices and the practice of business firms and banks, a difference that is correlated with another relating to fields covered by both types of contracts? The explanation essentially lies in the specific role of each instrument, even though it is also true that model and standard contracts stem from the same family – standard contracts sometimes identified as model contracts that have proved successful. A standard contract is a source of law of a higher level, a reference extending beyond the limits of the entity which uses it. Every French stakeholder on the currency market knows ISDAs and FBFs.

On the other hand, model contracts are internal references that crystallize the experience acquired by a bank or a law office on a type of contract.[7] As the survey shows, these contracts may be models for all sorts of activities for which a standard does not exist or even represent a specific adaptation of a standard contract, leading to a multitude of models. In the case of credit contracts, it is easy to identify the model contracts of a given bank or law office – the presentation of the contract, the order of its clauses, and so on, allowing a quick identification of its origin.

6 See 'Une nouvelle facette du metier d'avocat', *La Tribune*, 23 August 2006, p. 22.

7 Law offices have expressed an interest so great in models that new functions have appeared at their offices: Knowledge Manager Lawyer (KML) or Professional Support Lawyer (PSL). These specialized lawyers, with a minimum experience of six years, bring office doctrine to life, analyze and circulate new legislation or jurisprudence, and most of all, manage and update model contracts. Also of note: the use of models designed by lawyers, themselves advisors to bankers, results in reduced professional fees and costs ultimately payable by business firms.

If the development of model contracts by business firms is limited, it is mostly because in these firms, legal departments specializing in financial law are relatively recent, and so do not have a large experience of contract-making on which to base contract models. An even more decisive obstacle to the development of model contracts is the different role jurists play in business firms from that of jurists working in banks such as BNP Paribas or Société Générale which have over one hundred highly specialized jurists (for example, experts in option contracts with Japan). Among business firms, French groups with more than twenty jurists are rare. Consequently, jurists in business firms must first cope with the urgency of the multiple tasks for which they are responsible before being able to develop and manage genuine know-how. It is easier for them to use standard contracts when they exist.

The economic benefits of standard contracts, especially for business firms, are numerous. They ensure an equal and guaranteed level of quality. Drafting and negotiation are simplified because each of the parties is supposed to be familiar with the standard and the discussions are centred on a limited number of questions. Standardized documentation facilitates audits and thus reassures the risk committees of banks. It permits greater fluidity in secondary credit markets, for example with regard to debt transfers, securitization, and credit portfolio transfers achieved through ‘credit default swaps’ and other credit derivatives.

From an evolution of law and multijuralism perspective, standard contracts are more directly relevant than model contracts. The last question broached in this section, which we will revisit in the next section, is therefore especially significant for our purposes. How do we go from one or more model contract(s) to a standard contract? In the introduction, we noted that a major justification for standard contracts is that they fill a legal gap (this is the case for IPMA’s EMTN standards or ISDAs/FPFs for swaps). This is not the only justification, however. We also made mention of the diversity of models used in the domain of credit. This diversity has its drawbacks: it curbs the secondary credit market by increasing analysis time, risk, and so on. It is therefore understandable that this diversity is perceived as ground for the emergence of a standard contract. Indeed, the Loan Market Association is attempting to impose a single standard for syndicated credit – even though this is an area in which there are countless models and no gaps in the law.

Yet meeting a need is not enough. One question in the survey sought to identify what allows a model to be a standard and, more generally, what ‘law source’ can legitimize a standard. The answers to that question fall into two categories: one accepts the view that the proposed standard must stem from recognized professional associations, the other affirms that ‘practice determines it’. However, if it is true that ‘practice’, which in law is referred to as ‘custom’, is one of the sources of law recognized by legal theory, it must be pointed out that in financial matters, this ‘practice’ is never spontaneous but quite organized. Those who organize it are those who dominate and control the financial market – mainly banks and law offices.

Although standards are created by professional associations, they are developed using models created by banks and law offices with previous trading experience on the market.[8] Furthermore, it turns out that associations that have produced standard contracts, such as the ISDA or LMA – though they present themselves as neutral associations – in fact represent banks together with law offices working essentially for banks. To which one should add other standard contract-producing associations representing only banks and providers of investment services such as the FBF and the *Association Française des Établissements de Crédit et des Entreprises d'Investissement* (AFECEI). Business firms are generally absent from these associations, historically because of their lack of competency, currently due more to a lack of means and mobilization on the issue. In fact, a model will only become a standard contract if banks approve it as such.[9]

Relation with National Law and Implications for Multijuralism

Unlike early swap standard contracts (ISDAs and FBFs created in 1992), current standard contracts do not necessarily or primarily endeavour to fill a legal gap. Numerous standards, such as the LMA contract, appear in such classic fields such as syndicated credit. Responses to the survey point to the necessity of both complying with the mandatory provisions of existing national law and completing it through model and standard contracts. Below are two typical responses:

- Market contracts and model contracts enter into the existing legal framework and reiterate the mandatory provisions of French law, but they substantially complete this framework.
- The contracts are consistent with applicable legislation but generally contain provisions that go well beyond directly applicable prescriptions.

8 It is common in the world of finance for banks (and therefore, their lawyers) 'to hold the pen in hand', that is, offer the contract to be used as the basis for negotiation. Even though the best-structured business firms tend to oppose that practice, a consequence of it is that the models are known to all, including the business firms which had to negotiate them, and thus can easily become a standard.

9 It should be added, however, that some associations like the AFTE are trying to change this situation. Recent work by AFTE's legal commission was about a standard contract for syndicated credit conventions which could compete with that of the LMA. Its structure purported to be both better balanced for business firms and more respectful of French law. There is here the promise of a real revolution, a standard being offered by business firms for the first time.

In fact, the situation is much more ambiguous than these responses suggest. We may note the following points, based partly on collected answers:

Both Types of Contract have Significant International Dimensions

In its response to the questionnaire, a law office stated that its models are of local origin, but then specified that English models are used as a basis for developing local models where none exist. The distinction between local and global therefore fades in favour of the latter; this is a general phenomenon. For business firms, models are often created by the parent corporation's legal department and their use is more or less imposed on the subsidiaries if legally possible. This tends to generate a strong link between the structure of the entity surveyed and the use of global models. The more globally integrated the entity, the more global models dominate.

Most financial operations of a certain size pool national and international banks which has several consequences. Standard contracts are seldom purely national contracts. They are drafted in English, or at the very least contain many English terms, making English the language of finance. We have used many English terms in this study simply because no other terms exist and it is the custom to use them. The law selected is often English law or the law of one of the States of the United States. ISDA contracts, for example, can only be used if the law of the State of New York or English law is selected in the schedule. No other law can be applied to it (except for Japan). On the other hand, an FBF contract is only operable in French law; it must be noted that the FBF provides a poor defence for its use.

The selection of the applicable law has multiple consequences for a financial centre. The law must be consistent with the choice of jurisdiction. Even though theoretically a court may be asked to enforce a law which is not its own, the result is rarely satisfactory. Practically, litigation disputes which opt for the law of a foreign country are, as a result, subject to that country's jurisdiction. This has effects on a country. If cases are brought more frequently before the courts, this allows the courts as well as the lawyers pleading the cases to develop know-how. Decisions are then interpreted by the country's doctrine and studied in its law faculties. Conversely, knowledge – an asset central to finance and to society – is lost for the country neglected by standard contracts.[10]

Despite the International Dimensions, there is Little Recourse to Arbitration

One might have expected that parties to financial contracts would seek to avoid state courts in favour of arbitral agencies. In fact, all questionnaire answers

10 The fact that the Euromaster contract offers, as a competitor to ISDA, a contract model which authorizes the selection of any continental law does not seem able to change this situation: on the one hand, banks do not offer a Euromaster contract, and on the other hand, practitioners are little inclined to change their habits and certainties.

affirmed that authority is devolved to French courts, and particularly to commercial jurisdictions. Can this affirmation be attributable to France's specific situation in that it refers commercial matters to jurisdictions comprized of professionals? It is difficult to think so since commercial courts (*Tribunaux de Commerce*) have no division specializing in finance and have the same problems training their staff as courts exclusively comprized of professional magistrates. Most importantly, it appears that mistrust of arbitral agencies in financial law is an international phenomenon. Even for ISDA contracts, jurisdiction is given to the Court of the State of New York or Court of London, and not to some arbitral agency. Therefore, for the time being practice dismisses arbitration in a general way.

The financial world's mistrust of these jurisdictions can be explained in part by the cost of using them and the slowness of their procedures. It is also clear that organized arbitration divisions do not have any more specialists for the contracts in question than state jurisdictions.[11] We also note that one of the essential interests of arbitration is its confidentiality. Yet in the financial instruments field, the publicity enabled by the open-court principle tends to be an asset in the conflict, especially for business firms: because of that publicity, these firms can use the lever of a breach of the professionals' obligation to counsel. Another advantage of the open-court principle, this time at the collective level, is that there is a known problem in the training of magistrates who know little of financial matters. It is therefore the role of lawyers and doctrine to inform them but, in return, the public nature of state rulings permits models to evolve.[12]

International Practices Tend to be Adopted Even Though they are Illegal

The following example illustrates this phenomenon. We often see ISDA contracts being entered into between a bank and a business firm, both French, even though, because of the choice made by the association that created them, the contracts are subject to English law. This practice, however, is a breach of article 3 of the French civil code, which does not permit foreign law in this configuration – that is, when there is no foreign element in the contract. Banks are well aware of this since they propose to include a London subsidiary in the contract. Here, the legal arguments do not weigh sufficiently to prevail over the contract's appeal.

---

11 A more general problem is that of training. The university system, in France at least, offers little teaching on derivatives. It would be helpful if the university system opened itself to forms of learning involving professionals as a complement to the teaching of 'contract law'. Students would benefit thus from a first approach to these contracts, and become consequently more rapidly able to negotiate them.

12 In fact, in the future, recourse to alternative dispute resolution (ADR) procedures might develop. The recent creation in Paris of Euroarbitrage, which wants to be an arbitration chamber specialized in financial law both prompt and cost-effective, could announce this, even if banks with major influence in the Paris market have up to now preferred state jurisdictions.

A somewhat different example is provided in the area of syndicated credit by the version of the LMA contract that is subject to French law. This version contains two clauses that contravene French law: one allows for contract termination in the event of filing for bankruptcy; the other, in the event of a new tax, requires a debtor to refund a creditor an amount equivalent to the said tax ('tax gross-up' mechanism or '*brutage*' in poor French). The first clause is illegal because only the judicial administrator may rule on contract continuity. The requirement stipulated in the second clause is not operable in French law because the tax base would change together with the new payment and so on, in a never-ending mechanism. Yet this draft standard contract includes these two clauses and makes the debtor declare that all contract clauses are 'legal, valid and binding' (the contract having been written in English). Banks interrogated on this point answer that international practice requires this kind of clause. International influence is such that the default clause in the event of filing for bankruptcy is found in many domestic contracts between French business firms.

International Practice Induces Changes in National Law

To the question relative to a desired change in French law, only 30 per cent of the answers pointed to a desire for change, mostly about technicalities. One of the banks cited a possible reason for this lack of interest: 'since French law is (with regard to financial law) 90 per cent transposed or derived from European community law, there is little margin for change at the local level'.

This being said, we can easily find examples where French law has changed under the pressure of international practices, with competition between legislations being as constraining as economic competitiveness. In the name of competitiveness, French law introduced two provisions that were completely contrary to its principles. As of 1996, standard contracts are no longer vulnerable to the filing of bankruptcy and the suspension of any payment normally associated with it by French law. Thus, a swap contract signed under the FBF standard may have a default clause in the event of filing for bankruptcy which allows for compensation with amounts normally due to the non-defaulting party pursuant to the same contract. This derogation was essential so that standard conventions relative to derivatives could retain French law. In the same context, the introduction into French law of 'global close-out netting' or multilateral compensation in the event of default, makes it possible to compensate accounts receivables and debts from all the contracts of this type that would fall at the same time as an effect of the 'cross-default' technique.

Conclusion

The foregoing analysis may be interpreted as shedding light on the elements of a process of progressive easing of the ties established between the rules and conventions of financial law and any one State of origin. A first tie that slackens with any State of origin involves the training of specialists. Learning legal theory remains an essential basis of their training, but that theory can be learned in any civil law or common law country and does not provide true knowledge of the contracts which make up financial law. The training of specialists in the field is a matter above all for practice, not for universities. This is confirmed by the answers to the questionnaire. As the answers also show, state jurisdictions are certainly unanimously valued in financial matters to the detriment of arbitration. However, this preference does not necessarily establish a link with the State of origin because it extends to foreign state jurisdictions such as the State of New York and the City of London. It also appears that the practice of standard contracts has developed outside any state framework or any specific national law. Though English influence is strong, the same applies to American law and even continental law in certain aspects. Multijuralism is the general principle here. In a similar way, even though model contracts in major law offices or banks are globally created for all subsidiaries or partners belonging to the network, they must be adapted to local law, thereby creating a 'feedback' effect towards the original contract. Thus the latter may become richer and gradually detached from any national framework.

This legal corpus, enshrining a custom heavily inspired by the banking world and its satellites, constitutes a specific set which:

- is multijural, requiring practitioners to go beyond the perimeter of their national law;
- exercises its influence right down to national laws thanks to the competitiveness requirement;
- develops through multilateral associations such as the ISDA, and
- is learned by practice and not at the university.

Insofar as this corpus loses any connection to a particular jurisdiction, it could breathe new life into a legal concept which seemed like a purely theoretical and artificial construct when considered in the area of international commerce but which, in financial matters, might acquire an unparalleled magnitude: the concept of *lex mercatoria*.

Appendix

List of Law Offices, Banks, and Corporations Contacted:

Law Offices:

Allen & Overy
Clifford Chance
Denton Wilde Sapte

Freshfields
Gide Loyrette Nouel
Herbert Smith
Landwell & Associés
Latham & Watkins
Linklaters
Lowells
Orrick
Simmons and Simmons
Sherman & Sterling
Skadden Arps
White & Case

Banks:

ABN AMRO
BNP PARIBAS
CDC IXIS
CREDIT AGRICOLE INDOSUEZ
SOCIETE GENERALE

Business Firms:

Chargeurs
EADS
France Telecom
PSA Peugeot Citroën
Total
Vivendi Environnement

Chapter 9

Strategies of Displacement and Other Violations of Territoriality: Cybercrime, the World Wide Web and the Ambit of Criminal Law

Gareth Sansom*

Introduction

Computer-related crime[1] and, more specifically, crime perpetrated through the Internet, poses distinct challenges which fall into two broad classes. First, there are technological issues associated with the detection and tracing of the criminals responsible for the acts. Criminals can take advantage of Internet addressing systems and the protocols associated with addressing (such as the Domain Name System) for purposes such as the misdirection of their victims or to avoid being traced by the authorities. Much of the digital evidence in this regard derives from *transmission data*[2] from which can be unravelled the complexities of Internet addressing and one can then begin to resolve the questions of attribution by linking the addressing information to *subscriber information*.[3] Second, there are

* This chapter represents the views of the author and may not reflect the views of the Department of Justice Canada.

1 The scope of computer-related crime and its various types are tackled in Sansom (2006a).

2 'Transmission data' can be defined as data that relate to the telecommunication functions of dialling, routing, addressing or signalling and that (a) are transmitted to identify, activate or configure an apparatus or device, including a computer program, in order to establish or maintain access to a telecommunication for the purpose of enabling a communication, or is generated during the creation, transmission or reception of a communication and identifies or purports to identify the origin, type, direction, date, time, duration, size, destination or termination of the communication; and (b) do not reveal the substance, meaning or purpose of the communication. For further analysis see Sansom (2006b).

3 According to Article 18 of the CoE *Convention on Cybercrime* (Council of Europe, 2001) 'the term 'subscriber information' means any information contained in the form of computer data or any other form that are held by a service provider, relating to subscribers of its services other than traffic or content data and by which can be established: (a) the type

legal challenges arising from jurisdiction because computer-related crime is often *transnational crime* and, in some cases, is transnational *organized crime*. Those who perpetrate computer-related crimes often launch their activity from a country which is not their own, seek advantage from targets in one or more other countries and may reap the proceeds of crime in a country unrelated to any of the preceding steps. In broad strokes, this circumscribes the picture of transnational, organized, computer-related crime that underpins the Council of Europe's *Convention on Cybercrime*.

In this chapter, I shall demonstrate that computer-based, transnational organized crime is characterized by two governing strategies:

1. increasing fragmentation and specialization of the criminal activity; and
2. territorial dispersal of the elements of crime.

I will show how each of these governing strategies develop over time, changing the *modus operandi*, and adapting different criminal activities to different circumstances. It will also become clear how these governing strategies can interact with each other: the increasing fragmentation of the criminal activity further facilitating the territorial dispersal of the elements of the crime.

I will also illustrate how these governing strategies exacerbate the relationship between the technological challenges of the Internet and legal challenges, specifically in terms of *the problem of different kinds of space*. The ambit of criminal law is fundamentally, although not exclusively, predicated on the notion of *territoriality* which is a legal concept of space consonant with geopolitical space. The Internet functions within multiple spaces: some physical and some virtual. The technological challenges on which I shall focus in this chapter centre on this multiplicity of spaces and schemes to subvert jurisdiction through *strategies of displacement*.

Imagine five sheets of paper each with a checkerboard pattern. Let us put forward that the bottom sheet represents territoriality and the four sheets above each represent a different Internet space. Take a pencil and poke a hole through one of the squares, piercing all five sheets – at this point, with the pencil removed, the holes in each of these sheets line up perfectly. Now imagine shifting the sheets, one to the right, one to the left: the holes no longer line up. If at the outset, instead of a single act the process can be fragmented into multiple acts there would have been a handful of holes through the sheets of paper. Assuming one could not simply re-stack all the sheets, after the sheets had been shifted, it would have been even more difficult to determine quickly which hole on one sheet lined up with

of communication service used, the technical provisions taken thereto and the period of service; (b) the subscriber's identity, postal or geographic address, telephone and other access number, billing and payment information, available on the basis of the service agreement or arrangement; (c) any other information on the site of the installation of communication equipment, available on the basis of the service agreement or arrangement.'

which hole on another sheet. If one did not see the sequence in which the holes were punched, one would not know which checkerboard square was the first and which was the last. This is the problem that investigators face in tracing criminal activity on the Internet. Thus, my purpose is to explore how computer-based, transnational organized crime attempts to create that sort of shift or displacement between different kinds of space, possibly to avoid detection or identification but ultimately to avoid prosecution because the latter flows from a jurisdiction which is significantly (although not exclusively) dependant on territoriality.

Considerations

All human acts are social, even when they are solitary. None of us need reminding that what those acts mean is different in one culture than in another, nor that these acts and the artefacts they may leave behind are historically determined. Complex questions in terms of the emergence and construction of diverse discursive forms and the understanding of artistic or at least *cultural 'genres'* in a given historical conjuncture are outside the scope of the present chapter. Yet, to the extent that I will be considering the World Wide Web, particularly in relation to so-called 'content crimes', I cannot avoid the fact that this issue is intimately linked to the history of technology. The novel and (what came to be called after the fact) the 'pornographic novel' were made possible by technology in an age of mechanical reproduction. As mechanical reproduction is supplemented with the new technologies of digital reproduction, we would be blind if we did not acknowledge that a phenomenon such as the availability of pornography (how much and at what cost) was significantly determined over hundreds of years by such means of production as the printing press, etching techniques, the still camera, the motion picture camera, videotape, VCRs, camcorders, scanners, and digital cameras. In addition to the means of production and reproduction, and putting to one side the thorny question of consumption, the availability of pornography is also dependent on the means of distribution, indeed on changes in transportation itself: in maritime shipping followed by the introduction of railways to move goods (such as books and magazines); the invention of the automobile and its extension into the trucking industry; the emergence of national postal systems; the introduction of broadcast television and satellite capability; and the proliferation of computer networks culminating in today's Internet.

This analysis will return repeatedly to certain kinds of social acts, acts that sovereign states assert fall within the ambit of criminal law. It has been said that 'a state is sovereign within its borders', indeed 'territorial jurisdiction refers to the competence of a state to exercise control over events, [persons, and property] ... within the confines of its own boundaries' (Williams and Castel, 1981, p. 3). So I began naïvely wondering one day whether the new diagram that maps crimes committed through the Internet engendered violations of territoriality.

My initial starting point is that events occurring in or through the Internet occupy a number of different spaces that are physical (in various respects) and even when virtual are not amorphous. Consequently, whatever my ideological reaction might be to the *Communications Decency Act*, I am not entirely comfortable with such descriptions of the Internet as those in *ACLU v. Reno*, 217 F.3d 162 (3rd Circuit, 2000):

> The Internet has an international geographically-borderless nature. With the proper software, every website is accessible to all other Internet users worldwide ... Indeed, the Internet negates geometry ... it is fundamentally and profoundly antispatial. You cannot say where it is or describe its memorable shape and proportions or tell a stranger how to get there. But you can find things without knowing where they are. The Internet is ambient – nowhere in particular and everywhere at once (at 169).

Although from the perspective of the Internet user (often in the mode of consumer, window-shopper or spectator), the Internet experience may seem even less geographically-embedded than watching television in the living room (where some channels herald municipal, regional or national identities), this is to slide into the naïve perspective of the bored browser or to adopt actively a 'willing suspension of disbelief'. Below the surface of triviality and visual pleasure, it is essential to bear in mind the underlying idea that *the Internet is a network of networks*. This means that at the physical level of computers, servers, wires and cables, the geography of the Internet is constituted by the physical arrangement of those elements in the individual networks comprising the Internet and the points of interconnection between the networks. Some of these networks are global, owned by the transnational Internet Service Providers (ISPs) that dominate the worldwide flows of packets. Other networks are regional, spanning continents. Next one encounters ISPs with national networks and then another plane made up of the many thousands of local networks owned by a plurality of corporations, organizations and institutions.

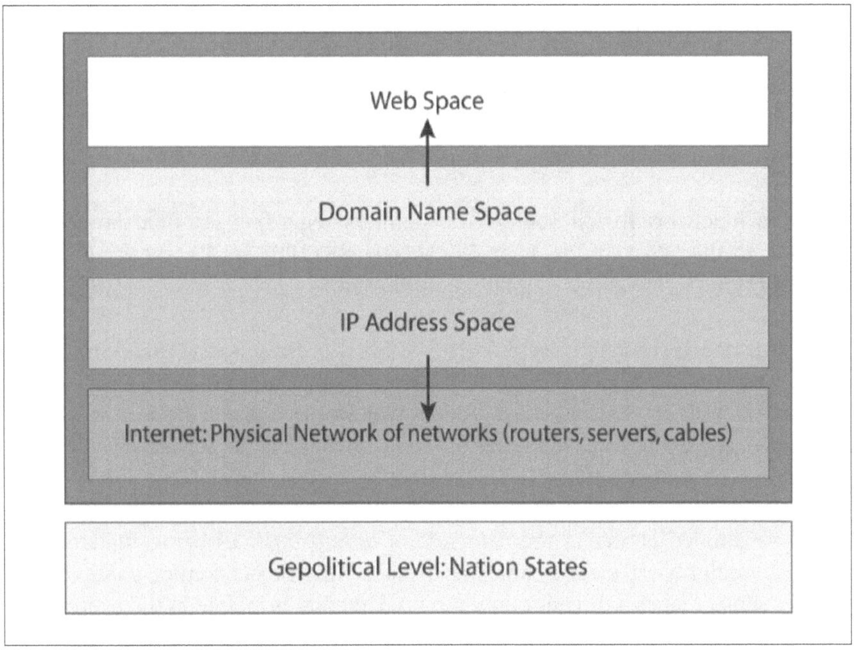

Figure 9.1 Different types of space

Yet equally important for today's analysis is the fact that this physical geography of interconnecting networks is embedded in another geography: the geopolitical configuration of nation states and their territorial boundaries. Contrary to the description in *ACLU v. Reno*, it is not that the Internet is profoundly antispatial but that there is an excess, a plurality of spaces – web-spaces, name-spaces, address-spaces ... physical spaces occupied by technological infrastructures, geopolitical spaces articulating relations of power, and social spaces of daily practices (workplaces, bedrooms, cyber-cafés, and so on). And it is not borderless as such, the networks have their own borders that may not be contiguous with geopolitical borders but are not devoid of any relation to them. For there is not an equal or uniform diffusion of physical networks and their elements across geopolitical space: there are concentrations and vacuums that are the artefacts of history, a plurality of digital divides tracing complex contours that correspond not only to the relative wealth and poverty of nations but also to the advantaged and disadvantaged within nations.[4] If one watches where the Code Red worm spreads,[5]

4 In the context of computer-related crime see Sansom (2005).

5 See CAIDA (2007) at http://www.caida.org/research/security/code-red/ for the Code Red worm and for the animated map of its geographic spread see CAIDA (2001) at http://www.caida.org/research/security/code-red/newframes-small-log.gif.

one can see a fairly accurate geographic map of the Internet, for where the worm cannot travel there is no 'Net'.

The Ambit of Criminal Law

I want to touch briefly on some basic pointers regarding criminal law before returning to the World Wide Web. Michael Hirst (2003, p. 2), speaking of the ambit of criminal law in the English tradition, said:

> The *actus reus* generally consists not only of proscribed conduct and (sometimes) of the proscribed results of that conduct, but also of the circumstances in which that conduct, etc., is committed. The location or place of the conduct or its results, and/or the status of the person who is committing the conduct, may be relevant circumstances for this *actus reus*.

I have alluded earlier to the *principle of territoriality* as being fundamental to the sovereignty of a state, and this from a host of economic, political and military considerations. It is not only the fundamental principle in the exercise of domestic criminal law but also in international law. Yet, as the Permanent Court of International Justice ruled in 1927, adjudicating between France and Turkey in the *Lotus Case*, the circumstance of criminal conduct being committed within one's territory is not the only consideration:

> It does not ... follow that international law prohibits a state from exercising jurisdiction in its own territory, in respect of any case which relates to acts which have taken place abroad, and in which it cannot rely on some permissive rule of international law. Such a view would only be tenable if international law contained a general prohibition to states to extend the application of their laws and the jurisdiction of their courts to persons, property and acts outside their territory, and if, as an exception to this general prohibition, it allowed states to do so in certain specific cases. But this is certainly not the case under international law as it stands at present. Far from laying down a general prohibition ... it leaves them in this respect a wide measure of discretion which is only limited in certain cases by prohibitive rules ... This discretion left to states by international law explains the great variety of rules which they have been able to adopt without objections or complaints on the part of other states.[6]

Williams and Castel (1981, pp. 7-9) have summarized the principals underlying these rules in much the same manner as were fully expressed in a landmark 1935 Harvard Law document:

---

6 *The Case of the S.S. 'Lotus'*, PCIJ, Ser. A., No. 10, 1927.

> The five principles upon which claims have been made to prescribe conduct are: (1) the territorial principle, which relates to the place where the crime is committed; (2) the nationality, active nationality or personality principle which relates to the status of the alleged offender; (3) the passive nationality or personality principle which relates to the status of the victim of the offence; (4) the protective principle which relates to the national security of the state affected by the offence; and (5) the universal principle which relates in practice to jurisdiction because of custody over the offender. Recently a possible sixth principle has been added: that jurisdiction can also be based on the principle of convenience.

It should be noted that not all of these principles have the same force and their application can differ from one country to the next and in one circumstance from another. For example, the majority in *R v. Cook* [1998] 2 S.C.R. 597 clarified their analysis of detectives from Vancouver (Canada) collecting evidence from a murder suspect in New Orleans (United States) by observing that in the case at issue: 'Jurisdictional competence under international law to apply the *Charter* to the actions of law enforcement authorities gathering evidence abroad rests in this instance not on the principle of territoriality, but of nationality' (para. 41). This finding on the jurisdictional basis of nationality was not in contradiction with two other Supreme Court cases which, rather than dealing with Canadian law enforcement officials, involved the actions of U.S. authorities:

> In our view, *Harrer* and *Terry* do not stand as authorities for the proposition that the *Charter* is absolutely restricted in its application to Canadian territory. Rather, the guiding principles to be gleaned from these cases are that (1) the *Charter* cannot apply to actions which fall beyond the purview of s.32(1) [of the *Charter*]; and (2) the *Charter* cannot be applied extraterritorially to govern the conduct of criminal proceedings by foreign authorities in another state since to do so would violate the principle of state sovereignty (para. 44).

The nationality principle has also been one of the ways to address child sexual exploitation, particularly by wealthy visitors to the Third World. In the context of child sex tourism, for example, a number of states have exercised the active nationality principle assuming both moral and legal responsibility for the actions of their citizens abroad.[7]

Although the principle of territoriality retains its dominance as grounds for establishing jurisdiction, over the course of the twentieth century many countries

7 Germany took the lead on this in September 1993 but, following the first World Congress against the Sexual Exploitation of Children, held in Stockholm, Sweden (August 27-31, 1996), a growing number of countries followed suit and introduced legislation with extra-territorial reach – the first wave including Ireland (December 1996), Austria (March 1997), Canada (May 1997) and the United Kingdom (May 1997).

began to adapt their conception of the conditions under which a criminal offence was subject to the jurisdiction of their courts. In the case of certain crimes straddling multiple states, the geographic restrictions of territoriality had to be re-thought and transborder jurisdiction became a legitimate dimension of principled national jurisdiction, although caution was exercised not to intrude unduly upon the sovereignty of other states. An illustration of this can be found in the Canadian Supreme Court ruling in *Libman v. The Queen* [1985] 2 S.C.R. 178, a case in which a Canadian, operating out of a telephone sales 'boiler-room' in Toronto, chose to defraud not Canadians but residents of the United States by enticing them to buy worthless shares in two Central American mining companies. The Americans who purchased the shares were directed to send their money to offices in Costa Rica and Panama. The accused sought to have the committal for trial quashed on the ground that the alleged offences occurred outside Canada, specifically that 'the deprivation of the victim was an essential element or gravamen, of the offence of fraud, and that any deprivation suffered by the purchasers of the shares ... had occurred outside Canada' (para. 6). The judgment concluded that Canada would have territorial jurisdiction if '... a significant portion of the activities constituting that offence took place in Canada ...' or expressed in another way '... it is sufficient that there be a 'real and substantial link' between the offence and this country ...' (per LaForest J, at p. 213). It is perhaps worth noting that under Canadian law this conception of transborder jurisdiction is not the same as asserting extra-territorial jurisdiction, because the *Libman* case interprets section 6 of the *Criminal Code* (the requirement for an offence to be committed in Canada), rather than section 7 of the *Criminal Code* (which deals explicitly with offences that occur outside Canada).

It is against the subtleties of this legal backdrop that I will explore criminal offences involving the World Wide Web. In recent years, a number of international fraud cases have involved the Internet generally[8] and the World Wide Web in particular.[9]

The world of online fraud is often wrapped in confusing jargon that sometimes seems to change with the flavour of the month. There are a number of different types of online fraud, ranging from 'click-fraud' (associated with the online advertising sector) to online auction fraud (including misrepresentation of goods or services; non-delivery of goods or services; non-payment for goods or services delivered). One type that has drawn considerable attention in the last few years comes under many names, such as 'identity theft', but is essentially online fraud associated with *credential goods* (Abad, 2005). The two main kinds of credential goods are *identity credentials* (passport, driver's licence, birth certificate, social security

8 Consider the $60 million dollar Internet scam involving the Tri-West Investment Club which defrauded approximately 15,000 investors between 1999 and 2001 and was cracked by a cooperative effort involving the United States, Costa Rica and Canada.

9 See for example Zeller (2006). Following Shadowcrew, other Web-based fraud sites to emerge include Carderplanet.com (a predominantly Russian site) and Darkprofits.com and Stealthdivision.com.

card)[10] and *financial institution credentials* (that is, debit cards and credit cards). The general public does not appear to have a clear understanding of the online fraud economy in credential goods as there is often no unified or coherent picture presented in mainstream media, so I would like to present a generic model. As with other economies, it is composed of various social networks of buyers and sellers of credential goods. The sellers of credential goods may have acquired the goods themselves or from a number of sources (in the underground they could come from individuals or groups with particular specialities, for example, 'phishers' or 'bot herders'). Sellers and buyers of credential goods need to have some meeting place to exchange their goods and conduct their transactions. In cyberspace, the online meeting place and market place can be a Web site (such as shadowcrew.com) or virtual chat rooms (on chat networks such as IRC for example).[11] The buyers of financial credential goods are often known as 'cashers' and they typically buy credentials in bulk (for example hundreds or thousands of pieces of cardholder information) and they may take a commission on the extracted funds (for example, debit card withdrawals) or barter exchanges of goods and services. The 'cashers' in turn, usually rely on 'money mules' (sometimes called 'cyber mules') who go from city to city with dozens or hundreds of cards and withdraw cash from ATMs or purchase goods with fraudulent credit cards.[12]

It may be instructive to consider a particular high-profile example such as the Shadowcrew case which was the focus of the US Secret Service's Operation Firewall as well as law enforcement actions in eleven other countries. A concise summary can be found in the indictment of 19 individuals, *United States v. Andrew Mantovani and others* (October 28, 2004), brought forward in the United States District Court (District of New Jersey), which states:

> a) Shadowcrew was an international organization of approximately 4,000 members which promoted and facilitated a wide variety of criminal activities including, among others, electronic theft of personal identifying information, credit card and debit card fraud, and the production and sale of false identification documents.

---

10 See NIST (National Institute of Standards and Technology) (2006).

11 Internet Relay Chat (IRC) is actually more like Citizens Band radio in which there are many different 'channels' on which people communicate, except that with IRC people type rather than speak. 'Chat rooms' are private channels, not really rooms. Abad (2005) has presented an interesting social network analysis of chat rooms in the economy of phishing. See also Symantec (2006).

12 For a recent overview of this process see Zetter (2007); for money mules see Zetter (2006); also Naraine (2006). For Eastern European money mules operating in the United Kingdom see 'Four charged in landmark UK phishing case' *The Register*. October 15, 2004.

> c) Shadowcrew members collectively trafficked and made unauthorized use of at least 1.5 million stolen credit card numbers, resulting in actual losses in excess of $4 million to credit card companies, financial institutions, and credit card holders. (Count 1)

Both (a) and (c) speak to the *actus reus*. Although some details have been contested,[13] it is acknowledged that this substantial, hierarchical enterprise operated between early 2002 and October 2004 by providing fora to exchange information about criminal activities as well as a clearinghouse for online auctions (based on a review process) of false identification documents, personal information and the building blocks for fraudulent credit and debit cards (such as plastic blanks for credit cards complete with hologram logos). In terms of the issue at hand, it is important to draw attention to clause (b) in Count 1, which states:

> b) Shadowcrew operated and maintained the Internet web site www.shdowcrew.org … in Seacaucus and New Jersey, as a communications medium to facilitate the commission of their criminal activities.

The specification of the place in which the server is located is an explicit assertion predicated on the principle of territoriality to establish jurisdiction within the District of New Jersey by the United States District Court. The physical location of infrastructure elements, such as servers, is one factor that can satisfy claims of territoriality but, as we shall see, the absence of Internet infrastructure elements in a given territory has not been sufficient to foreclose on an assertion of jurisdiction. Overall, the Shadowcrew case is an example of the typical exercise of jurisdiction in cybercrime contexts: at the international level, other participants who carried out Shadowcrew fraud schemes in various localities appear to have been charged and prosecutions carried out in a number of countries outside the United States (for example, the fraud ring in Argentina, headed by Marcelo Del Mazo of Buenos Aires), consistent with the principle of territoriality.

Generic Model for 'Commercial' Child Pornography

The distribution of child pornography has changed over the past 50 years: from the small commercial trade in child pornography magazines of the 1960s to 1970s (prior to the legislative introduction of child pornography offences in North America and Europe) to the peer-to-peer (P2P) computer networks of today. The distribution of

---

13 It has been suggested that Shadowcrew's 4,000 members did not equate to 4,000 actual individuals because many individuals registered under multiple nicknames and over more than two years many accounts were inactive but even if the number of individuals involved was only half the contended size it represents a significant number of hackers, carders and hangers-on.

child pornography via the Internet in particular is a complex phenomenon. Having analysed this issue for more than a decade, I reached the conclusion that not only is it crucial to distinguish among different Internet services (that is, networks in the technological sense) but to recognize that these different computer networks have been adopted and adapted by different kinds of social networks engaged in the production, distribution and consumption of child pornography. In the past decade, the distribution of child pornography on the Internet and other computer networks has been conducted using diverse services – Usenet newsgroups, email, Internet Relay Chat (IRC), P2P networks such as KaZaA and Gnutella (US GAO, 2003; Mehta, Best and Poon, 2002) and more recently hidden labyrinths created by botnets.[14] These different vectors of distribution range from the overt and publicly accessible to the covert and highly secretive. The different social networks involved with child pornography (which I would argue map to the technological networks) are characterized by a variety of different exchanges: obviously there are exchanges of child pornography images or videos but not all of these social networks involve monetary exchanges (and this is one of the crucial differences[15]

14 Botnets (that is 'roBOT NETworks') are networks created by compromising dozens or thousands of computers and placing them under remote control without their owners' knowledge or permission. Botnets are best known for being used in distributed denial of service (DDoS) attacks. By creating a large, geographically dispersed army of bots (sometimes called 'zombie machines'), an attacker has the ability to launch DDoS attacks, sending billions of requests from valid source addresses against a target computer, effectively preventing it from functioning. Botnets have many other criminal uses including identity theft, extortion, click-fraud, and, more recently, serving as labyrinths to evade authorities or as a network of multiple drop sites to hide illegal material such as child pornography.

15 There are many cases that prove that the distribution of child pornography using computer networks meets the definition of organized crime. Consider for example the W0nderland Club targeted by Operation Cathedral in a coordinated international operation on September 2, 1998. Operation Cathedral involved arrests and conviction of individuals in more than a dozen countries (including the United States, the United Kingdom, and Australia). Press stories around the world reported that W0nderland (named after Lewis Carroll's novel) was comprised of at least 180 members. This clearly meets the threshold of 'a *structured group of three or more persons*, existing for a period of time and acting in concert with the aim of committing one or more serious crimes or offences established in accordance with the Convention, in order to obtain, directly or indirectly, a financial or other material benefit' *(United Nations Convention against Transnational Organized Crime*, Article 2(a)). W0nderland also indicates another feature that is common to many such cases, namely that we are dealing with a *transnational* phenomenon. Paedophile social networks such as W0nderland (which centered on IRC) differ from other social networks involved with child pornography (such as those that form around pay-per-view Web sites) in a number of respects: the W0nderland type of network involved individuals who already had massive collections of child pornography (that is, each member had many thousands of images); it had a comparatively small number of members (a couple of hundred rather than a few thousand), and had a very high percentage of members who were also producers of child pornography (that is, who were actively abusing children and making a record

among these social networks). As such, at least two different supply side/demand side economic models would need to be developed. In addition different social groups engage in a variety of exchanges of information, some of it not surprisingly designed to support or justify behaviour that is regarded as deviant outside these communities, whereas other information exchanges, depending on the type of group, may centre on technical or computer-related advice (how to avoid detection by hiding one's originating IP address or how to use encryption or other means of concealing child pornography).

A 'pay-for-view' child pornography Web site has a number of different elements that need to be distinguished as each of the elements could result in charges for different offences. Some elements are involved in the production of child pornography, other elements are involved in the distribution of child pornography, and at the consumer end the charges may be restricted to possession of child pornography (assuming the consumer is not a contact offender). Finally, it should be pointed out that one or more of the elements may have no knowledge of the criminal activities at all. A generic model should distinguish between the following different elements:

- the producer or producers of the child pornography who create(s) the primary commodity and – with the exception of those who produce works of the imagination – are directly involved in the sexual abuse of children;
- the Webmaster who possesses the child pornography and creates the Web site (the html pages). Note that the Webmaster seeks to populate the website quickly, remotely, and may do so repeatedly. In a larger operation, with multiple Websites there could also be multiple independent Webmasters;
- a hosting provider or a Web server which provides the server space where the Web site resides and bandwidth for connectivity from the Web site out to the customers on the Internet. This could take a variety of forms including a virtual host (a single web server which hosts a large number of

---

of the abuse). The pay-per-view Web sites involve monetary payment (and hence are an adaptation of traditional profit-based organized crime networks), whereas other paedophile social networks do not involve monetary transactions. For example, my research on Usenet child pornography newsgroups reveals that it is not an economy based on capital (like the pay-per-view websites) but rather an economy based on prestige (and hence is more akin to conspicuous gift-giving or the model of potlatch in George Bataille's work). The Usenet child pornography newsgroups manifest an observable hierarchy predicated on different activities having different values within those particular newsgroup communities. This *hierarchy of status or prestige* places individuals who post (that is, give away) new material (child pornography images or videos) at the top of the pyramid.

sites) or a web-hoster (typically a company that has thousands of servers and provides services to tens of thousands of websites).

- a payment provider who processes the credit card payments for sales and who typically operates independently from the website or websites, and
- the customers who pay to access and download the child pornography.

Commercial, pay-for-view child pornography Web sites can thus be seen to involve potentially multiple individuals and possibly multiple companies or commercial entities, often located in different countries. What is being called the 'payment provider' may actually be one or more companies each of which could provide different components of the subscription and payment process. The more companies involved and the greater the distance from the source, the greater the chance their knowledge of the criminal activity is limited. At one end of the continuum, a payments processing service could actually be a legitimate processing company that handles payments for many thousands of other companies and has no knowledge of any illegal activity.

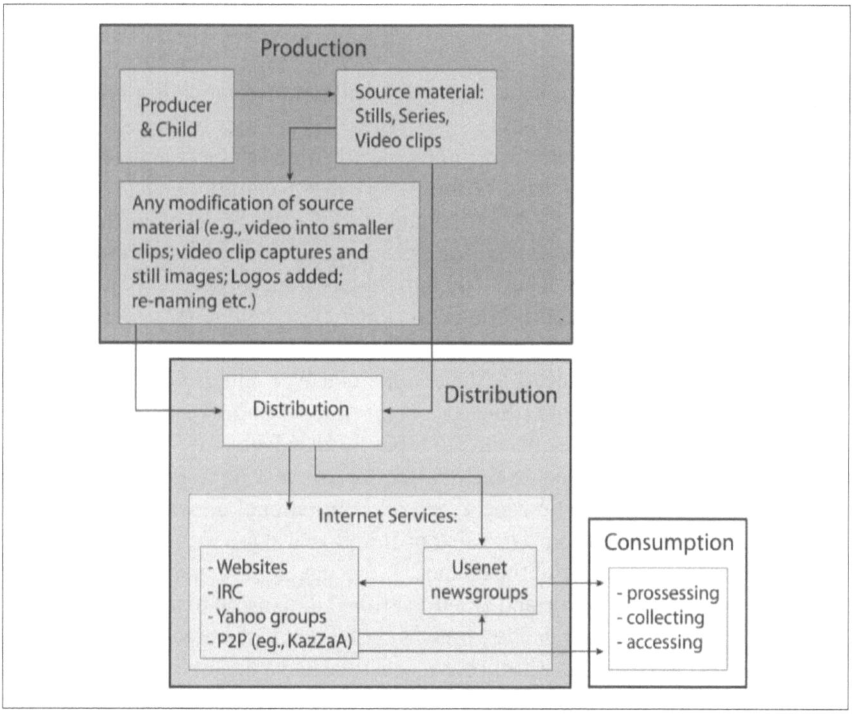

Figure 9.2 The production, distribution and consumption of child pornography

Similarly the Web host could be a legitimate company hosting tens of thousands of Web sites for tens of thousands of companies or individuals and may have no knowledge of the contents of any individual site (particularly if, as in the case of some sophisticated commercial child pornography Web operations, the child pornography is only on the host provider for hours or days before being moved to another host site). This generic model took slightly different forms in the real world. It was refined overtime in order to become more effective at profit generation and more resistant to takedown by law enforcement. I will present two case studies that illustrate different stages in its development.

'Commercial' Child Pornography: Case 1

The first case history we shall consider centres on a company called Landslide Productions. It is helpful to divide the analysis into the three phases of the investigation and prosecution: the first two phases involved what was called in the United States, Operation Avalanche. The third phase, targeting the consumers of child pornography internationally, involved a plurality of countries and went under many different names. The first phase of Operation Avalanche centered on the takedown of Landslide Productions and the laying of charges against the persons running the business, which Chief Postal Inspector Kenneth Weaver described as 'the shutdown of the largest known commercial child pornography enterprise in the history of the United States' (Press Conference, August 8, 2001), a description that continued to be echoed in newspapers and subsequent press releases. The second phase of the two-year-long, multi-agency Operation Avalanche was the arrest of 100 individuals (who were resident in the United States and subscribers to Landslide) for trafficking in child pornography through the mail and via the Internet. These 100 individuals were subsequently targeted in undercover operations including 'stings' in which these individuals received child pornography through the mail.

In the first phase, two aspects of the commercial Web enterprise were targeted: (a) Landslide Productions Inc., owned and operated by the Texas husband and wife, Thomas and Janice Reedy, and (b) three foreign Webmasters (on which we shall focus later). With respect to the distribution of child pornography there was both a United States domestic aspect, and an international dimension. Yet if the involvement of foreign Webmasters demonstrates that there was an international dimension to the supply side of the operation, it is equally imperative to recognize that there was both a domestic and an international dimension to the demand side. In important respects the Landslide case was significant in the broader sociological and criminological context precisely because it revealed a disturbing phenomenon: the relatively easy accessibility of child pornography via the Web seemed to make possible a world-wide market of thousands of consumers apparently willing to pay for images of child pornography. There is some justification to suppose that at that point in time (1999-2000), the widespread adoption of the World Wide Web was one of the primary factors that transformed the conditions of the accessibility of child pornography, broadening it wider than in it had been for two decades[16] and possibly returning this marginal market to the shape it had during the 1968-1980 period in which child pornography magazines were in circulation (perhaps even making it bigger, although further analysis would be required to prove that there was in fact a proportionate increase).

Although the size of this market was larger than many observers had imagined (numbering in the thousands instead of the hundreds), it should also not be overstated (it was not hundreds of thousands and it is orders of magnitude smaller than the millions of consumers who form the demand side for the legitimate and legal market for pornography). In order to avoid exaggeration from a social policy perspective and to help clarify some of the legal questions pertaining to jurisdiction it is necessary to look more closely at the nature of Landslide and its market. Landslide itself was a company that 'provided a computerized credit card verification service used by various webmasters whose websites contained adult and child pornography' (*United States v. Reedy*, 304 F.3d 358 (5th Circuit, 2002) at 362). Landslide offered the public a Web site that provided customers with a means of obtaining two main subscription services for which payment was made by the customers using their credit cards: the adult verification system ('AVS') and the 'KeyZ' system.

> AVS subscribers paid $19.95, which provided six months' access to all the websites under the AVS umbrella. The websites accessed through AVS offered adult pornography only.
>
> KeyZ subscribers purchased access to specific sites at $29.95 per month. Landslide retained a portion of the money collected, and the webmasters received the rest (*Reedy*, at 362).

---

16 The conditions of accessibility have a number of different parameters: the adult bookstores of the late sixties and early seventies had constraints on the point of purchase (that is, the customer had to travel physically to a certain neighbourhood, usually in a metropolitan area and be seen publicly entering the premises, rather than accessing a site via the *perceived anonymity* of a computer in the bedroom); as well as constraints on the distribution networks that the adult bookstore established with magazine wholesalers (with the attendant physical controls of goods by Customs agents). Although there are some parallels to the 'underground' mail order business of the Seventies and Eighties, the closest precedent to the World Wide Web is probably the small subset of adult computer bulletin board systems (BBSs) of the early 1990s which distributed some child pornography (mainly images of teenagers). A small number of these BBSs (for example, BAMSE BBS in Denmark, which also catered to bestiality and other extreme forms of pornography, or Amateur Action BBS in the United States) had roughly five thousand subscribers but, because they were accessed via modems over telephone lines, long distance charges were sufficiently high that the majority of their subscribers were at the national level and international subscribers numbered in the hundreds, not the thousands. See Sansom (2002).

Hence Landslide had two basic elements: a Web portal that offered a computerized verification system and acted the role of a payments provider through the customers' or subscribers' credit cards. Moreover, it is absolutely essential to distinguish between these two sets of subscribers, otherwise the number of people believed to be interested in child pornography is massively inflated. Conflation of the two services is, however, difficult to unravel: Landslide 'offered the AVS and KeyZ codes to 250,000 subscribers who could then access over 5,000 adult sites'. Although this references 5,000 adult sites, the largest number of child pornography sites cited in any of the court documents is 28 Web sites.[17] We do know that AVS subscribers accessed adult pornography the vast majority of which is not illegal. It is not clear whether all KeyZ subscribers were only accessing child pornography or only some KeyZ subscribers were accessing child pornography. If, as we shall see, there were 37,000 subscribers to child pornography in the United States, approximately 7,200 in the United Kingdom, and approximately 2,200 subscribers in Canada (giving a total of 46,400 subscribers as well as a much smaller number from other countries) it seems unlikely that the global total would exceed 100,000 subscribers – a significantly larger number simply would not correspond with computer-mediated pornography consumption patterns in general.[18]

It is true that Chief Postal Inspector Kenneth Weaver on August 8, 2001 stated that Landslide 'was a multi-million dollar enterprise', and continued: 'The vast majority of this money was from subscriptions to child pornography websites'. However, the 'vast majority' is not 'all'. William C. Walsh of the Dallas Police Department's Internet Crimes against Children (ICAC) Task Force who co-managed Operation Avalanche (along with Postal Inspector Ray Smith of the U.S. Postal Inspection Service) clearly distinguished between the income from adult pornography and the separate service for accessing child pornography. With respect to the child pornography service he stated: 'This service proved to be the greater source of income for Landslide' (see Walsh, 2002). The official press release at the time of sentencing makes one wonder whether there is still room for clarification: 'An investigator testified at trial that Thomas Reedy told him that Landslide

17 'In April 1999, United States Postal Inspector R.C. Adams contacted Detective Steve Nelson of the FBI's Crimes Against Children Task Force assigned to the Dallas Police Department's Child Exploitation Unit. Adams requested Nelson's aid in investigating an Internet website named 'kintamani.com,' which linked to another website named 'Lolita World.' Nelson agreed to access the website as part of an undercover investigation' (*United States v. Reedy*, 304 F.3d 358 (5th Circuit, 2002) at 361).

'Under the KeyZ system, Nelson found twenty-eight websites depicting child pornography. These websites included Lolita Hardcore/Fucking Little Kids, Blackcat Lolita, Children of God, Children Forced to Porn, Just Grow Up, Child Rape, Children Playground, Innocent Lolita, Fantastic Site, and Special Site' (*ibid* at 362).

18 Interestingly, one of the last references I found postulates such a figure: 'In July 2001, the husband and wife team who owned Landslide were sentenced to life imprisonment and 14 years respectively. Landslide's servers contained the names of around 100,000 people from more than 60 countries who had bought child pornography.' (Carr, 2002).

provided customers access to approximately 5,700 websites that offered a variety of pornography and that between 30 and 40 per cent of Landslide's business came from providing access to websites containing child pornography' (Press Release: U.S. Department of Justice, United States Attorney, Northern District of Texas, August 6, 2001). In fact, based on the Court of Appeal decision (August 26, 2002) citing the auditor's report, Landslide's profit for the two year period of September 1997 to August 1999 was $2,968,422. of which $1,290,422. was derived from the eleven child pornography Web sites named in the indictment of May 17, 2000. Note that this figure (which comes to 43.5 per cent of the profit) is not far from the voluntary statement given by Thomas Reedy as testified by the postal inspector at trial. This figure does not constitute the 'vast majority' but is in fact somewhat less than the majority.

The international aspect of the demand side of Landslide's business was addressed by a series of domestic law enforcement actions in multiple countries. In Canada it went under the name Operation Snowball (there were potentially 2,200 subscribers – between 50 and 100 persons were arrested). In the United Kingdom it was known as Operation Ore (there were potentially 7,200 subscribers of whom 1,300 had been arrested as of January 2003). In this regard, although Landslide provides an example of criminal activity on the World Wide Web that was international in scope, from the perspective of attacking the demand side (that is, the consumers) the domestic law enforcement operations did not really compromise or subvert the territorial principle and did not raise jurisdictional issues.[19] A proposition for further analysis is that it may be easier to address the territorial dispersal of the *instances* of crime (for example, multiple counts of possession in different jurisdictions)[20] as compared to the territorial dispersal of the *elements* of crime (that is, fragmenting distribution and compensation into multiple elements distributed across multiple agents in multiple countries).

Let us turn now to the issue of the three foreign Webmasters.[21] In one respect, their role raises the kinds of legal issues that have surfaced in other cases involving

---

19 The second case I will consider later in the paper (that is, RegPay) is, however, more complex and raises its own jurisdictional issues.

20 Multiplying the instances of crime is not problematic in circumstances where the crime is possession of child pornography, where the actor and the action are in proximity. Multiplying the instances of crime where the actor is geographically far removed from the crime may be more problematic from an enforcement standpoint.

21 The foreign nationals were charged by the Grand Jury (United States District Court for the Northern District of Texas, Fort Worth Division) with two counts of conspiracy associated with the distribution of child pornography (Count 1 and Count 45). For example, Count 45 is conspiracy 'to transport and cause to be transported in interstate and foreign commerce by various means, including by computer, visual depictions of child pornography'. In addition, there were a number of specific charges of distributing images of child pornography. The first set of charges were for violations of Title 18, *United States Code*, Sections 2252 and 2 and, for the same images, a set of charges for violations of Title 18, *United States Code*, Sections 2252A and 2: the defendant from Russia, Boris

'content crimes' on the Internet, for example, the challenges of prosecution when illegal content is hosted in a location outside the prosecuting country's jurisdiction. Consider, for example, cases involving the publication of obscenity: on a domestic level, existing laws could adapt through statutory interpretation or be adapted by amendment to the Internet in a fairly straightforward manner. In the United Kingdom, for example, the question of whether placing material on a Internet-accessible site constituted 'publication' was dealt with by the Appeals Court in *R. v. Fellows and Arnold*, [1997] 2 All ER 548.[22] Counsel for the accused submitted that 'publication' within section 1(3) of the *Obscene Publications Act*, requires some form of active conduct and that providing access to the Internet archive was 'passive' conduct only'. The Appeals Court ruled against this argument,[23] and thereby established that placing digital material on an fpt (File Transfer Protocol) archive constituted publication (a ruling that easily extends to other Internet forms of communication such as Websites). As far as the publication of obscenity was concerned, cases could be prosecuted where residents of the United Kingdom data stored on Internet-accessible computers located in the United Kingdom. In some cases, we can also see that jurisdiction may be extended beyond the borders, for example, when a resident the United Kingdom publishes illegal material on a server located in the United States. Although jurisdiction in such circumstances could perhaps be justified pursuant to the active nationality principle, in actual cases this has not been the legal rationale. For example, in *R. v. Waddon*, [2000] E.W.J. No. 2095, the defendant conceded that he was himself, or through his

---

Greenberg for 7 images from the site named 'Lolitas Land' (Counts 31 through 37 and Counts 75 through 81) and the defendants from Indonesia: R.W.Kusuma: for 5 images from the site named 'Fantastic Site' (Counts 26 through 30 and Counts 70 through 74) and Hanny Inggnata for 7 images from the site named 'Special Site' (Counts 38 through 44 and Counts 82 through 88).

22 'The *Obscene Publications Act 1959*, as amended in 1964, makes it an offence to publish an obscene article (s. 2(1)). Section 1 defines both 'article' and 'publishes' in terms which, for obvious reasons, do not provide expressly for the computer technology which was available to the first appellant in 1994. He contends therefore that his computer-based activities did not constitute an offence under the 1959 *Act*, as amended in 1964. Further amendments have been made to this *Act*, as to the 1978 *Act*, by the *Criminal Justice and Public Order Act* 1994, and it is unnecessary for present purposes to determine whether or not the amended wording could cover the present case' (*R. v. Fellows; R. v. Arnold*, [1997] 2 All ER 548).

23 The Court ruled that if some active conduct was necessary, there was evidence of such: 'it seems to us that there was ample evidence of such conduct on his part. He took whatever steps were necessary not merely to store the data on his computer but also to make it available worldwide to other computers via the internet. He corresponded by e-mail with those who sought to have access to it and he imposed certain conditions before they were permitted to do so. He gave permission by giving them the password. He did all of this with the sole object of allowing others, as well as himself, to view exact reproductions of the photographs stored in his archive.'

agents, involved in the transmission of pornographic material to a website in the United States and its transmission back again to England. In what appears to have been an *obiter dictum*, Rose L.J. ruled:

> As it seems to us, there can be publication on a Website abroad, when images are there uploaded; and there can be further publication when those images are downloaded elsewhere. That approach is, as it seems to us, underlined by the provisions of Section 1(3)(b), as to what is capable of giving rise to publication where matter has been electronically transmitted (para. 12).

Although this did not definitively establish United Kingdom law on whether publication extends to those cases where material is uploaded from the United Kingdom to a server in another jurisdiction, such as the United States,[24] the courts continued to rule in this direction. In the interesting case of *R. v. Perrin*, [2002] E.W.J. No. 1328, the accused, who was a director and/or majority shareholder of one or more US companies involved in operating a website from the United States, was charged and convicted of publishing 'obscene articles' (Web pages with pornographic images of coprophilia and coprophagia). The circumstances begin to show extension: pornographic material was accessed by a police officer in London, Perrin was a French citizen, and the Website was hosted in the United States. To the extent that the charges were contrary to section 2(1) of the *Obscene Publications Act*, the motivating question is once more whether the Website pages in these circumstances constituted a publication under English law. The Crown made no attempt to challenge the appellant's assertion that 'the major steps involved in publishing the Web page that resulted in his conviction were in a jurisdiction where the material published was lawful' (*Perrin*, para. 32). Indeed, the Appeals Court ruled quite forcefully: 'We reject the suggestion that it is ever necessary for the Crown to show where the major steps in relation to publication were taken' (*ibid.*, para. 52). As such it would appear that the location of the Web server did not matter as far as the Court was concerned[25] and, to the extent that Perrin happened to be residing in London at the time, the question

---

24 The court declined to rule upon what the position might be in relation to jurisdiction if a person storing material on a Website outside the United Kingdom intended that no transmission of that material should take place back to the United Kingdom. Rose L.J. said that the issues would 'no doubt … depend upon questions of intention and causation in relation to where publication should take place ...' (quoted in Hirst 2003, p. 189).

25 Hirst (2003, pp. 189-190) has respectfully suggested that the rejection of the steps involved in Internet publication in *R. v. Perrin* is problematic and follows from an insufficiently attentive reading of an *obiter dictum* in *R. v. Waddon* (2000) which, moreover, may have different fact circumstances. It should be noted that this objection arises in the context of U.K. case law and interpretation of the statute in question. Hirst (2003, p. 191) notes that child pornography in the United Kingdom falls under the *Protection of Children Act 1978*, and as such the legal construct of 'publication' would not be raised if the material were child pornography rather than obscenity.

at least remains open whether in the cases of both *Perrin* and *Waddon*, the act of publication is predicated to some degree on these persons having *uploaded material from England* to servers in the United States. The fact that the court in both cases also acknowledged that the receiving (downloading) of such material in England by a police officer constituted an act of publication puts matters on much more precarious footing, because essentially this would mean that if any citizen in any country placed material on a Website, located outside the United Kingdom, that contravened the laws of the United Kingdom, that person could be charged, for example, with the publication of obscenity. In the first decade of the new millennium, this approach to Websites outside a state's territory was taken not only for the publication of obscene material by the United Kingdom but in relation to Nazi and Holocaust revisionist material by both France[26] and Germany, and in relation to child pornography by the United States. For example, Frederick Toben, an Australian citizen residing in Australia, was charged in Germany for posting pro-Nazi and Holocaust revisionist material on a Website being hosted in Australia. Toben appealed the November 1999 lower court ruling (which had resulted in a sentence of ten months in prison), arguing that the Website located in Australia was not subject to German law. The appeal was heard by Germany's highest court, the *Bundesgerichthof*, which ruled in December 2000 that 'the laws prohibiting racial hatred clearly apply to Internet material created outside of Germany and stored on servers outside the country, but which is accessible to German Internet users'.[27]

In the latter half of the 1990s, similar questions regarding jurisdiction in Internet cases were being grappled with in the sphere of private law. In the United States, for example, the basis for personal jurisdiction had been established in *International Shoe Co. v. Washington* which determined that 'a court can exercise jurisdiction over a non-resident defendant if that defendant 'has certain

26 In this regard attention is drawn to the Yahoo! Case concerning Internet access to auctions of Nazi memorabilia in France. The case is quite complex. It began with a case in France, *Ligue contre la racisme et l'antisemitisme et Union des étudiants juifs de France c. Yahoo! Inc. et Société Yahoo! France* (*LICRA v. Yahoo!*), concerning actions ultimately ruled contrary to Article R645-2 of the French Criminal Code. The French court rendered an interim judgement (*LICRA et UEJF c. Yahoo! Inc and Yahoo France, Tribunal de Grande Instance de Paris* (Superior Court of Paris)), on May 22, 2000 ruling Yahoo!'s activities contravened French law. Following another order on August 11, 2000, a team of experts was convened by the court and an injunction rendered on November 20, 2000. Yahoo! brought a case to trial in the United States District Court for the Northern District of California, San Jose: *Yahoo! Inc. v. La Ligue contre le racisme et l'antisemitisme*, 145 F. Supp. 2d 1168 (2001), which ruled that the French action was inconsistent with the First Amendment to the Constitution of the United States. LICRA and UEJF appealed the decision and the U.S. Court of Appeals for the Ninth Circuit, reversed the ruling on August 23, 2004. The United States Court of Appeals from the Ninth Circuit rendered a lengthy decision on January 12, 2006.

27 Gold (2000).

minimum contacts with [the forum] such that the maintenance of the suit does not offend traditional notions of fair play and substantial justice".[28] In 1996, a decision regarding personal jurisdiction was rendered in an important trademark infringement case, *Inset Systems, Inc. v. Instruction Set, Inc.,* in which the latter Massachusetts company (ISI) established a Website in its home state using the domain name 'Inset.com', which the Connecticut-based Inset Systems, Inc. claimed was a trademark infringement. The court decided that a Website was akin to a continuous advertisement directed to every state and hence the exercise of long-arm jurisdiction by the state was proper, the minimum contacts test was met, and the Connecticut venue was appropriate.[29] This decision followed the type of reasoning underlying criminal law cases such as *Perrin* and *Waddon* in the United Kingdom or *Toben* in Germany. Yet within the legal study of personal jurisdiction, debate begins to mount because it seemed potentially problematic to conclude that merely uploading information to a Website constituted the purposeful availment of every jurisdiction, such that every court, everywhere, could assert jurisdiction.

The core of the Landslide case regarding the three foreign Webmasters role is summarized in the U.S. Department of Justice press release:

> Along with the Reedys, foreign webmasters, R.W. Kusuma and Hanny Ingganata of Indonesia and Boris Greenberg of Russia, were charged with Sexual Exploitation of Minors and Distribution of Child Pornography in the April 2000 indictment. Warrants have been issued for their arrest and the United States will seek extradition. These webmasters designed, launched and maintained websites that offered pictures and movies of minors engaging in sexually explicit conduct.
>
> … Testimony at trial revealed that between 1997 and 1998, Landslide netted more than $1 million and the Reedy's paid Kusuma, Ingganata and Greenberg approximately two-thirds of the money they collected. (Press Release: U.S. Department of Justice, United States Attorney, Northern District of Texas, August 6, 2001)

---

28 Geist (2001), quoting *International Shoe Co. v. Washington,* 326 U.S. 310 (1945).

29 'In the present case, Instruction has directed its advertising activities via the Internet and its toll-free number toward not only the state of Connecticut, but to all states. The Internet as well as toll-free numbers are designed to communicate with people and their businesses in every state. Advertisement on the Internet can reach as many as 10,000 Internet users within Connecticut alone. Further, once posted on the Internet, unlike television and radio advertising, the advertisement is available continuously to any Internet user. ISI has therefore, purposefully availed itself of the privilege of doing business within Connecticut. The court concludes that since ISI purposefully directed its advertising activities toward this state on a continuing basis since March, 1995, it could reasonably anticipate the possibility of being hailed into court here' (*Inset Systems, Inc. v. Instruction Set, Inc.,* 1996).

From a criminological perspective the situation highlights a familiar pattern in commercial child pornography: it appears to be an attempt to bypass jurisdiction by compromising the territoriality principle. It is common in the past six years to find that the Webmasters who control the commercial trade in child pornography, as well as designing and maintaining the Websites, are located outside 'first world' countries.[30]

It is apparent that the United States exercised extra-territorial jurisdiction with respect to charging the foreign Webmasters. Unlike *R v. Perrin* and the other U.K. obscenity cases considered above, the accused were not resident in the jurisdiction laying the charges. Significant questions of international law can be raised in light of the fact that there were conflicting domestic laws among the jurisdictions concerned: arguably, there was no crime committed in the jurisdictions where Kusuma, Ingganata and Greenberg were resident. For example, it is important to recognize that, at the time,[31] the Russian Federation's law did not have a concept of 'child pornography', nor was pornography as such qualified as relating to children in any way (a circumstance not ameliorated by age of consent provisions also in force prior to 2003). In addition, the pornography offence was punishable by fairly mild sanctions, ranging from fines to a maximum of two years imprisonment, which may have fallen below the threshold for extradition (see specifically Article 241 of the *Criminal Code of the Russian Federation*; Tjurjukanova *et al.*, 2003). Similarly, with respect to Indonesia:

> The *Criminal Code* does not specifically address child pornography. The *Child Protection Act* also lacks criminal offences on child pornography. Thus, there is no legal definition of child pornography in Indonesia. The *Child Protection Act* contains no provisions related to distributing and possessing child pornography (Arna and Bryneson, 2004, p. 33).[32]

30 Much of the child pornography could be produced in other jurisdiction for a variety of reasons, some of which may be due to legal regimes but also due to poverty, the relative level of human rights conditions, or the lack of policing.

31 On December 8, 2003 the Russian Federation introduced Federal Law No. 162 which, among other things, modified Article 242 into a provision to specifically address the production and distribution of child pornography by prohibiting the use of children in the manufacture of pornographic products. The new amendments also raised the age of consent and increased penalties from two years to a maximum of six years.

32 Criminal Code of Indonesia (Ch. XIV, Art. 282) 'includes offences on dealing in indecent material'. While it does not define what constitutes 'indecent', any material with child pornographic images would likely be within the scope of the provisions when such material contains nudity. The general prohibition covers indecent material in the form of writings, portraits or objects. As the provision was enacted long before the advent of modern forms of communications, there are no provisions concerning videotapes, audiotapes, or digital media, and it is uncertain whether this law applies to indecent material distributed or contained in such media. The law prohibits producing, disseminating, distributing, storing,

In extradition cases, many jurisdictions require dual criminality. In this regard, one of the most significant issues is that one could argue that neither the Russian Federation nor Indonesia had a domestic offence that was equivalent to the United States' provisions pertaining to the distribution of child pornography over the Internet and conspiracy to distribute child pornography. Even more problematic from a practical standpoint is the fact that Indonesia is one of the countries with which the United States does not have an extradition treaty. Ultimately, it appears that the Indonesian and Russian Webmasters were never brought to trial.

'Commercial' Child Pornography: Case 2

The indictment of Regpay Co. Ltd. and related defendants on January 15, 2004 by the United States District Court for New Jersey, reveals the evolving face of commercial child pornography. The RegPay case is similar in many respects to the Landslide case but raises even more acutely questions of the extraterritorial application of law not least because the principal defendants, rather than being residents of the United States, were citizens of Belarus (a country with whom the United States does not have an extradition treaty), and the defendants were lured[33] to and subsequently captured in jurisdictions (France and Spain) with which the United States had extradition treaties. At the core of the case one finds the familiar building blocks of transnational, Web-based, pay-per-view child pornography. As with Landslide there is a Web portal (in this case www.redlagoon.com) which provided access to a number of child pornography sites and a subscription or membership system. There is also a payment system underlying this operation; this was, however, far more sophisticated than that in Landslide and bears a strong resemblance to the complex payment systems associated with those forms of

---

importing or exporting indecent material; displaying indecent material in public; or offering such material for sale' (Arna and Bryneson, 2004, p. 34).

33 The extraterritorial projection of state power draws attention to factors both of fairness toward the individuals impacted and of comity between the sovereign states implicated. The potentially controversial law enforcement tactic of luring targets from one jurisdiction where they cannot be prosecuted into another jurisdiction where they can be prosecuted (or from which they can be extradited), was also employed in the case of Alexey Ivanov and Vasiliy Gorshkov of Chelyabinsk, Russia (See http://www.cybercrime.gov/gorshkovSent.htm). The Russian computer hackers were enticed into U.S. territory in November 2000 to be hired for lucrative positions at a computer security start-up company, Invita, which was actually a front created for the FBI sting. In response, Russia's Federal Security Service (the FSB) filed criminal charges in August 2002 against Michael Schuler, the 'FBI agent it says lured two Russian hackers to the United States, then illegally seized evidence against them by downloading data from their computers in Chelyabinsk, Russia'. See http://www.msnbc.msn.com/id/3078784/.

computer-related crime that feed profit-motivated transnational organized crime. Not surprisingly, money-laundering charges were also laid by the United States.[34]

American authorities first encountered the activities associated with this illicit enterprise under the name Trustbill. Bryan-Low reported in *The Wall Street Journal* that Trustbill 'changed its name to Regpay after receiving two cease-and-desist notices from the Michigan attorney general's office in August and September 2002, according to an affidavit by Internal Revenue Service agent Maria Reverendo attached to a July 2003 complaint against Messrs. Zalatarou and Boika' (Bryan-Low, 2006). The principal parties associated with RegPay Co. Ltd. (located in Minsk, Belarus) were all residents of Belarus: Yahor Zalatarou (age 25, president of RegPay), Aliaksandr Boika (age 29, RegPay's technical administrator), Alexei Buchnev (age 26, RegPay's marketing director) and Tatsiana Sienko (age 25, RegPay's administrative and financial assistant). United States Attorney, Christopher J. Christie (2006) testified before a U.S. Senate Subcommittee that in early 2003 that:

> federal agents made undercover purchases of monthly subscriptions to numerous child pornography websites in an effort to track down the producers of the material and the operators of the sites. The investigation revealed that a company based in Belarus, which called itself RegPay, operated several commercial child pornography websites and processed credit card fees for more than 50 other similar sites. The investigation also determined that credit card payments for access to these sites were being processed through a company based in Ft. Lauderdale, Florida known as Connections, USA. Agents also executed search warrants on computer servers in Texas and Virginia that RegPay had leased, and

34 The United States laid charges pertaining to a money laundering conspiracy involving RegPay and Connections USA, Inc., a credit card processing company based in Ft. Lauderdale, Florida which provided internet billing services to RegPay: 'It was part of the conspiracy that defendants YAHOR ZALATAROU, ALIAKSANDR BOIKA, ALEXEI BUCHNEV, TATSIANA SIENKO, and REGPAY CO LTD., obtained the services of defendant CONNECTIONS USA, INC., in order to process credit card transactions for the sale of memberships to websites containing child pornography as described in Counts Three through Eight. In this manner, defendants were able to conceal their involvement in these transactions from the major credit card associations. Defendant Connections received a commission in excess of eleven percent of the funds received from this scheme.' (*United States of America v. Yahor Zalatarou and others*, Count 9, para. 6)

The effort to hide the money trail has been described by Bryan-Low (2006): 'Connections, which had a legal business in online and telephone dating services, had signed up as a merchant in credit-card networks … The money was transferred from a Morgan Stanley account – apparently the business account for Connections – to a Deutsche Bank AG account and from there to Aizkraukles Bank in Riga, Latvia, according to the IRS agent's affidavit … Regpay also used another U.S. company, LB Systems Inc. run by a Belarussian man living in Los Angeles, to transfer funds to a Regpay account in Latvia, according to the indictments'.

> recovered extensive databases documenting credit card transactions involving approximately 90,000 customers worldwide.[35]

As noted, the United States does not have an extradition treaty with Belarus and consequently, American authorities mounted an undercover operation to lure the principals outside their country. As United States Attorney Christie (2006) testified:

> To pursue the operators of RegPay, agents first executed a search warrant at Connections, USA in Ft. Lauderdale. Upon executing the search warrant, agents learned of an ongoing financial dispute between Connections USA and the operators of RegPay relating to an outstanding debt of more than one million dollars supposedly owed to RegPay. Agents were able to assume the role of Connections USA to broker a meeting in Paris between the operators of RegPay and Connections USA, ostensibly to resolve the ongoing dispute and to set the groundwork for future financial cooperation between the companies.

The undercover operation led to the arrest and extradition of the RegPay principals.[36]

Pursuing justice through the exercise of criminal law in a case such as this is evidently predicated on a demonstrable threat to the public good. The parties upholding the administration of justice in the United States must have made a determination that the actions of the principals located in Belarus, ultimately constituted a threat to children in the United States brought about through the distribution of child pornography. Consequently, although the customers who

---

35 According to Laura H. Parsky (2006), Deputy Assistant Attorney General: 'The Regpay investigation spawned the U.S. Immigration and Customs Enforcement's Operation Falcon, an international child pornography trafficking investigation that so far has resulted in 448 open investigations, 130 search warrants in the U.S., 191 domestic and approximately 767 foreign arrests (in Australia, Denmark, Finland, Hong Kong, Liechtenstein, Netherlands, Norway, Scotland, Sweden, Switzerland, and the United Kingdom), and 47 domestic indictments, generating 14 convictions'. The law enforcement operations directed at child pornography subscribers (the demand side of the market) such as Operation Auxin in Australia – are similar to earlier operations such as those stemming from the Landslide case and generally do not raise jurisdictional issues.

36 As *The Wall Street Journal* reported: 'Posing as Mr. Levinson, federal agents began communicating with Mr. Zalatarou, the Regpay president, and others at the company via email and phone about payment arrangements … An agent met with Mr. Zalatarou and Mr. Buchnev, the translator, at the restaurant of the Hotel Concorde La Fayette in Paris on July 30, 2003. Following the meeting, French police arrested the two men in the hotel's lobby. Two days later, Interpol officers arrested Mr. Boika, the Regpay software expert, at a hotel [in Tarragona] on the northeast coast of Spain, where he was on vacation with his wife. Spain and France have since extradited the three men to the United States' (Bryan-Low, 2006).

accessed child pornography were located throughout the world, it is significant that almost half were from the United States and, of these, a certain portion were from the state of New Jersey, where the trial was being held.[37]

We noted earlier that in the area of private law, the latter half of the 1990s revealed an increasing sensitivity in North America and elsewhere to find reasonable tests to establish jurisdiction. The most widely analyzed of these cases was the *Zippo* test (Geist, 2001; Dauterman, 2002; Greenstein, 2007) which appeared to provide a more nuanced way to understand Internet-mediated communications than the uncontrollably ubiquitous approach of the 1996 *Inset* decision. In *Zippo Manufacturing Co. v. Zippo Dot Com, Inc.*, 952 F. Supp. 1119 (W.D. Pa., 1997), the court identified a sliding scale for websites going from passive to active:

> At one end of the spectrum are situations where a defendant clearly does business over the Internet. If the defendant enters into contracts with residents of a foreign jurisdiction that involve the knowing and repeated transmission of computer files over the Internet, personal jurisdiction is proper. At the opposite end are situations where a defendant has simply posted information on an Internet Web site, which is accessible to users in foreign jurisdictions. A passive Web site that does little more than make information available to those who are interested in it is not grounds for the exercise of personal jurisdiction. The middle ground is occupied by interactive Web sites where a user can exchange information with the host computer. In these cases, the exercise of jurisdiction is determined by examining the level of interactivity and commercial nature of the exchange of information that occurs on the Web site (at 1124).

Although a test determining the appropriateness of jurisdiction based on a Website's degree of activity (from passive to active) put into question the one-dimensional assumption that the mere existence of a Website entailed global consequences stemming from the purported global accessibility of the material, the degree of 'interactivity' has proven not to be the most appropriate metric (Geist, 2001; Paterson, 2004; Spencer, 2006).[38] As the 1990s ended and the new millennium dawned, the *Zippo* 'sliding scale' approach was supplemented with additional considerations, ultimately forming a body of legal reasoning referred to as 'targeting-based analysis'. For example, a federal appeals court addressed the issue of personal jurisdiction in *Cybersell, Inc. v. Cybersell, Inc.*, 130 F.3d 414

37 Bryan-Low (2006) reported: 'The probe has discovered the names of some 40,000 Americans who downloaded child porn and led to more than 1,400 arrests world-wide including about 330 in the U.S. At least three users arrested in the U.S. have committed suicide.'

38 Although there have been criticisms directed at the *Zippo* decision on the grounds that it is not technology-neutral these may be overstated, particularly to the degree that similar lines of argument can be found in *Burger King Corp. v. Rudzewicz*, 471, U.S. 462 (1985).

(9th Circuit, 1997), noted that the defendant's Website was essentially passive but clarified that what was relevant regarding the lack of activity was that the court could not 'see how from that fact alone it can be inferred that [the defendant] deliberately directed its merchandising efforts toward [forum] residents' (at 419). Further clarification was provided in a Fourth Circuit decision, *ALS Scan, Inc. v. Digital Service Consultants, Inc.*, 293 F.3d 707 (4th Circuit, 2002), which underscored that *Zippo* model had to be adapted:

> [A] State may, consistent with due process, exercise judicial power over a person outside of the State when that person (1) directs electronic activity into the State, (2) with the manifested intent of engaging in business or other interactions within the State, and (3) that activity creates, in a person within the State, a potential cause of action cognizable in the State's courts (at 714).

The indictment in the RegPay case emphasized a number of elements which are consistent with targeting-based analysis. The indictment, while confirming that the company was not American and that the individuals controlling the portal site were neither citizens of nor residents in the United States, nonetheless contended that constituent elements of the offences were based in the United States, a line of argument which is consistent with the territoriality principle, particularly in transborder criminal cases. First, the Redlagoon Web portal, which advertised the sale of memberships to Websites containing child pornography, was evidently hosted in the United States.[39] Second, the billing service used by the defendants stored transaction records for the consumers of child pornography in databases hosted in the United States.[40] Third, some of the child pornography Web sites

---

39 'It was part of the conspiracy that defendants YAHOR ZALATAROU, ALIAKSANDR BOIKA, REGPAY CO LTD., and others, used the services of computer hosting companies located in the United States to maintain the Redlagoon website enabling individuals located in New Jersey, the United States and throughout the world to obtain access to the website over the internet … It was further part of the conspiracy that defendants … maintained and operated the Redlagoon website remotely from Belarus and other locations outside the United States.' (*United States of America v. Yahor Zalatarou and others*, Count 1, paragraphs 6 and 8)

40 'It was part of the conspiracy that defendants YAHOR ZALATAROU, ALIAKSANDR BOIKA, ALEXEI BUCHNEV, TATSIANA SIENKO, REGPAY CO LTD., and others, provided billing services for individuals and/or companies offering over the internet access to over fifty (50) websites containing child pornography. Access to each of these websites was available to individuals purchasing a membership to the site. In this manner the defendants obtained personal information from individuals located in New Jersey, the United States and throughout the world, seeking to purchase access to these websites with a credit card. It was further part of the conspiracy that after obtaining personal and credit card information from prospective customers … [the defendants] ran a series of internal checks on the credit card before approving the transaction. If a transaction was approved, the defendants sent the purchaser an e-mail containing among other information,

were hosted in the United States, even though these were maintained and operated remotely from Belarus.[41] These elements demonstrate that although the principals were located abroad, Regpay manifested the intent of engaging in business or other interactions within the United States, and as such, American jurisdiction was proper.[42]

Uncontrollably Ubiquitous Communication and the Universal Principle: Questions of Limits

The view that any Website with 'illegal content' is an example of uncontrollably ubiquitous global communication that could effect harm in any state and thereby satisfy the jurisdictional tests of any state, seemed to underlie certain cases in the past decade pertaining to child pornography, the publication of obscenity and hate crime in countries such as the United Kingdom, France, Germany and the United States. In the area of private law in North America, although the presumption of uncontrollably ubiquitous communication appeared in the mid-1990s it was to some degree superseded by tests which determined jurisdiction according to 'target-based analysis'.

---

a password and user name enabling the customer to access the website containing child pornography for a specified period of time. It was a further part of the conspiracy that … [the defendants] used the services of computer hosting companies in the United States to maintain a database of transactional information regarding the above described purchases. These computers were also used to send the above described e-mail notices to individuals purchasing access to the websites containing child pornography' (*United States of America v. Yahor Zalatarou and others*, Count 2, paragraphs 5-7).

41 'It was part of the conspiracy that defendants YAHOR ZALATAROU, ALIAKSANDR BOIKA, REGPAY CO LTD., and others, maintained and operated at least four websites containing child pornography which were available over the internet to individuals located in New Jersey, the United States and throughout the world. These websites included www.darkfeeling.com, www.lust-gallery.com, www.lolittles.com, and wwww.veiledpages.com (hereinafter the 'Regpay websites'). It was a further part of the conspiracy that … [the defendants] used the services of computer hosting companies located in the United States to maintain the Regpay websites enabling throughout New Jersey, the United States, and foreign countries to obtain access to them over the Internet. It was further part of the conspiracy that … [the defendants] maintained and operated the Regpay websites remotely from Belarus and other locations outside of the United States' (*United States of America v. Yahor Zalatarou and others*, Count 2, paragraphs 8-10).

42 In other words, the indictment sought to establish, what in Canadian criminal context associated with transborder cases was a 'real and substantial link' between the offence and the forum state (*R. v. Libman*).

There are a number of technological considerations regarding websites that put into question the presumption of uncontrollably ubiquitous communication. Simply publishing a Website does not entail that anyone beyond its creator knows the content is available, does not ensure that anyone will visit the site, and certainly does not guarantee that anyone from a specific state will visit the site in a manner that constitutes harm. Some authors regard the progeny of *Zippo* and subsequent target-based analysis as constituting a legal wrong-turn and revert to the view that 'unrestricted Web publishing knowingly and immediately pushes material to computers in every state' (Spencer, 2006, p. 96): such a position is not only overstated it is outright false. Although the World Wide Web is in some respects a web, not all the strands are equal – some are major, some are minor, and others are so intermittent as to be almost invisible. Some strands are highly interconnected to major thoroughfares and others are dusty paths leading to cul-de-sacs; some do not connect to the core Web at all (Broder *et al.*, 2000).

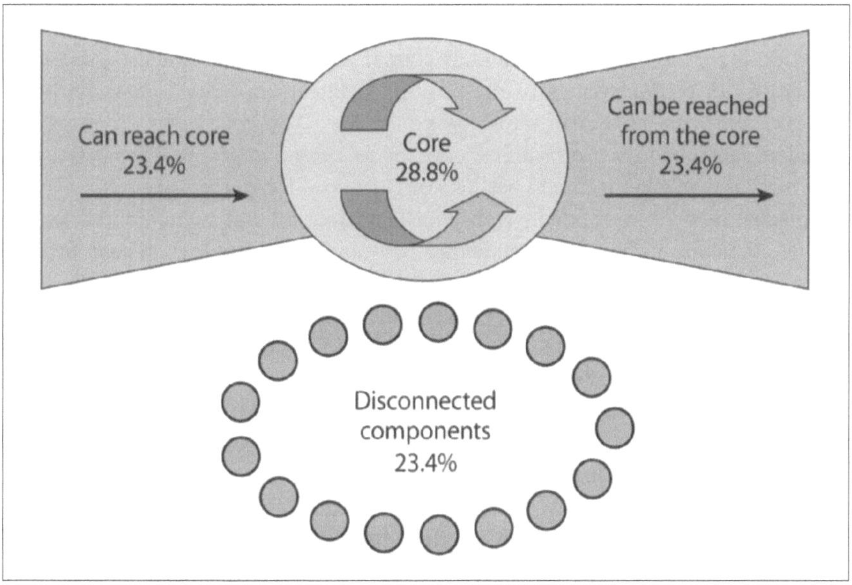

Figure 9.3 Bow-tie shape of the web
Source: Levene and Poulovassilis (2001); Broder *et al.* (2000).

Studies of the shape or topology of the World Wide Web by Broder *et al.* (2000) revealed that the core of the Web (about 56 million nodes of their sample, or just under 30 per cent) was highly interconnected, meaning there was a directed path from any node in the core to any other node in the core. The left bow of the Web (about 23 per cent of the Web) was made up of Web pages that could reach the core via a directed path but could not themselves be reached by pages in the core. The right-hand bow (also about 23 per cent) can be reached from the core by a directed path but cannot themselves reach the core. Finally, the remaining 23 per cent cannot be reached from bulk of the Web (the bow-tie) via a directed or undirected path – these sites are essentially disconnected from the Web – isolated archipelagos, tiny islands of data. It has also been reported that 75 per cent of the time there is no directed path from one random Web page to another random Web page (Levene and Poulovassilis, 2001, p. 3). Thus there are serious grounds to believe that the presumption of uncontrollably ubiquitous communication is not supported by scientific evidence. Moreover, other studies have demonstrated that from a geopolitical perspective the Web is highly heterogeneous in its connectivity: some countries have high densities of Web sites and hyperlinks and other countries not only have few sites and few hyperlinks but are significantly less connected to the Web (Brunn and Dodge, 2001). Webspace is, to some degree, influenced by the underlying conditions of the infrastructure, as evidenced by the 'digital divide' (Sciadas, 2003) – which manifests through the characteristics of the host provider in terms of geographic location in the 'real' world, the provider's connectivity (to whom do the telecommunications lines connect upstream and downstream), and the bandwidth characteristics of the provider's lines (how much data can flow, how fast, and with what error rates). Not only does Webspace have a topography that adapts and changes to a significant degree according to the interconnections of hypermedia itself (that is, the hyperlinks or Universal Resource Locators, URLS), the 'reachability' of any node in Webspace is profoundly influenced by the search engines, their algorithms, their indexing bots and their rankings. These factors undermine the presumption of uncontrollably ubiquitous communication.

Although the mere publication of a Web site in one state should not automatically expose it to liability in any state, the inverse should not be automatically assumed (as it was in some post-*Zippo* cases in private law): simply because a Web site is 'passive' and not located in the forum state, it should not automatically be exempted from jurisdiction. For example, would it be reasonable to conclude that some forms of content are so heinous that any state could choose to exert jurisdiction extra-territorially by invoking the universal principle? Normally, invocation of the universal principle is restricted to crimes against humanity such as genocide. Could one argue that there is a class of expression that falls within this ambit? Some might contend that child pornography offences could be a potential candidate, citing as justification the United Nations *Optional Protocol to the Convention on the Rights of the Child on the sale of children, child prostitution, and child pornography* (adopted May 25, 2000; entered into force January 18, 2002). 'Content crimes', however, must be weighed in the balance against rights to freedom of expression. Many states have constitutional protections for freedom of expression and, at the international level, there are guarantees of freedom of expression embodied in the United Nations *Universal Declaration of Human Rights* (UDHR, 1948), the *Convention on the Elimination of all Forms of Racial Discrimination* (the Discrimination Convention; 1965), and the *International*

Covenant on Civil and Political Rights (ICCPR; 1966). It is evident, however, that legal constraints such as 'obscenity', despite the redefining of censorship practices in the latter half of the twentieth century, differ from state to state even among Western liberal democracies.

The other major class of 'content crime', hate speech (xenophobia and racist material), appears to be so deeply imbricated in the cultural and historical experiences of specific regions or nations (for example, contrast the United States and Germany) that attempts to formulate and apply a universal principle seem unlikely in the foreseeable future. If the tension between freedom of expression and classes of communication such as hate speech cannot be resolved in the same manner in all jurisdictions (even, for example, within the context of those states that have ratified the Council of Europe *Convention on Cybercrime* but are unable to sign or ratify the *Additional Protocol*), does that mean that too much weight has been accorded to freedom of expression? Although such pronouncements have been enlisted occasionally in rhetorical strategies, they do not reflect the pragmatic realities of the practice of international law. A systematic review of the cases[43] does not necessarily dissuade one from concluding along with Dauterman (2002, p. 218) that 'International declarations and covenants such as the UDHR, the Discrimination Convention and the ICCPR which deal with freedom of expression issues essentially give state actors a blank check to curtail freedom of expression'.

Conclusion

It has been stated that the ambit of criminal law is fundamentally, although not exclusively, predicated on the notion of *territoriality* which is a legal concept of space consonant with geopolitical space. We have demonstrated that computer-based, transnational organized crime is characterized by two governing strategies: (1) increasing fragmentation and specialization of the criminal activity; and (2) territorial dispersal of the elements of crime. From our review of case law we have seen that these criminal strategies are ultimately directed at undermining investigation and frustrating prosecution not simply by dispersing the elements of the crime across multiple geopolitical territories but also by creating displacements

43 Dauterman (2002, p. 217) notes specifically that '... the UDHR, the Discrimination Convention, and the ICCPR place few, if any, restrictions on states to curtail individual freedom of expression in cases of pornography and hate speech. The margin of discretion standard expounded by the HRC in *Hertzberg and Others v. Finland* is so deferential to state authority that states can censor almost any kind of communications that they label to be pornographic. Likewise in the case of hate speech, the UDHR's public safety, morals and general welfare exception plus the HRC's holdings in cases like *M.A. v. Italy* and *J.R.T. and W.G. Party v. Canada*, proves that hate speech is outside the realm of expression to be protected by these international agreements.'

or slippages between different spaces (for example, between IP space and domain name space using dynamic DNS).[44] Interestingly, many of the criminal strategies have not frustrated jurisdiction as such, for we have seen a willingness by various states to exert jurisdiction, particularly in the area of 'content crimes' (as opposed to crimes against the confidentiality, integrity, or availability of computer systems and data).[45] Yet we have seen that the underlying technology may put into question the legitimacy of asserting jurisdiction over Websites located in other countries when jurisdiction is predicated on the presumption of uncontrollably ubiquitous communication. This does not mean that jurisdiction cannot be asserted at all – in some cases, such as the distribution of child pornography, it may be reasonable to invoke the universal principle (although the latter may not be suitable for other 'content crimes' such as obscenity or hate speech[46] which may be more culturally

44 One of the 'next generation' strategies for organized criminals seeking to profit from commercial child pornography was the deployment of websites with transitory hosting which exploits *dynamic DNS*, that is the fact that the domain name can remain the same but a dynamic DNS service provider permits one to change rapidly and repeatedly the IP address in the DNS record. This simple change, however, has profound consequences: the IP address which pointed to a host server physically located in one country is replaced with an IP address that points to a different host server located in another country. The Webmaster simply leases Web space from a new hosting company, then uploads the Web pages and digital data to the new host. When everything is ready on this second host, the DNS entry is changed, and the Web address now points to the second host rather than the previous host. From the point of view of the subscribing customers, nothing has changed: they continue to type the same URL into the browser and everything looks exactly the same on their computer screen. The tactic, however, would appear to violate jurisdiction based on the principle of territoriality: the child pornography that was hosted in one country is now hosted in another country … and the following week it could be in a third country. This tactic also thwarts routine responses such as IP-blocking (designed to disrupt access to child pornography) and makes legal takedowns of the Web sites potentially trivial interruptions or even ineffective altogether.

45 In the area of computer-based economic crime, crimes arising from the use of botnets (networks of compromised computers that are used to commit acts such as identity theft, click-fraud, and so on) infringe upon the spirit of criminal law by being a unique adaptation that instantiates a paradox of surplus and deficiency. Although one could remark that botnet crimes constitute a violation of territoriality because they are transnational and offer themselves up to a plurality of nation states to exert their jurisdiction, it is more significant that this *very surplus of jurisdictional possibilities* is undermined by *the deficiency or poverty of the constituent crime itself*: the botnet is established by hundreds or thousands of low-level criminal acts that flit across the sovereign state like a cloud of flies, ignored by maintaining an existence beneath the threshold of significance and hence below any serious response.

46 Consider the difference of positions between Germany and Iran: for example, on December 11, 2006, President Mahmoud Ahmadinejad of Iran opened a two-day conference explicitly intended to put into question the 'official version' of the Holocaust. The conference featured speeches by such Westerners as former Ku Klux Klan leader David

specific). In some criminal cases, it may be appropriate to establish jurisdiction by pursuing the kind of 'target-based analysis' that has developed in the area of private law in North America in the past decade. Principles of law, however, should be developed and articulated for computer-related crimes that have extra-territorial dimensions lest we collapse into the principle of convenience, where law reverts to expediency becoming merely the will to exercise power coupled with the resource capacity to sustain the long arm of the law.

References

Abad, Christopher (2005). 'The Economy of Phishing: A Survey of the Operations of the Phishing Market', *First Monday*, **10**(9), at: http://firstmonday.org/issues/issue10_9/abad/index.html.

Arna, Antarini and Mattias Bryneson (2004). *Report on Laws and Legal Procedures Concerning the Commercial Sexual Exploitation of Children in Indonesia*, Bangkok: ECPAT International.

Binational Working Group on Cross-Border Mass Marketing Fraud (2006). *Report on Phishing: A Report to the Minister of Public Safety and Emergency Preparedness Canada and the Attorney General of the United States*, at: http://www.psepc-sppcc.gc.ca/prg/le/_fl/Phishing%20for%20CBCF%202006-en.pdf.

Broder, Andrei, Ravi Kumar, Farzin Maghoul, Prabhakar Raghavan, Sridhar Rajagopalan, Raymie Stata, Andrew Tomkins and Janet Wiener (2000). 'Graph Structure in the Web', Paper presented at the Ninth International World Wide Web Conference, Amsterdam, at: http://www9.org/w9cdrom/160/160.html.

Brunker, Mike (2002). 'FBI agent charged with hacking', *MSNBC News*, 15 August, at: http://www.msnbc.msn.com/id/3078784/.

Brunn, Stanley D. and Martin Dodge (2001). 'Mapping the "Worlds" of the World Wide Web: (Re)Structuring Global Commerce through Hyperlinks', *American Behavioural Scientist*, **44**(10): 1717–1739.

Bryan-Low, Cassell (2006). 'Dangerous Mix: Internet Transforms Child Porn into Lucrative Criminal Trade', *The Wall Street Journal*, 17 January, A1.

Carr, John (2002). 'A force to be reckoned with', *GuardianUnlimited*, 12 November, at: http://www.guardian.co.uk/technology/2002/nov/12/childrensservices.crime.

Christie, Christopher J. (2006). *Sexual Exploitation of Children over the Internet*, Statement before the Committee on Energy and Commerce Subcommittee on Oversight and Investigation, 10 July at: http://energycommerce.house.gov/reparchives/108/hearings/07102006hearing1973/christie.pdf.

Duke, Frederick Toben, who had been incarcerated under German law for his Australian Holocaust revisionist Website, and Robert Faurisson (who has been convicted five times in France for Holocaust-related denials). http://abcnews.go.com/International/WireStory?id=2715610&page=1.

Council of Europe (2001). *Convention on Cybercrime*, at: http://conventions.coe.int/Treaty/EN/Treaties/Html/185.htm.

Cooperative Association for Internet Data Analysis (2001). *Animated gif of geographic spread of Code-Red worm*, at: http://www.caida.org/research/security/code-red/newframes-small-log.gif.

Cooperative Association for Internet Data Analysis (2007). *CAIDA Analysis of Code-Red*, at: http://www.caida.org/research/security/code-red/.

Dauterman, Walter C. (2002). 'Internet Regulation: Foreign Actors and Local Harms – at the Crossroads of Pornography, Hate Speech, and Freedom of Expression', *North Carolina Journal of International Law and Commercial Regulation*, **28**(Pt 1): 177-220.

Geist, Michael (2001). 'Is There a There There? Toward Greater Certainty for Internet Jurisdiction', *Berkeley Technology Law Journal*, **16**(3): 1345–1406.

Gold, Steve (2000). 'German Landmark Nazi Ruling', *Newsbytes*, 12 December.

Greenstein, Richard K. (2007). 'The Action Bias in American Law: Internet Jurisdiction and the Triumph of Zippo Dot Com', *Temple Law Review*, **80**(1): 21–51.

Hirst, Michael (2003). *Jurisdiction and the Ambit of the Criminal Law*, Oxford: Oxford University Press.

Kohl, Uta (2004). 'The Rule of Law, Jurisdiction and the Internet', *International Journal of Law and Information Technology*, **12**(3): 365–376.

Kozierok, Charles M. (2005). *The TCP/IP Guide: A Comprehensive, Illustrated Internet Protocols Reference*, San Francisco: No Starch Press.

Levene, Mark and Alexandra Poulovassilis (2001). 'Web Dynamics', *Computer Networks*, **39**(3): 221–223.

Leyden, John (2004). 'Four charged in landmark UK phishing case', *The Register*, 15 October, at: http://www.theregister.co.uk/2004/10/15/phishing_charges/.

Mehta, Michael D., Don Best and Nancy Poon (2002). 'Peer-to-peer sharing on the Internet: An Analysis of how Gnutella networks are used to distribute pornographic material', *Canadian Journal of Law and Technology*, **1**(1), at: http://cjlt.dal.ca/vol1_no1/articles/01_01_MeBePo_gnutella.pdf.

Naraine, Ryan (2006). '"Money Mule": The Hidden Side of Phishing', *eWeek*, 16 October, at: http://www.eweek.com/article2/0,1759,2029953,00.asp.

National Institute of Standards and Technology (2006). *An Ontology of Identity Credentials – Part One: Background and Formulation*, U.S. Department of Commerce, available online at: http://csrc.nist.gov/publications/drafts/sp800-103-draft.pdf.

Parsky, Laura H. (2006). *Statement before the Committee on Commerce, Science and Transportation, United States Senate, Concerning Protecting Children Online*. 19 January, at: http://commerce.senate.gov/pdf/Laura%20Parsky%20Testimony.pdf.

Paterson, Mary (2004). 'Following the Right Lead: Gutnick and the Dance of Internet Jurisdiction', *Canadian Journal of Law and Technology*, **3**(1): 49–56.

Taylor, Max and Ethel Quayle (2003). *Child Pornography: An Internet Crime*, New York: Routledge.

Sansom, Gareth (2002). 'Child Pornography: From Commercial Collapse to Computer-Mediated Consumption', *mimeo*.

Sansom, Gareth (2005). 'Computer-related Crime in the Context of the Digital Divide', Paper presented at the Eleventh United Nations Congress on Crime Prevention and Criminal Justice, Bangkok, 18-25 April.

Sansom, Gareth (2006a). 'Towards a Typology of Computer-Related Crime', *Expert Group Meeting on the Development of Virtual Forum against Cybercrime Report*, Seoul: Korean Institute of Criminal Justice Policy and the United Nations Office on Drugs and Crime, 91–124.

Sansom, Gareth (2006b). 'Privacy with Precision: Search and Seizure in the Context of Diverse Data Types', Paper presented at the National Symposium on Technological Crime and Electronic Evidence, 9 December, Toronto.

Sciadas, George (ed.) (2003). *Monitoring the Digital Divide ... and Beyond*, Montreal: Orbicom.

Spencer, A. Benjamin (2006). 'Jurisdiction and the Internet: Returning to Traditional Principles to Analyze Network-Mediated Contacts', *University of Illinois Law Review*, (1): 71–126, at: http://home.law.uiuc.edu/lrev/publications/2000s/2006/2006_1/Spencer.pdf.

Symantec (2006). *DeepSight Threat Management System Research Report: Online Fraud Communities and Tools*, 24 January, at: http://www.securitymanagement.com/archive/library/symantec_techink0506.pdf.

Tjurjukanova, Elena, Maja Rusakova and Viktoria Sakina (2003). *Analysis of the Situation and Institutions in the Field of Commercial Sexual Exploitation of Children (CSEC) and Counter-CSEC Activities in Russia*, ECPAT International, at: http://www.ecpat.net/eng/Ecpat_inter/projects/monitoring/Russia/Situational_Analysis_Research__Russia_Feb2004.pdf.

United Nations (2000). *United Nations Convention against Transnational Organized Crime*, at: http://www.uncjin.org/Documents/Conventions/dcatoc/final_documents_2/convention_eng.pdf.

United States Attorney's Office for the District of New Jersey (2004). *Indictment – United States v. Andrew Mantovani and others*, 28 October, United States District Court (District of New Jersey), at: http://www.usdog.gov/usao/nj/press/files/pdffiles/firewallindct1028.pdf.

United States Attorney's Office for the District of New Jersey (2004). *Indictment – United States v. Yahor Zalatarou and others*, 15 January, United States District Court (District of New Jersey), at: http://www.usdoj.gov/usao/nj/press/files/pdffiles/regpayindict.pdf.

United States Attorney's Office for the Northern District of Texas (2001). Press Release – *Thomas Reedy Sentenced to Life Imprisonment in Child Porn Case*, 6 August. United States Department of Justice (2001). *Operation Avalanche Press Conference* [transcript], 8 August.

United States Attorney's Office for the Western District of Washington (2002). *Press Release – Russian Computer Hacker Sentenced to Three Years in Prison*, 4 October, at: http://www.usdoj.gov/criminal/cybercrime/gorshkovSent.htm.

United States General Accounting Office (2003). *File-Sharing Programs: Child Pornography is Readily Available over Peer-to-Peer Networks*, testimony before the Committee on Government Reform, House of Representatives (GAO-03-537T), 13 March.

Walsh, William C. (2002). *Testimony on Virtual Child Pornography: The Impact of the U.S. Supreme Court Decision in the Case of Ashcroft v. Free Speech Coalition*, for the U.S. House of Representative, Judiciary Committee, Subcommittee on Crime, 1 May, at: http://www.judiciary.house.gov/legacy/walsh050102.htm.

Williams, Sharon A. and J.-G. Castel (1981). *Canadian Criminal Law, International and Transnational Aspects*, Toronto: Butterworths.

Wilson, Paul (2005). *The Geography of Internet Addressing*, Asia Pacific Network Information Centre, at: http://www.apnic.net/archive/news/hot-topics/internet-gov/internet-geography.pdf.

Zeller, Tom Jr. (2006). 'Web's Main Mugger's Still Out of U.S. Reach', *International Herald Tribune*, 3 April, at: http://www.iht.com/articles/2006/04/02/business/data.php#end_main.

Zetter, Kim (2006). 'Confessions of a Cybermule', *Wired News*, 28 July, at: http://www.wired.com/politics/onlinerights/news/2006/07/71479.

Zetter, Kim (2007). 'I Was a Cyber-Crook for the FBI', *Wired News*, 30 January, at: http://www.wired.com/politics/onlinerights/news/2007/01/72515.

Zook, Matthew A. (2003). 'Underground Globalization: Mapping the Space of Flows of the Internet Adult Industry', *Environment and Planning A*, **35**(7): 1261–1286.

Legal Cases

Permanent Court of International Justice

The Case of the S.S. 'Lotus', PCIJ, Ser. A., No. 10., 1927

Canadian Cases

Libman v. The Queen, [1985] 2 S.C.R. 178
R v. Cook, [1998] 2 S.C.R. 597

American Cases

International Shoe Co. v. Washington, 326 U.S. 310 (1945)
Burger King Corp. v. Rudzewicz, 471 U.S. 462 (1985)

Inset Systems, Inc. v. Instruction Set, Inc., U.S. Dist. Lexis 7160, 937 F. Supp. 161 (D.Conn., April 17, 1996)

Cybersell, Inc. v. Cybersell, Inc., 130 F.3d 414 (9th Circuit, 1997)

Zippo Manufacturing Co. v. Zippo Dot Com, Inc., 952 F. Supp. 1119 (W.D. Pa., January 16, 1997)

ACLU v. Reno, 217 F.3d 162 (3rd Circuit, 2000)

Yahoo! Inc. v. La Ligue contre le racisme et l'antisemitisme, 145 F. Supp. 2d 1168, (N.D. Ca., September 24, 2001)

United States v. Reedy, 304 F.3d 358 (5th Circuit, 2002)

ALS Scan, Inc. v. Digital Service Consultants, Inc., 293 F.3d 707 (4th Circuit, 2002)

United Kingdom Cases

R. v. Fellows; *R. v. Arnold*, [1997] 2 All ER 548

R. v. Waddon, [2000] E.W.J. No. 2095

R. v. Perrin, [2002] E.W.J. No. 1328

French Cases

LICRA et UEJF c. Yahoo! Inc and Yahoo France, Tribunal de Grande Instance de Paris, May 22, 2000.

Index

Numbers such as 217n33 mean page 217 note 33.